Managing Change/Chan

The topic of change management presents students with many challenges. One of the most challenging is making sense of guru and hero-manager literature, of which there is a plethora.

Managing Change/Changing Managers is an innovative textbook that encourages readers to question rigorously popular management theory, presenting a challenging review of existing literature in the change management field. The author brings together an overarching perspective on the most influential writings in the area, but, unlike other textbooks, provides a much-needed critique of the material and its implications for management practice.

Arguing that the majority of management guru literature makes the art of managing change appear simple and foolproof when it is not, this text is refreshingly critical, guiding and enhancing the reader's own criticality. The book also draws the best practice out of the traditional theory, using cases to illuminate the practical side to change management.

Primarily a guide for managers and postgraduates entering the territory of change management, this invigorating book is essential reading for all those studying or working in the field.

Julian Randall is Director of Programmes at the Centre for Business Education, St Andrews University.

Managing Change/ Changing Managers

Julian Randall

Routledge
Taylor & Francis Group

LONDON AND NEW YORK

First published 2004
by Routledge
11 New Fetter Lane, London EC4P 4EE

Simultaneously published in the USA and Canada
by Routledge
29 West 35th Street, New York, NY 10001

Routledge is an imprint of the Taylor & Francis Group

© 2004 Julian Randall

Typeset in Perpetua and Bell Gothic by
Florence Production Ltd, Stoodleigh, Devon
Printed and bound in Great Britain by
TJ International Ltd, Padstow, Cornwall

British Library Cataloguing in Publication Data
A catalogue record for this book is available from the British Library

Library of Congress Cataloging in Publication Data
Randall, Julian, 1945–
    Managing change, changing managers/Julian Randall.
        p. cm.
    Includes bibliographical references and index.
    1. Organizational change – Management.   2. Industrial management.
    I. Title.
    HD58.8.R347 2004
    658.4'06 – dc22   2003023749

ISBN 0–415–32311–8 (hbk)
ISBN 0–415–32312–6 (pbk)

Contents

CONTENTS

Figures

Tables

Boxes

Acknowledgements

There should be an award for academics who have an open door policy to the many callers who come from the publishing houses on the off-chance that a worthwhile interchange may be possible with their usually evasive quarry, for it was during one such encounter that I owned up to running a module entitled the Management of Change.

The discussion that followed included the usual question of the textbooks used and I allowed myself the self-indulgence of complaining that there were so many different books needed to cover a complex and diverse set of literatures, each of which included theory and empirical work. My visitor without hesitation suggested I should write a book to bring some of those diverse themes together. The result is the present volume. I am indebted to Catriona King who was responsible for this invitation.

I would also like to thank the three anonymous reviewers who commented on my sample chapter. Two of them offered positive suggestions, which I was pleased to follow up and include in the present volume. The third said it should be strangled at birth. I will leave the reader to decide whether this recommendation should have been implemented by my publisher.

Formatting and reading text is a tedious and unrewarding part of writing and one that I find somewhat uncongenial. For her commitment and helpful comment, together with her comprehensive knowledge of computers and the potential of their software, I am indebted to my wife, Pauline.

A first attempt at publishing requires a sympathetic manager, mentor and guide to the many considerations of layout, drafting and permissions. It has been an interesting and useful learning journey for me. For fulfilling that role with good humour and giving constant encouragement, I am indebted to Rachel Crookes of Routledge.

Finally, I am grateful to Professor Sandra Nutley, the colleague whose course I ran for three years, during which time I was able to fine-tune some of my material and observe its impact on three years of honours students. She was always willing to loan her books, offer advice and read my final efforts. She has been a good friend and great colleague.

This book is dedicated to my late mother, Hyacinth Irene Randall, who died just as the book was being completed at the end of July 2003. I am indebted to her for her support, encouragement and inspiration in the many things I tried to take on and complete in my life.

Introduction

In nearly twenty years of management consultancy work in the UK and abroad, I have experienced the management of change in different initiatives in over 300 companies. In 1993 I embarked on an MSc in Human Resource Management and discovered that theory can appear to conflict with assumptions born of previous consultancy practice. Sometimes the academics teaching us found the older, experienced learners in the class less inclined to accept the prescriptions offered by the textbooks. We in our turn had to learn that, in order to contribute to learning, it is necessary first to listen to the general debate contained within a literature before attempting to make a contribution through research and dissertation.

Many textbooks approach their subject by addressing the theoretical principles underlying each topic before offering empirical evidence or case study to illustrate and develop the critical points being made in the text. A different approach seemed appropriate for experienced students and postgraduates. As a management trainer, it had always been my experience that subjects raised with managers benefit from reflection and active discussion of practice encountered and then addressing the implications for underpinning theory. The problem for a book attempting to replicate this approach lies in the difficulty of simulating such reflectiveness in the written text.

Most managers probably read popular management books, broadsheet newspapers or professional journals on the subject of managing change at work. The articles are usually current, topical and well written. However, they can sometimes leave more critical questions either unanswered or only briefly addressed. Besides journalistic contributions there is a range of books which includes what David Collins refers to as guru/hero manager texts together with more closely argued academic works and scholarly monographs.

The layout of each chapter has therefore been planned to enable the reader coming back into study or embarking on postgraduate study to read each chapter in a discursive way. The first section includes popular readings and poses questions arising from the approach taken by the contribution. The critical points arising then lead on to a second section in which the theory underpinning the topic is examined in greater detail together with accounts from practitioners. A third section includes examination questions and offers an opportunity to consider possible structured answers. Finally, a fourth section contains references drawn on throughout the chapter and attempts to include a representative selection of the different books and journals that might offer a point of departure for further study.

It has always been my experience that students with previous working experience enhance the learning that can be offered on a postgraduate course of study. It is the hope of the present author that this book may make the challenging topic of the management of change more accessible to those who come to it from that background of experience and facilitate their contribution to research and the development of the theory which underpins it.

Chapter 1

Finding your way in

Managing change or changing managers

TOPIC HEADINGS

- Current issues in the management of change
- The different literatures contributing to the management of change
- The theoretical assumptions underpinning the management of change
- Sociological paradigms and organizational analysis
- Historical human relations background to change interventions

INTRODUCTION

The Management of Change is a subject that is destined to be with us for many years to come, while people adjust to a world of work that is likely to be more fragmented than previous generations had come to expect. In the middle of the last century it would be fair to say that most people expected to choose a trade, profession or occupation and, if they wanted to, stay in it until retirement. Popular authors frequently refer to a period of stability after the Second World War when full employment was the objective of governments, whether in the Western world or in the more managed economies to be found elsewhere.

If we accept the findings of Expectancy Theory (Vroom, 1964), we would anticipate that most individuals looked forward to a stable experience of employment, which started with specific qualification levels and induction training and then proceeded through various promotions, accompanied by appropriate incremental pay rises. For many, the prospect of working for one employer enabled individuals to plan their lives, and to invest in a family and property with the security of feeling that they could discharge these responsibilities with a reasonable prospect of consistent success. Individuals might freely embark on change should opportunity arise elsewhere or an alternative offer be made in the same sector. One well-known popular writer in management summarizes what many might have felt then:

> Thirty years ago I started work in a world-famous multinational company. By way of
> encouragement they produced an outline of my future career — 'This will be your life,'

3

they said, with titles of likely jobs. The line ended, I remember with myself as chief executive of a particular company in a particular far-off country. I was, at the time, suitably flattered.

(Handy, 1989, 5)

However, the author continues to consider the changes that have broken into the world of work since that time. We can note that it has given rise to much reassessment by individuals of how they will manage their lives to take account of different, sometimes imposed and unplanned breaks in what would previously have been a seamless experience. The post-war consensus of providing employment for all broke down and the assumptions that underwrote motivation at work and career development came to be questioned.

Interestingly, the full development of the all-providing organization had emerged in the terms of Human Resource Management (HRM) (Beer, 1984). It could be said that traditional personnel management during the twentieth century had offered the prospect of managed motivation leading to productivity and achievement of organizational objectives (Storey, 1989; Sisson, 1994). However, now there came a philosophy that was far more comprehensive and combined performativity with personal commitment to the organization (Fournier and Grey, 2000). The outcomes of HRM could be listed:

- Quality
- Flexibility
- Commitment
- Strategic integration.

(Guest, 1989)

There were even those who saw a psychological contract in which transactional elements (money in return of work and effort) were balanced by relational elements (loyalty and trust), which would explain the internal calculation that an individual might make during his or her experience at work (McNeil, 1985; Rousseau, 1998).

This obligingly cohesive and easily managed world could not be expected to survive what was to be a decade of monetarism in which businesses were projected into a financial accountability, which would find them struggling to survive without radical downsizing or merger. The alluring prospect of reducing what for most businesses accounted for 75 per cent of overhead – staff costs – could only lead to the competitive drive to become lean and risk averse (Peters and Waterman, 1985). Excellence came at a price and the right formula for a company's survival could well mean reduction in numbers and arbitrary termination of employment contracts. The effect of this on individuals became the focus of increasing research (Jahoda, 1982; Little, 1976; Smith, 1985; Swinburne, 1981). The consequences were found to impact on not just workers directly affected in this way, but also those employees who remained in work and had witnessed how their peers had been treated (Hallier and Lyon, 1996; Hallier and James, 1997).

The implications of this imposition of change also affected the rationale of much public sector employment. Governments were not slow to see the value of reducing head-count in sectors for which they were responsible. Performativity could offer the prospect not just of reduction of overhead but also the functional flexibility that unionized environments had precluded in the past. The debate about the rights of private profit makers to undertake publicly funded services is with us still. But the drive for what was sometimes referred to as New Public Sector Management is unlikely to recede (Fox, 1991; Pollitt, 1993).

MANAGING CHANGE

The claim that change at work can be managed is not a new position. The history of industrialization offers myriad examples of organizations evolving in all sectors. New technologies have always driven the search for new applications, which in turn provide the competitive advantage to those who first implement them. Unsurprisingly, it often meant for workers increased productivity imposed with no necessary compensating benefits (Littler, 1985; Melling and McKinlay, 1996; Gall, 2003). Into that world of change came initiators, inventors and managers of change who offered business owners new ways of implementing such competitive advantage. Taylorism is a prime example of Ford's investment in performativity linked to production, but following this application of derived productivity to systematic management were many others whose names are equally well known. Most students of social sciences will have heard of Lewin (1947) who addressed the forces for and against change and attempted to manage the process with groups of workers using group work. His research influenced many practitioners who took part in facilitating that work and who went on to research and write in the field of management and motivation in their own right. Among them were such well-known names as Argyris, Schein and McGregor, to name but three of those who continued and developed his work.

However, it took the excellence literature to bring popularity to writings on the management of change. Academics such as Porter and Kanter became household names among the advocates of proactive intervention and positive interpretation of the imposed management of change. Practising managers and students alike found such contributions accessible and readable. They often reinforced an optimistic belief that it was possible to bring about change at work without inducing resistance or alienation in those on whom it was imposed.

Not surprisingly a range of texts appeared for students and managers wanting to investigate good practice and the theoretical principles that underpin the practice of change management (Burnes, 1992; Carnall, 1999; Wilson, 1999; Collins, 1998; Williams *et al.*, 2002; Darwin *et al.*, 2002; Hayes, 2002; Jick and Peiperl, 2003). They balanced the theoretical and the empirical using different approaches, sometimes illustrating theory with practical examples or alternatively offering case study-led comment on practical contributions to an exponentially burgeoning literature on the successful implementation of change.

At the foundation of such theorizing lie the findings of researchers. Such contributors, mostly academics, enter into the world of work carrying with them a set of tools and a set of assumptions (Weick, 1995). Some come from the Labour Process tradition, which has its roots in the assumption that the employer–employee relationship is inherently exploitative. Others have a more critical approach, perhaps accepting the necessary interaction of worker and manager whilst seeking to evaluate critically the outcome of management strategies and their intervention in the workplace. Such work often finds its initial publication in periodicals and journals and in edited volumes of assembled contributions (McKinlay and Starkey, 1998).

5

EXAMINING DIFFERENT CONTRIBUTIONS

In the first section of this chapter we will attempt to give the reader examples of these different types of contribution. Popular writers can provide compelling reading, particularly when consultancy has provided them with examples which give their texts both credibility and currency. It can sometimes be difficult for the general reader approaching such literature to identify the theoretical assumptions being made by the writer. Perhaps the pace of the narrative overtakes the need to be analytical and, on occasion, critical of claims being made about effectively managed change and its impact on the individuals involved. The examples used offer opportunities to examine the assumptions made by the writers.

In the second section we will look at the theoretical assumptions underlying the management of change in greater detail, for the impact of change on individuals has its base in the discipline of psychology, in which there is a very full literature addressing change and its impact on individual subjects both in laboratory and in fieldwork. But individuals usually work with others and this brings us into the areas of group work and the ever-popular emphasis on teams. Here we are entering into the more sociologically based literatures of group dynamics and team roles. Finally, once we embark on organizational studies there are other debates that need to be addressed. These are both definitional – what is an organization – and also conceptual – how do we think about the dynamics which underpin the disciplines we are studying during change?

In the third section we will look at the historical evolution of traditions, which have been significant contributors to the way we think about change and the assumptions that may be made about it. We will consider the background of those who would see organizations as almost mechanical in the way they operate. There are still many practitioners and consultants who would see their work as diagnosing problems arising from the way an organization is structured and staffed. Organization Development as a discipline has its roots in such a functionalist view.

The alternative tradition of perceptions of individuals as the critical factor in managing change in organizations derives from an interpretist tradition. Contributions range from the Human Relations school to later work on climate and culture, in which the way individuals interpret change depends on the basic assumptions they hold about themselves, their jobs, their career and the organization. Here we are at the heart of the structure and actor debate, which surfaces along the interface between personal and corporate constructs (Balnaves and Caputi, 1993). The debate will endure and reflects the distinct contributions that psychology and sociology have made to the management of change. We have allowed that distinction expression in the alternate parts of the title of this book, for structuralists will usually be more comfortable with *managing change* as a process, whereas interpretists will be more comfortable starting from the premise that *changing managers'* attitudes is what actually underlies the claim to be effective in the management of change.

The fourth section of this chapter will address the practical considerations of those embarking on academic, postgraduate courses. You will probably be confronted by requirements to produce essays, assignments and eventually a dissertation. Getting back into the ways of writing extended prose composition can be trying for those whose lives are more dependent on minimal e-mails and bullet-point lists.

6

So, here is the opportunity to examine the conventions required to be successful, and the form and content, which should make it easier to write and gain reasonable marks from academics who, as a race, can be remarkably insistent on the requirements of parsing, analysis and the grammatical conventions sometimes left behind at school by those involved in everyday management practice.

In this first chapter we will look at the structure of assignment and examination questions and the methods to follow in putting together your answer. Writing is a discipline which, like any other, should become easier with practice. However, some ground rules may make it easier to judge how closely your work has come to best practice. In subsequent chapters we will use the fourth section to examine how to develop questions which can arise in exams and assignments.

DIFFERENT VOICES IN THE MANAGEMENT OF CHANGE

The most accessible works for a general readership interested in entering the world of the management of change are usually popular to-do books. Their titles often give them away. We will notice the inclusion of 'how to' and 'to do' phrases included in the title. Academic students are often warned off using such books as frequently very little is offered to the reader by way of Index or References. This makes the work, however well written, difficult to link to other contributors and can become a monologue of the author's personal opinion backed by anecdote and selective quotation from sympathetic sources. However, for those looking to break into the subject there is sometimes a value in reading to identify what the basic assumptions of the writer are and whereabouts on a spectrum of contributors he or she would be sited. With this in mind we offer the following extract as not untypical of such general works. It comes from a book entitled *Effective change: twenty ways to make it happen*:

Search for initial solutions
Faced with a complex situation requiring change a common management reaction is 'Where do I begin?' Successful change efforts suggest that a change should start at those points in the system where some stress and strain exist, but not where these are the greatest. Strain causes dissatisfaction with the status quo and thus becomes a motivating factor for change in the system. Look carefully at the recipient of the proposed changes, to see if they can be grouped or segmented so as to benefit from slightly varying change strategies.

Stagnating organisations develop many layers of filters to keep out the external world. One solution may be to deliberately introduce conflict. This can stimulate the creation of mutual goals and values, integrating individuals into the groups. Confrontation meetings, for example, can ensure that problems are aired along with alternative solutions.

Problem recognition narrows the task, putting crucial not marginal issues on the agenda for action. At this stage you are only looking for an outline of possible action and this must reflect:

■ Available resources
■ An acceptable time scale.

It is no use, for example, devising a major change programme, which cannot be properly financed. Similarly, there is no point planning a major change programme lasting too long.

At this early stage in the process of organising the change effort you should also identify how much commitment to change exists. The retailer's survey, for example, revealed that there was widespread staff support for it:

The smaller the commitment, the more intense
The change effort required.

(Leigh and Walters, 1998, 114)

Before we move on consider the following questions:

1 What sort of stress and strain is the author referring to?
2 How does strain become a motivating factor?
3 On what basis would change recipients be grouped or segmented?
4 How would you identify a stagnating organization?
5 What examples would typify layers of filters?
6 How do you deliberately introduce conflict?
7 How can you gauge commitment to change prior to its taking place?
8 What comment would you make about the final statement 'the smaller the commitment, the more intensive the change effort required'?

The use of this excerpt is not intended to suggest that the work from which it is derived is unworthy in any way. There are many ways of gaining interest and commitment to a subject and popular or journalistic articles will be used throughout this book because they are often insightful and can be stimulating. However, the reader embarking on an academic course now needs to be more critical in the best sense. Criticism here does not mean being negative, but it does mean asking questions to clarify statements or concepts that may be unclear.

So, in the above passage we can ask what the author means by 'stress and strain' and how it becomes a motivating factor. Sometimes an example would have sufficed. Here, it is not given. The tenor of the excerpt is anecdotal in style. It passes uncritically over assertions that do not offer a clear definition to allow us to identify, for example, what is a 'stagnating organization'. It offers general prescription in a definitive way, for example, suggesting that deliberately introducing conflict and confrontation meetings would facilitate the formation of consensus. The final summaries about time and resources would seem unexceptionable and the quotation at the end has a surface validity, which scarcely needs stating but frustratingly offers no specific example.

TEXTBOOKS

Here is another excerpt, this time from a well-known textbook, which offers both references and tools for considering the phenomena involved in thinking about the stages that might comprise change and allows us to think more clearly about how they interface with each other:

Change and transition model

If the concept of change can be examined from an internal, external or proactive set of viewpoints, then the response of managers has to be equally as widespread. Buchanan & McCalman (1989) suggest that this requires a framework of 'perpetual transition management'. Following from Lawler's (1986) concept of the lack of a visionary end state, what appears to be required is the ability within managers to deal with constant change. This transition management model, although specifically related to large-scale organizational change, has some interesting insights into what triggers change in organizations, and how they respond. It suggests that four interlocking management processes must take place both to implement and sustain major organizational changes. These processes operate at different levels, and may involve different actors in the organizational hierarchy. The four layers are:

- *Trigger layer* Concerning the identification of needs and openings for major change deliberately formulated in the form of opportunities rather than threats or crises.
- *Vision layer* Establishing the future development of the organization by articulating a vision and communicating this effectively in terms of where the organization is heading.
- *Conversion layer* Setting out to mobilize support in the organization for the new vision as the most appropriate method for dealing with the triggers of change.
- *Maintenance and renewal layer* Identifying ways in which changes can be sustained and enhance belief, reinforce and justify change and avoid regression by using, say, ritual.

(Paton and McCalman, 2000, 10)

We can contrast our first excerpt with the second by considering the more structured layout of the content. Many textbook writers include diagrams and outlines to guide the reader through processes, steps or stages, which make the material they feature appear more logical in sequence and therefore easier to follow.

The links to previous contributors allow the student to identify the authors whose work may have provided the basis for the inclusion of the model or diagram. They may also offer critical comments and questions themselves, as is the case here:

Transition management suggests that organizations have to plan for, divert resources to, and implement four sets of interlocking processes. These are designed to implement, to sustain, and to build on change and its achievements in an attempt to address the issues associated with change over time. The argument here is that these layers – trigger, vision, conversion and maintenance and renewal – are necessary processes that occur in change management. The respective emphasis and priority attached to each of them will alter over time, but recognition of their existence goes a long way to determining the management action needed.

The model of perpetual transition management starts out with a number of questions. How do we explain successful change? How do we explain attempts at change that is initially successful but wanes or fizzles out halfway through? Effective large-scale change demands a series of management actions linked to four interlocking layers or processes.

(Paton and McCalman, 2000, 11)

9

LEARNED ARTICLES AND PERIODICALS

All serious students at postgraduate level will be guided towards the sources of research from which theory is derived and developed. Reading excerpts as we are at present and as is offered in textbooks, is no substitute for consulting original research at source and intact. For most students this is by far the hardest part of the work and will become increasingly so if a dissertation is to be embarked upon.

It may be useful to consider an example of what could be described as empirical evidence simply offered and linked to a general theme, which has been part of a topical debate for some years now: the Learning Organization. The authors of our excerpt have surveyed 92 managers from 14 public and 14 private-sector organizations. Explanations for differences in experience and perception are considered along with their implications. The authors identify what they believe are the significant differences, which need not detain us here. However, their final paragraph may give an idea of the conclusions of their study:

> It therefore seems that the unanticipated can, in principle, be predicted. If the concept of the learning organization were to be taken seriously in this context, then what is conventionally regarded as 'planning error' in change implementation could be regarded instead as a platform for discussion, argument, learning and debate, addressing the fresh issues uncovered. If change were indeed an orderly and predictable process, would 96% of respondents to this survey have been able to claim that change for them was a valuable learning experience? The principle of the learning organization appeared to find some fragile support in the findings of this survey. It would appear, therefore, that establishing specific organizational learning mechanisms could contribute significantly to improvements in both the process and outcomes of the organizational change implementation process.
>
> (Doyle *et al.*, 2000, S73)

A reader familiar with the ongoing debate on Learning Organizations might be reinforced in their belief that a question had been raised – that question is clearly there in the final paragraph. But how far the findings were significant would be a reasonable question. The authors themselves seem somewhat tentative in their claims here. Perhaps it is a question of more research needing to be done.

Compare this piece of scholarship with an excerpt from an author who is well known for her writings on corporate transformation. Following members of staff through their experience of change in one organization, she examines how far the findings of the research support the idea of the emergence of a post-industrial, 'post-occupational' social solidarity:

> As the new technologies integrate and inform more and more of the production process, the social technologies are similarly organized to facilitate the integrated flexibility and democratizing capacities of the technologies. It is indeed possible that employees could appropriate the new culture to genuinely transform the institutions of work. However, what is happening now is a nostalgic restoration of the effect of industrial solidarities and pre-industrial mythical memories of family and belonging, to hold together the social sphere and to ensure production for the time being. It is an effort to shore up against

But what other assumptions might practising managers be making? Experience suggests that most of us are realists: we feel that there is a world that we can intervene in and control, otherwise why would we be attempting to make things happen in a particular way? We might also believe that the world is a predictable place and that there are laws, like the law of gravity, which govern what we see occurring before our eyes. We may have embarked on an academic or postgraduate course because we think there is some knowledge based on experience and good practice, which will make us more effective in our attempts to bring order out of chaos at work. In this regard we might feel that there are factors that can be measured which would enable us to understand what underlies our experience and would enable us to work more efficiently if we were able to implement them in our working lives.

If we had to summarize that position we would wittingly or unwittingly have adopted a position that could be described as modernistic: a view of the world which is fully in tune with the tradition of scientific rationalism, which has been the vehicle for the practices which underwrite the progress of industrialization. But there are alternative approaches and they are sometimes summarized and represented in a tradition referred to as postmodernism.

Before we get too deeply into the terminology it would be as well to examine on what basis there might be an alternative perspective of analysing human experience. Dealing with people in a management situation should have alerted us to the uncertainties of making things happen through people. If only it were just as easy as the theory sounds. However, experience suggests that what one person thinks is a good business idea may well be viewed differently by those on whom it is visited. So, why does the same objective piece of information come to be interpreted in two or more different ways by different people involved? The answer may be something simple like: the people being managed had their own way of interpreting change. Looked at more closely, this statement may mean that these individuals had a different set of expectations, which were not met by the plan produced by others. So, what happens to individuals depends on how they interpret what is done to them. We will be addressing exactly how this occurs later in this book when we deal with culture and cultural change management initiatives. For the moment, though, it is sufficient that we accept diversity of view as a common occurrence in everyday experience.

THE SUBJECTIVE–OBJECTIVE DIMENSION

What we are accepting at this point is a world which is not as measurable and predictable as is sometimes suggested. Human beings have a propensity to behave in unpredictable ways or do not accept the rationality imposed by others. To find out about this would be more difficult for us than just measuring, say, productivity factors or working out statistical inferences on profit projections and share yields. But, more than that, our calculations on the hard facts might well be dependent on a world of feelings and opinions, which suggests a world of knowledge that is variable rather than constant – an existence that is not so hard and fast as first appears.

At this point we can usefully look at a book which made quite an impact when it appeared in 1979. It was entitled *Sociological paradigms and organisational analysis*. The authors, Gibson Burrell and Gareth Morgan, refer to this spectrum of ways of interpreting the world around

13

us as the subjective–objective dimension and they offer a diagram which offers what they describe as 'a scheme for analysing assumptions about the nature of social science' (see Box 1.1).

If you are not familiar with these concepts you could be forgiven for thinking that, while offering explanation of ways of thinking about the world around us, they also make it more difficult to express clearly what should be simple for managers to understand. Do practising managers really need to know this? Is this not a case of explaining the obscure by the more obscure? In some ways, we could say 'yes' to the last question. And yet in our previous discussion we have accepted that what managers become involved in is not just confined to the right-hand side of the diagram. If human beings were automatons then we might accept a deterministic view of managing them. But even those who work in closely determined control and command environments know that human beings can appear to give consent and 'go through the motions' while believing something different; in other words, experience suggests a voluntaristic aspect to the experience of managing working life.

Similarly, when we manage others we can measure what they achieve at the end of a shift and give performance-related pay as agreed with them beforehand. This kind of measurement would be part of a positivist approach. But how can we measure effort? We really have little idea what efforts individuals make, any more than we can know what pain another individual suffers. Pain and effort thresholds are alike in being purely subjective and therefore non-positivistic – there is no reliable way of measuring them, still less of comparing them between individuals.

So, too, a researcher can use methods of measurement which seem very objective and therefore fair. These are referred to as nomothetic – the Greek word *nomos* suggests that there are laws surrounding that sort of measurement, which make the results quantifiable. On the other hand, if we want to find out what individuals think, we would have to ask them. The problem is that they may not tell us everything we want to know. The more people we interview, the more opinions we will receive: as in the Latin phrase *tot homines, quot sententiae* – there are as many opinions as there are people. The researcher cannot compare these results between individuals very easily and, sometimes, not at all. This tradition of research is ideographic – it is qualified rather than quantified research.

Finally, we need to look again at the world itself. If you incline towards realism then, like Samuel Johnson, you will kick a stone and declare, 'I refute him thus'. However, there

BOX 1.1 KEY PHILOSOPHICAL IDEAS IN SOCIOLOGY

The subjectivist approach to social science		The objectivist approach to social science
Nominalism	Ontology	Realism
Anti-positivism	Epistemology	Positivism
Voluntarism	Human nature	Determinism
Ideographic	Methodology	Nomothetic

Source: Burrell and Morgan (1979, 3)

is just the problem of some of the realities we talk about and refer to, which are not quite as physical as the stone. How often have we talked about 'mental faculties' and 'mind'? These things are incorporeal. We can observe the activity of the brain, but we cannot deal as directly with concepts that are abstract: beauty, goodness, truth – these are ideas. We see or experience a good person or drink a good wine, but goodness is an abstract concept. It relates to a nominalist world – it is a name, label or concept. We can think about it but cannot demonstrate it in a way that physical artefacts would allow us to do.

ORDER AND CONFLICT

Following their examination of the subjective–objective dimension, Burrell and Morgan identify another critical distinction in assumptions about the nature of society. They identify a view of society which emphasizes stability, integration, functional coordination and consensus. This they describe as an 'order' or 'integrationist' view. They contrast this view with a 'conflict' or 'coercion' view, which emphasizes change, conflict, disintegration and coercion (1979, 13). They finally label these contrasting theories as 'regulation' and 'radical change'. At first sight the term theory seems to suggest that these are opposing poles and that it would be difficult to hold both views simultaneously. And yet, perhaps it could be argued that management is itself a battle ground between those elements which tend towards either a steady-state view of organizations or a sporadic almost anarchic radicalism. Certainly, we might identify bureaucratic tendencies as part of a colonizing attempt to impose order and direct acceptable outcomes in a proactive way. We might then compare that to the tendency to impulsiveness, randomness, surprise and reaction to events, which can characterize the reality of the daily conduct of business.

However, whatever we consider about the dimension itself and how comparable it is to the subjectivist–objectivist dimension, Burrell and Morgan combine the two to form what they describe as four paradigms (see Figure 1.1).

If we take the bottom right-hand quadrant first we can see that the term Functionalist is applied to those who take an objectivist and regulatory view of the conduct of academic

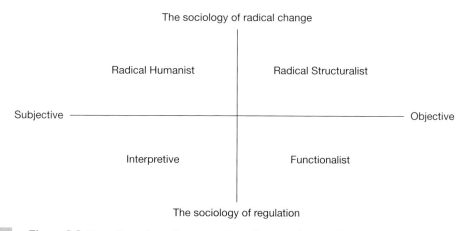

Figure 1.1 Two dimensions, four paradigms for organizational analysis

sociology in the study of organizations. That would relate most easily to the common sense approach we described earlier, which many management practitioners might be expected to espouse. Burrell and Morgan would expect the standpoint of such an observer to be realist, positivist, determinist and nomothetical. They see the founding fathers of the discipline of sociology as emanating from this perspective. Such theorists would be Auguste Comte, Herbert Spencer, Emile Durkheim and Vilfredo Pareto (1979, 26). The desire to objectify and make comparisons may well reinforce the perception of control and the focus on the physical aspects of reality in the management of work.

But, as we noted above, it is difficult to remain totally focused on the objective and the regulated where human beings are involved. Those who are convinced by the arguments of the behaviourist school may find a deterministic view of individuals convincing (Skinner, 1974). However, for most managers, experience suggests that members of staff may be less amenable to direction than to persuasion and influence. The study of motivation, which underlies the practice of management, would suggest that a more voluntaristic approach is likely to make managing people easier. Indeed, the lower left-hand quadrant now brings us into the field of Interpretation. How individuals interpret what they experience opens up the prospect of an inner world of the subjective, which the authors associate with phenomenology, hermeneutics and the 'intersubjectively shared meanings' that link into symbolic interactionism. There is an important link here between the personal and the corporate or group perception of reality. This inner life is still grounded in the social context.

If we move to the upper quadrants we are presented first with the Radical Humanist paradigm. Burrell and Morgan refer to this paradigm as Anti-organization Theory and associate it with Critical Theory and French existentialist writers, some of whom we will come to in more detail later in the book. The name of Foucault would be well known among them, offering us very different premises from which such commentators begin their quest to make sense of outside controlling factors impinging on the freedom of the individual and the techniques used to gain and keep control of individuals. Such power/knowledge constructions then govern the behaviour and attitudes of individuals within a managed world of imposition and discipline (Foucault, 1977). The quest to deconstruct this ordered social prison is one from which the only escape is into possible emancipation and the prospect of reconstruction in more congenial discourse. Such relations of power are constructed in the very discourse that governs social conventions, say, between doctor and patient or warder and prisoner (Clegg, 1989). Even something as apparently benevolent as HRM can be seen as another form of panopticon, whose tools become a means of monitoring and surveillance of the individual at work (Townley, 1994).

This brings us to the final quadrant, the Radical Structuralist paradigm. The Marxian analysis of capitalism as the dominant socio-political model is based on the assumption that the employer–employee relationship is inherently exploitative. It gives rise, therefore, to resistance from the worker and ultimately to alienation. But the revolution that would end this servitude would require the overthrow of the structural constraints put in place by owners of capital, land and labour, so that these important elements of social organization would be reconstructed in an equitable, free and fraternal way for the proletariat.

THE CONTEXT OF CHANGE LITERATURE

Thus far we have spent some time in identifying a framework which may help us to place the context of different contributors whose diverse literatures impinge on the management of change. It may assist us to be aware of the tradition in which a writer stands and therefore the standpoint from which he or she writes. The question of how to relate the different traditions has given rise to a separate debate entitled 'incommensurability', in which it is sometimes argued that it is not possible to range across the borders of the paradigms. At this stage it is not necessary for us to examine this debate in detail. What is important is our ability to understand the tradition from which writers contribute their understanding of the theoretical assumptions that underlie our subject and its implications for the management of change.

A HISTORICAL PERSPECTIVE ON THE MANAGEMENT OF CHANGE

One way of seeing how writers fit into the historical perspective of the management of work is to place them in a historical context. So, in this section we will offer some guidance on significant innovation and the names associated with it. It is not our intention to replicate the many historical surveys, some of which can be found in authors offering textbooks both on the subject of the management of change (Hayes, 2002) and on Human Resource Management (Armstrong, 2001). However, some pointers will be useful to link to our previous section on paradigms and also into our continued tracking of underlying theoretical assumptions that govern academic debates.

Most people will have heard of Taylor and *scientific management*. The early twentieth century saw the organization of work pioneered by Henry Ford, who used Taylor to analyse optimum working practices among workers and combine this information with the traditional concept of the division of labour. In a sense we could say that Taylor would be associated with structural functionalism, in that his work certainly focuses on the objective factors of production and they in turn concern the regulation of work around the productivity factors of time, quality, quantity and cost. The manufacturing sector was not slow to learn from the application of these principles in the deliberate way that Taylor employed them. Thereafter mass production adhered to assembly line techniques pioneered by Ford during the 1920s.

That decade offered another significant development that has impressed itself on a wide readership: the Hawthorne experiments and Elton Mayo. As is well known, deliberate changes made during experiments to the environment affecting workers were accompanied by improvements in productivity rates. This caused a discussion, which has continued since, about managers' ability to modify the ergonomics affecting workers in an attempt to increase their satisfaction and therefore effect an improvement in their productivity. It could be said that this initiative triggered an ongoing debate with an underlying assumption: how far can managers manipulate motivation by modifying the external working environment, including offering incentives and rewards to affect productivity in a positive direction?

So, we can track the inception of the welfare approach to managing workers from that early period of the twentieth century, which was to see the birth of such organizations as the Institute of Personnel Management. During the 1950s the *human relations* approach inspired the work of the Tavistock Institute and the many initiatives which attempted to involve workers in decisions affecting the conditions of their working environment and the decisions affecting the challenges and risks faced by them at work. A fuller history can be found of these initiatives and those associated with them in most standard textbooks (Burnes, 2000, 57ff.; Collins, 1998, 16). Our purpose here is to point out that this tradition moves the focus of the debate about the management of change away from structural factors alone and into the area of motivation which has traditionally been the preserve of psychology rather than sociology.

THE MANAGERIAL PARADIGM

The concept of management seems to be absent from the early part of industrialization. More often texts speak of the owners and their helpers with more references to supervisors – the often local foreman whose expertise put him or her in a position of obvious advantage in controlling others. Increasingly in the twentieth century an ordered way of approaching the planning and implementation of working objectives became part of an emerging body of knowledge which could, therefore, be learned by those who wanted to become more effective in directing the labours of others efficiently. Analysing how individuals were successful at this task and what internal steps they took to become effective became the basis for a developing body of knowledge which could be cascaded to others. Well known among them would be Fayol, a French theorist who ordered the steps into a classic list:

- Planning
- Organizing
- Command
- Coordination
- Control.

Allied to this is the work of another European theorist and contemporary of Fayol, the German theorist, Weber. He focused on the bureaucratic structures used in the control of many individuals by the few and, indeed, eventually just one leader. Here the development of levels of responsibility devolve and at each level require the designation of roles and functions for each individual so that together the sum total of their efforts will be a predictable and consistent outcome for the organization. A fuller description of Weber's contribution can be found in Burnes (2000, 44).

Thus far we have the constituent elements of a continuing debate between those who would concentrate on reorganizing structures during change and those who would see the people-acceptance side as being more important. Whether we identify them as structural functionalist or interpretist, it is clear that we have two approaches that the manager of change needs to take account of.

One strand of research, which seems to offer connections between individual and organization is *symbolic interactionism*. The work of such individuals as W.I. Thomas, James Dewey, G.H. Mead, R.E. Park, E.W. Burgess and E. Faris, in the Department of Sociology at

Chicago University, made an important contribution to a strand of research which owed more to social anthropology than to psychology. Without going deeply into the detail of the theories that lie behind this tradition, we can acknowledge the importance of symbol in society for conveying meaning and values. The symbolic not only conveys direction and the means of imposing or offering acceptable interpretation to an individual within a wider society, but also links into an emerging concept which will dominate much rhetoric in management practice and the theories and propositions underlying change: culture. We will deal in greater detail when we look at the claims of cultural management and culture change later in this book. But suffice it to say here that this language emerges again in that more predictive period of 1980s' management when the symbolic was sometimes claimed to have an important part to play in the management of change. It also offers a possible link between the individual and the formation of meaning and values during the early periods of socialization and this again we will examine in the chapter on culture and change management. A fuller account of symbolic interactionism can be found in Burrell and Morgan (1979, 78ff.).

INTERVENTIONAL APPROACHES

Another famous name associated with the management of change is that of Kurt Lewin. His work in 1947 marked the beginning of taking working groups and conducting sensitivity or T-groups. This open approach combined the confessional with the counselling mode and sought to unfreeze worker attitudes before moving them to a new perception and acceptance of change in working practices. In some ways it was the beginning of a bottom-up approach to change, which sought to ameliorate the impact of imposed change by allowing individuals within their working groups to come to terms with change.

In a similar way, several researchers focused on the resistance encountered from workers who are subjected to change at work. There is an enduring tradition that individuals will adapt and eventually adopt new working conditions. They may modify their expectancies when change triggers cognitive dissonance (Festinger, 1957); they may have their own perceptions of the likely outcomes of change (Becker, 1964); they may go through some sort of cognitive calculus (Rusbult and Farrell, 1983; Lazarus and Folkman, 1984); but usually they will come to terms with the change in the end. Indeed some researchers identify a stepped approach in which initially resistance is eventually accepted and the new ways internalized (Nicholson and West, 1988; Isabella, 1990).

Such approaches at least begin to address the actor side of the debate between structure and actor. However, the structural side still tends to be in the ascendant. This mechanistic approach to organizational change as the basis of management intervention is sometimes referred to as a *classic* approach. Such contributors as Burnes and Stalker represented an approach which could be summarized as having the following characteristics:

- The specialisation of tasks.
- Closely defined duties, responsibilities and technical methods.
- A clear hierarchical structure with insistence on loyalty to the organisation and obedience to superiors.

(Burnes, 2000, 76)

19

But, increasingly, the context in which change takes place became more dominant and authors such as Lawrence and Lorsch emphasized the relationship between structure and organizational environment. Underlying this is a move away from the mechanistic view of organization. The influences on people at work lie outside the workplace and are not just confined to what they do and the way they do it. So, as these individuals come and go, we could come to see the organization as something porous, or open. It is not a closed or hermetically sealed environment in which automatons conduct their work to the required standards and then return home, like working cogs in machinery. The logical progression of such perceptions can be found in Contingency Theory whose unifying themes can be summarized as:

- Organisations are open systems.
- Structure, and therefore performance, is dependent upon the particular circumstances, situational variables, faced by each organisations.
- There is no 'one best way' for all organisations.

(Burnes, 2000, 83)

The variance between the views of organizations as closed or open systems affects how far individuals working within it are passive or active agents of change and how far change needs to be bottom-up rather than top-down.

THE EXCELLENCE LITERATURE AND HUMAN RESOURCE MANAGEMENT

Peters and Waterman are iconic figures in the popular literature of management. Their book *In search of excellence* sold many millions of copies and brought a new enthusiasm to many managers about the prospect of generating commitment at work. The descriptors that they offer of the factors essential to the excellent company are simple enough to sound convincing and yet somewhat vague for accurate implementation. For example, 'stick to the knitting' sounds good advice until questions are raised about the content of competence and the requirement to develop new, customer-focused products and services. Change is often driven outside-in and then the question of whether workers have the requisite aptitudes to achieve success becomes the critical issue.

However, the formula of excellent companies fitted well with the new, comprehensive human relations model entitled Human Resource Management. It included the remit of traditional personnel and attempted to combine it with organizational commitment from the individual worker as part of mainstream management practice. But, if we examine the HR outcomes in detail, we can observe that the list of factors required of individuals is merely an extension of the productivity factors which management has always sought to control and improve:

- Quality
- Flexibility
- Commitment
- Strategic integration.

(Guest, 1989)

As we will see later in this book, there have been coordinated attempts to focus on quality in such movements as Total Quality Management. Flexibility was a primary objective of politicians and managers when faced with union-reinforced inflexibility protecting particular jobs or crafts. The commitment required was more than just coming to work and giving reasonable effort during a contracted time-frame. It was an internalization of the targets required by the organization, which was now committed to communicate what these targets were and reinforce them in the minds of all those involved in work endeavours – in other words, strategic integration.

THE RADICAL SHIFT TOWARDS INTERPRETATION

Two contributions have probably modified the structural focus towards a more actor-centred approach. First, Expectancy Theory (Vroom, 1964), which, as has been said, opens the door to subjectivity (Hassard and Parker, 1993). What individuals feel about themselves, their job, their work, their manager, the organization, is part of their own identity and in a sense is changing and emergent at any time. Second, there is the important question of emergent change (Pettigrew, 1991). If we accept that the context of working life is itself changing, then those within are subject to change themselves. This is an extension of the debate on organizations as open rather than closed or mechanical. Viewed in this way, organizations are not static and unyielding structures. They are much more ephemeral and, as such, unmanageable. Managers can impose structural change but cannot guarantee the effect this will have on those who can interpret the change and invest it with meaning and value.

UNDERLYING THEORETICAL DEBATES

Thus far, we have identified a number of underlying assumptions which are critical to the formulation of questions about the nature of change and how far it can be managed. It will be necessary to be specific about our definitions of key concepts and ideas before venturing into these debates.

We should perhaps begin with the question of organization. There is a list of definitions contained in Rosemary Stewart's book *Managing today and tomorrow* (1991, 40–41). They vary between attempts to describe functions, relationships and interrelated systems. More holistic approaches attempt to identify a minimum set of assumptions which one commentator lists as:

- Interdependency
- Synergy
- Boundary
- Binding ideology.
                    (Brown, 1992)

Interesting and insightful though these different elements are, they emphasize the problem we have in defining preset factors. We can accept that most organizations would require coordinated activity and that working together should give a result impossible to achieve without such synergy. However, when we get to the boundary, we come up against the open/closed debate again. How do you identify a binding ideology? Where would it lie inside the organization? Is it inherent in individuals, placed there through socialization, or is it a series of unrelated assumptions, which give surface validity to a consensus view, but in reality are only held by individuals in a fragmented or sporadic way?

This touches on the question of the organization as a system, or series of systems. Structuralists may often make assumptions about the organization being such an interface. It is easy to explain what occurs in organizations if it is possible to point to some pre-existent and designed, rational system, which accounts for what would otherwise seem random or arbitrary to an outside observer. An organization can then come to seem like a sentient and responding organism. Such statements as 'the organization decided to sack 10 per cent of the workforce' suggest that there is an impersonal decision-making process inherent in the structure itself. Thinking about organizations in this way makes it easier to see structural change as necessary and resistance as a temporary aberration of uncomprehending individuals. The perception of resistance runs like a fault-line through the management of change literature. For some commentators it is inherent in imposing change on individuals and may signal for them an alienation from accepting the legitimacy of management control. For others it is a temporary phenomenon, which careful managers of change can overcome (Nadler, 1993).

Finally, we return to the competing attentions of the structure–actor debate. Do these have to be contradictory positions or can we see a reasonable balance between them? There will be choices to be made between top-down imposition of change followed by picking up the pieces with the individuals affected, or bottom-up approaches which seek to involve those affected in the process of change – sometimes referred to as getting turkeys to vote for Christmas (Collins, 1998, 145ff.).

ADDRESSING SIGNIFICANT QUESTIONS

In the final section of each chapter it is our hope to address the question of writing assignments or answering examination questions. In order to attempt either task it is necessary to look at a possible framework for drawing up an answer.

Most questions will pose a problem/dilemma or offer a quotation and then invite you to answer in simple, direct and sometimes illustrated terms. It will be important to read the question carefully and examine its parts and their relationship to each other. Resist the temptation to download all that you know on receiving the one key word you happen to know something about.

Once you have identified the key words in the question, you may need to define clearly what you believe the terms mean or what you will take the term to mean as you offer your answer.

Mention the theoretical background and cite the main authors who have contributed to it.

Use examples, if appropriate, to illustrate where theory and practice support each other and where they do not.

Allow this variance between theory and practice to guide your discussion about how far each supports the other or does not.

Summarize and draw conclusions based on your discussion.

DISCUSSION QUESTIONS

1   'An organization is a social unit within which people have achieved somewhat stable relations (not necessarily face-to-face) among themselves in order to facilitate obtaining a set of objectives or goals' (Litterer, 1963).

   Is this definition comprehensive enough to cover all organizations?

This question allows you to look at definitions and discuss them more fully. Your first comment might point out that it is possible to apply the definition to a family or group outside work, though that may not invalidate it as a definition as such. However, the phrase 'somewhat stable relations' does invite further probing. So, also, does the word 'facilitate' – a word which means making it easy. How would we know when individuals have achieved this? Is it just a part of doing the job anyway? Finally, are these objectives and goals universal or do they break down into departmental goals and then into key tasks as classical management theorists sometimes suggest?

   The theoretical basis of the definition should allow you to enter into the structure–actor debate. Do you think this definition favours one position rather than the other? Or is it an attempt to offer a balanced definition? If so, how successful is it, in your opinion?

   Could you offer examples where such a definition would not apply and yet still includes a coordination of results? How, for example, would it explain a call centre? Some people might argue that the relationships are very unstable – at least that is how it may feel if you are a customer, since it is often difficult to speak to the same person twice. Perhaps this definition does not consider the customer as part of the dynamics described. In an increasingly service-based society, how realistic is this apparent exclusion? This could lead you into an interesting and important discussion about stakeholders and the porous boundaries of organization.

   Finally, go back to the original definition. Where is it weak? What are your conclusions about it as a definition of organization?

2   'Logic demands that for an organization to remain viable in the long term it must ensure all internal changes ultimately support long term survival in the environment in which it operates' (Stickland, 1998).

   How feasible is this definition for managers to implement?

Once again you will need to look closely at the different parts of the question. The way it is worded invites a comment from you on personification: organization cannot be the subject of the verb 'ensure' because the organization has no brain of its own with which to make such an assessment (Collins, 1998, 151). So, who in the organization might make that decision?

   Second, how far can 'all internal changes' be managed? Some of them are involuntary and will occur whatever managers do, e.g. retirements and staff leaving.

23

Third, unlike the first question, this one considers the 'environment in which it operates'. But how far is this environment manageable? What competitors do or customers demand is often outside the ability of managers to affect. They may well have to respond to them but it would be difficult to argue that this is management, if by that we are using Fayol's definition, which we saw above (see p. 18) as a predictive cycle of logical elements.

Finally, isn't this a question posed with hindsight? When we look back it may be possible for us to see what we did or did not do which contributed to our success or survival. In truth, at the time we may have got there by chance or just by responding reflexively in the right way.

Underlying this question, therefore, is the definition of management and how far it is possible to apply this to what occurs in organizations that ensures their survival. There are a number of definitions in Rosemary Stewart's book, this time on pages 19–20. One will suffice to illustrate the point:

> To carry out the task of ensuring that a number of diverse activities are performed in such a way that a defined objective is achieved.
>
> (French and Saward, 1983)

Forward planning can only take place if a certain set of assumptions are made about future outcomes. So, management is not just that aspect of forward planning, it also involves guesswork and sheer reaction when hit by the unknown.

The debate between structure and actor will be a constant in discussions about the management of change. The imposition of change will always involve one imponderable we cannot manage: how others will react or respond.

In the future chapters we will consider the factors which affect such management of change and the interaction between practice and theory.

REFERENCES AND FURTHER READING

Armstrong, M. *A handbook of human resource management practice*. London: Kogan Page, 2001.

Balnaves, M. and Caputi, P. Corporate constructs: to what extent are personal constructs personal? *International Journal of Personal Construct Psychology*, 1993: 119–138.

Becker, H. Personal change in adult life. *Sociometry*, 1964, *27*: 40–53.

Beer, M. *Managing human assets*. Boston: Harvard Business School, 1984.

Brown, R.K. *Understanding industrial organizations: theoretical perspectives in industrial sociology*. London: Routledge, 1992.

Buchanan, D.A. and McCalman, J. *High performance work systems: the digital experience*. London: Routledge, 1989.

Burnes, B. *Managing change*. London: Pitman, 1992.

Burnes, B. *Managing change: a strategic approach to organizational dynamics*. London: *Financial Times*/Prentice Hall, 2000.

Burrell, G. and Morgan, G. *Sociological paradigms and organizational analysis*. London: Heinemann, 1979.

Carnall, C.A. *Managing change in organizations*. London: *Financial Times*/Prentice Hall, 1999.

Casey, C. Corporate transformations: designer culture, designer employees and 'post-occupational' solidarity. *Organization*, 1996, *3* (3): 317–339.

Clegg, S. *Frameworks of power*. London: Sage, 1989.

Collins, D. *Organizational change: sociological perspectives*. London: Routledge, 1998.

Darwin, J., Johnson, P. and McAuley, J. *Developing strategies for change*. London: *Financial Times*/Prentice Hall, 2002.

Doyle, M., Claydon, T. and Buchanan, D. Mixed results, lousy process: the management experience of organizational change. *British Journal of Management*, 2000, *11* (Special Issue): S59–S80.

Festinger, L. *A theory of cognitive dissonance*. New York: Harper Row, 1957.

Foucault, M. *Discipline and punish: the birth of the prison*. Harmondsworth: Penguin, 1977.

Fournier, V. and Grey, C. At the critical moment: conditions and prospects for critical management studies. *Human Relations*, 2000 (January), *53* (1): 7–32.

Fox, N. Postmodernism, rationality and the evaluation of health care. *Sociological Review*, 1991, *39* (4): 709–744.

French, D. and Saward, H. *Dictionary of management*, 2nd edn. Aldershot: Gower, 1983.

Gall, G. *Union organizing*. London: Routledge, 2003.

Guest, D. Personnel and HRM. *Personnel Management*, 1989 (January): 48–51.

Hallier, J. and James, P. Middle managers and the employees' psychological contract: agency, protection and advancement. *Journal of Management Studies*, 1997, *34* (5): 705–728.

Hallier, J. and Lyon, P. Job insecurity and employee commitment: managers' reactions to the threat and outcomes of redundancy selection. *British Journal of Management*, 1996, *7*: 107–123.

Handy, C. *The age of unreason*. London: Hutchinson, 1989.

Hassard, J. and Parker, M. *Postmodernism and organizations*. London: Sage, 1993.

Hayes, J. *The theory and practice of change management*. New York: Palgrave, 2002.

Isabella, L.A. (1990) Evolving interpretations as a change unfolds: how managers construe key organizational events. *Academy of Management Journal*, 1990, *33* (1): 7–41.

Jahoda, M. *Employment and unemployment: a social psychological analysis*. Cambridge University Press, 1982.

Jahoda, M. and Fryer, D. The simultaneity of the unsimultaneous. *Journal of Community and Applied Social Psychology*, 1998 (March–April), *8* (2): 89–100.

Jick, T.D. and Peiperl, M.A. *Managing change: cases and concepts*, 2nd edn. McGraw Hill/Irwin, 2003.

Lawler, E.E. *High involvement management*. San Francisco, CA: Jossey Bass, 1986.

Lazarus, R.S. and Folkman, S. *Stress, appraisal and coping*. New York: Springer, 1984.

Leigh, A. and Walters, M. *Effective change: twenty ways to make it happen*. London: CIPD, 1998.

Lewin, K. Frontiers in group dynamics. *Human Relations*, 1947, *1*: 5–41.

Litterer, J.A. *Organizations: structure and behaviour*. New York: Wiley, 1963.

Little, C.B. Technical and professional unemployment: middle class adaptability to personal crisis. *Sociological Quarterly*, 1976, *17*: 262–274.

Littler, C.R. (ed.) *The experience of work*. Aldershot: Gower/Open University, 1985.

25

McKinlay, A. and Starkey, K. *Foucault, management and organizational theory*. London: Sage, 1998.

McNeil, I.R. Relational contract: what we know and do not know. *Wisconsin Law Review*, 1985: 483–525.

Melling, J. and McKinlay, A. *Management, labour and industrial politics in modern Europe*. Cheltenham: Edward Elgar, 1996.

Nadler, D.A. Concepts for the management of organizational change, in C. Mabey and B. Mayon-White (eds) *Managing Change*. London: Paul Chapman, 1993.

Nicholson, N. and West, M. *Managerial job change: men and women in transition*. Cambridge: Cambridge University Press, 1988.

Paton, R.A. and McCalman, J. *Change management: a guide to effective implementation*. London: Sage, 2000.

Peters, T.J. and Waterman, R.H. *In search of excellence*. New York: Harper & Row, 1982.

Pettigrew, A.M. and Whipp, R. *Managing change for competitive success*. Oxford: Blackwell, 1993.

Pollitt, C. *Managerialism and the public service: cuts or culture change in the 1990s*. Oxford: Blackwell, 1993.

Rousseau, D.M. The problem of the psychological contract considered. *Journal of Organizational Behaviour*, 1998, *19*: 665–671.

Rusbult, C.E. and Farrell, D. A longitudinal test of the investment model. *Journal of Applied Psychology*, 1983, *68*: 429–438.

Sisson, K. Personnel management in perspective, in K. Sisson (ed.) *Personnel Management*. Oxford: Blackwell, 1989.

Sisson, K. *Personnel management: a comprehensive guide to theory and practice in Britain*. Oxford: Blackwell, 1994.

Skinner, B.F. *About behaviourism*. New York: Knopf, 1974.

Smith, D. Job security and other myths: the employment climate. *Management Today*, 1997: 38–41.

Smith, R. What's the point, I'm no use to anyone: the psychological consequences of unemployment. *British Medical Journal*, 1985, *291*: 1338–1341.

Stewart, R. *Managing today and tomorrow*. Basingstoke: Macmillan, 1991.

Stickland, F. *The dynamics of change*. London: Routledge, 1998.

Storey, J. *New Perspectives in HRM*. London: Routledge, 1989.

Storey, J. *Human resource: a critical text*. London: Routledge, 1995.

Swinburne, P. The psychological impact of unemployment on managers and professional staff. *Journal of Occupational Psychology*, 1981, *54* (1): 47–64.

Townley, B. *Reframing human resource management*. London: Sage, 1994.

Vroom, V. *Work and motivation*. New York: Wiley, 1964.

Weick, K.E. *Sensemaking in organizations*. London: Sage, 1995.

Williams, A., Woodward, S. and Dobson, P. *Managing change successfully*. London: Thomson Learning, 2002.

Wilson, D.E. *A strategy for change*. London: International Thomson, 1999.

Chapter 2

Thinking about change
Stages, process or continuum

TOPIC HEADINGS

- The types of change
- Organizational Development
- The theoretical underpinnings of change
- Planned interventions and managed change
- Emergent change initiatives and the Learning Organization

INTRODUCTION

At the heart of the Management of Change as a subject is a series of claims about what causes change and what are the solutions for managing it effectively. The claims of those who know what these solutions are can be simply and directly put, but are sometimes more general than they are specific about the definitions on which these claims rely.

In this first section we intend to spend a little time examining some of these claims, allowing a discussion to take us back to the assumptions often made but seldom acknowledged and rarely challenged in popular writers on the subject.

Here is a useful quotation to set our discussion in motion:

Change becomes a constant
Change is the third C. We already know that customers and competition have changed, but so, too, has the nature of change itself. Foremost, change has become both pervasive and persistent. It is normality.

Moreover, the pace of change has accelerated. With globalization of the economy, companies face a greater number of competitors, each one of which may introduce product and service innovations to the market. The rapidity of technological change also promotes innovation. Product life cycles have gone from years to months. Ford produced the Model T for an entire human generation. The life cycle of a computer product introduced today might stretch for two years, but probably won't. A company in the pension business recently developed a service to take advantage of a quirk in the tax laws and interest rates. Its anticipated market life was exactly three months. Coming to this market late by just thirty days would have cut the company's selling time by a third.

(Hammer and Champy, 1995, 23)

The claims made here raise a number of questions:

- What change is referred to in 'the pace of change'?
- What exactly is the 'globalization' referred to?
- What comment might be made about the claims for the Model T Ford?
- How could an anticipated market life be measured as three months?
- How can we link together the different changes referred to?

As we have noted in the previous chapter, claims about change as an increasingly common event in the experience of business life are impossible to quantify in a comparative way. We cannot know what impact change has had during the early periods of industrialization, for example. And yet the drivers of technology and innovation may have been as disruptive then as at any time since.

Globalization is a recent word suggesting that there is a new cohesion in markets worldwide, which may imply that it is likely that change cannot be resisted or that the traditional local markets cannot be sheltered from the impact of such general change. Such claims might seem to have a surface validity. However, it is difficult to identify exactly how this interplay of forces is materially different from influences that have reinforced change in the past.

Initiators in any market may always appear to have an advantage. The Model T Ford is often cited as such a product. However, though its makers may have imagined that it would supply a generation, it was soon overtaken by the alternative supply of vehicles which captured the interest and commitment of buyers, now provided with more choice. The challenge faced by writers explaining the past will always be that what seemed quite uncertain at the time later becomes an assertion of fact. Outcomes of conflict always look certain once victory has been achieved. The reasons for success can then be analysed with assurance that the outcome cannot now be in doubt.

Finally, when we look at the different kinds of change alluded to we seem to be offered a series of different change events from product life cycle to market life change with no clear idea of how these different change events may link with and interact with each other.

DIFFERENT TYPES OF CHANGE

The way we define change depends on what we envisage change to be, how it fits into the model of 'organization' in use and the theoretical foundations from which the model or definition model is derived.

The simplest idea of change is probably the *incremental model*. Here, the shift is a change in process, perhaps associated with implementing productivity changes. Much that has passed for Total Quality Management during the years of its popularity could be seen within this type of change. In simple terms, there was the way the production process was organized before the change; the plan embodying the new method of production; a period of transition during which new procedures and equipment would be put in place; and the final new procedure reinforced by training and reward which would supersede previous practice and bring about the newly expected yields anticipated by the change in the first place (Burnes, 2000, 254).

Devolving a plan of action for such change underpins many different planned change schemas. They often involve steps which are offered to the prospective manager of change and relate quite well to problem solving schemas, too. It is a way of examining the management steps similar to Fayol's, which we saw in the previous chapter. Collins gives a typical example of such a schematic change model:

1   Develop strategy
2   Confirm top level support
3   Use project management support
    ■ Identify tasks
    ■ Assign responsibilities
    ■ Agree deadlines
    ■ Initiate action
    ■ Monitor
    ■ Act on problems
    ■ Close down
4   Communicate results.

(1998, 83)

It gives the impression of offering control based on predictive steps and conceals possible complexity at the level of identifying tasks. At this point we are presented with the *systemic approach* to change. If there is a system which underwrites any process, then it is possible to proceed in the way suggested. Any system, by definition, is designed in a way that makes it possible to follow a sequence and thereby replicate a result or intervene in the process in a predictive way. If we were changing a wheel on a car the steps would be as follows:

1   Loosen nuts on wheel of car
2   Affix jack to car chassis
3   Raise wheel until tyre is clear of the ground
4   Remove nuts from wheel
5   Remove wheel
6   Fit spare wheel to car
7   Tighten nuts to wheel
8   Lower jack and remove
9   Make final tightening adjustment to wheel nuts.

Collins deals with this type of change under the heading of 'under-socialized models of change'. Examples given are often mechanical and have been designed in a particular sequence. Those who know the sequence can solve any problem arising and they will do so by following the steps designed into the system.

A second type of change is referred to by some authors as *punctuated equilibrium*. It is associated with the work of Miller and Friesen (1984), Tushman and Romanelli (1985) and Gersick (1991). It is suggested that the idea of revolutionary or fundamental change is characteristic of the type of change. Its proponents see a similarity between the claims of evolutionary change in the natural sciences to the same kind of change process in organizations. The problem that we have with this descriptor is finding examples that will distinguish it from the previously discussed incremental change. Equilibrium as a word suggests that there is a steady state which is somehow disturbed – hence the punctuation leading to a new and different state of equilibrium following the change intervention. A simple example might be an aircraft in flight, which is acted upon by the four forces of flight that hold an aircraft steady in straight and level flight (see Figure 2.1).

Intervention on the controls by the pilot disturbs the equilibrium; the plane climbs or descends until the desired flight level is reached. The controls are set to normal and the plane resumes straight and level flight at a different altitude.

Another example might be the demand/supply curve. In position A the two curves intersect at one point indicating a price of x for the product. If supply falls then the curve moves to the left and settles at a point to the left of the demand curve, thus indicating a different price of y (see Figure 2.2).

This kind of change in each example suggests that there are predictive dynamics attached to the movement of the forces depicted in the diagrams. It also suggests that the interventions are regular and we can gauge what the likely outcomes will be from whatever inputs were made. The dynamics of each model are, therefore, predictive so that the interventions to be made can be learned.

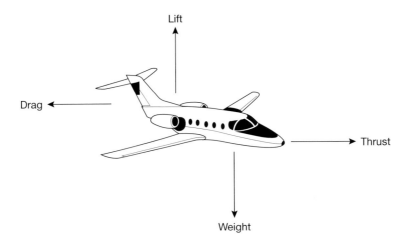

Figure 2.1 *Forces affecting flight*

So, in the example of the plane, a non-flier faced with a suddenly unconscious pilot could conceivably manoeuvre the controls in turn to discover how each intervention affects the flight. With the information derived from discovering the system designed into the controls, he or she could, in theory, land the plane (given direction from Air Traffic Control).

The structural argument that we referred to in the previous chapter would find itself attracted to the systemic view of organization and change. Those elements that are testable, measurable and concrete will always lend themselves to a predictive assessment of how to control and manage change. *Organizational Development* (OD) as a discipline would describe itself in such terms. Indeed the following is a typical example:

> Organizational development involves the long-term, system-wide application of behav-ioural science techniques to increase organization effectiveness. OD works on the idea that organization change involves improving the way people work in teams and the way team activities are integrated with organizational goals.
>
> OD is a continuing process of organization improvement usually involving a sequence of steps, or stages. The eight stages presented here are typical of most OD programs, but they are not always exactly followed, since a change program is an unpredictable and turbulent thing. The stages may not occur in the sequence described or some of the stages may occur simultaneously, but they can be regarded as an ideal or a typical model rather than as the actual representation of every OD program. The objective of OD is a payoff in increased adaptability and productivity.
>
> (Harvey and Brown, 1992, 81 from *An experiential approach to organizational development*, 4th edn. With kind permission of Pearson Education)

The idea of structure emerges in the first paragraph here. Organizational objectives devolving into departmental goals and then finally embodied in individual key tasks has about it a predictiveness that assumes hierarchy and a systematic world governed by targeted work for individuals who contribute to departmental targets. These departments work together to support the organizational objectives (Drucker, 1992, 94).

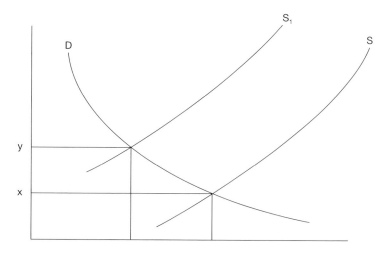

Figure 2.2 *Demand/supply curves*

Interestingly, the eight steps are similar to the stages we examined above, though in this case the author alerts us to the variable nature of their occurrence. They are not quite as predictable as the steps involved in changing the car wheel, though the reasons for this are not discussed at this point in the book.

A third category for describing change is contained in the *continuous transformation* model of change. This gets closer to the anecdotal style of popular claims that change is a series of challenges to established order and a constant in the business environment that characterizes modern global industries. We will be looking more closely at the claims of authors who define the new competencies required to sustain this vision of individuals who are functionally flexible and organizations which support constant learning on the job to transform work to meet evolving targets over a long-cycle working life. Some authors refer to this phenomenon as 'an improvisational model for managing change' (Jick and Peiperl, 2003, 14). The authors explain it as follows:

> The model rests on two major assumptions that differentiate it from traditional models of change: First, the changes associated with technology implementations constitute an on-going process rather than an event with an end-point after which the organization can expect to return to a reasonably steady state. Second, all the technological and organizational changes made during the on-going process cannot, by definition, be anticipated ahead of time.
>
> Given these assumptions, our improvisational change model recognises three different types of change: anticipated, emergent and opportunity based. The three types of change build on each other iteratively over time. While there is no predefined sequence in which the different types of change occur, the deployment of new technology often entails an initial anticipated organizational change associated with the installation of new hardware and software. Over time, however, use of the new technology will typically involve a series of opportunity-based, emergent and further anticipated changes, the order of which cannot be determined in advance because changes interact with each other in response to outcomes, events and conditions arising through experimentation and use.
>
> (Jick and Peiperl, *Managing change: cases and concepts*, 2003, 15.
> Reprinted with permission of The McGraw-Hill Companies)

The first paragraph here agrees with those who see change now as continuous, presumably because the technology which drives change shows no signs of abating – rather the reverse, in fact. But the second paragraph seems to suggest that the effect of this implementation of new technology is not certain in its consequences. As such we cannot predict the outcomes and therefore the management and control are not as predictable as the previous mechanistic models of incremental and punctuated change seemed to suggest.

THEORETICAL UNDERPINNINGS OF CHANGE

We have already noted that Change Management as a discipline draws on three different theoretical bases: first, we are dealing with individuals and therefore the perceptions that they have must form a significant foundation of any attempt to manage change. We will see, in subsequent chapters, how difficult it is to assume that imposed change will be predictable in terms of the responses of individuals affected. The ways in which individuals interpret their experiences depend on the expectancies they hold and, as we shall see, the ways in which these expectancies are affected by imposed change may radically alter perception and future expectancies as well.

Two approaches to the individual aspect of change are often mentioned: Behaviourism and Gestalt-Field psychology (Burnes, 2000, 258). In general terms we could say that behaviourists have a functional view of human behaviour. In this view individuals are thought to be conditioned to behave according to the training that they have received or assumptions they internalized in early social conditioning. So, to implement change means reconditioning these assumptions or schemas, as they are sometimes referred to (Schanck and Abelson, 1977). This view of individual behaviour would be similar to the functionalist view of organizations in which external interventions are the primary means of effecting change. In this view, the individual is conceived of as a compliant body awaiting external stimulus in order to make change possible (Skinner, 1974).

The alternative view is based on the belief that behaviour is not just a function of the external stimuli or the environment of the individual but depends on his or her responses to that external influence and on the way that it is interpreted, for from this arise the judgements made about values and outcomes. What is valued, then, is a function of the basic assumptions held and the way in which these taken-for-granted beliefs have been acquired and modified over time by a combination of conscious and unconscious assimilation. At this point we are closer to the interpretist paradigm, and the actor side of the structure–actor debate, which we discussed in the previous chapter. For proponents of this viewpoint, the question of managing change becomes an immediate source of uncertainty and concern. How will individuals respond to the change stimulus? The more individuals become the focus of the change, the more disparate, it might be thought, would be the individual responses. In motivational theory the research conducted on responses to external stimuli are referred to as extrinsic, and individual responses as intrinsic, factors of motivation. Much of the research into these factors forms the basis of the psychological literature, which is sometimes drawn on to explain the possible effects on individual responses.

But, as soon as we begin to think of people at work, then we need to embark on a journey, which extends beyond personal perceptions and how they are derived and sustained into the social world of interaction and negotiation brokered between individuals. Some contributors refer to this in terms of personal and corporate constructs (Balnaves and Caputi, 1993). Corporate constructs are considered more dependent on the peer group for the perceptions derived. This area of research is sometimes referred to as Group Dynamics and has exercised a significant influence on the way managers think about their work with groups. When we come to look at individual contributions to facilitating change through group work, then the name of Lewin (1947) features prominently. Inherent in his work was the assumption that, just as groups have probably had a significant influence on the way values and beliefs are reinforced in early work experience by the peer group, so they will be more readily modified through the influence of the working group itself. We will examine the content of his contribution in more detail on the n-step approach to change. Suffice it to say here that Lewin made the group the primary vehicle of achieving individual change of attitude and the assimilation of required beliefs about prospective changes at work.

33

Managers are well used to the concepts of working in teams, managing teams and the critical nature of teamwork for achieving competitive success and much popular management literature asserts that belief, sometimes quite uncritically (Hamel and Prahaled, 1994). However, analysis of what is written on teams and their management relies on the roles played by individual members and the interaction that may occur when different groups containing those different role players work together (Belbin, 1980). There is logic in the belief that flexibility of roles is essential for successful teamwork (Allen and Van der Vliert, 1984), but there is less certainty about how such dynamics work during enforced change at work. Often the interventions most favoured are those of training and development. Here is an excerpt from one such example:

> Management were treated like clerks, being conditioned to handle systems, procedures, stock and property. People were to be manipulated and disciplined. Creativity and initiative had neither been expected nor rewarded. The survey results indicated a heartfelt cry from all staff to return pride and confidence in working for Woolworths. Fundamental perceptions had to be changed about what it meant to manage people. The behaviour of a great many people had to be modified.
>
> To get action the top management decided to send a signal across the company: management means doing things right, leadership means doing the right things. All 1,200 managers were to be given training spread over three years. The first year would emphasise leadership and the team; the second leadership and the customer and the third leadership and the business. The aim was to revitalise leadership skills, sharpen awareness of customers and improve managers' perceptions of the whole business, not just their own part in it.
>
> (Leigh and Walters, 1998, 111)

There is here an assumption that managers' attitudes affect team performance and that training may improve the competence with which managers embark on these perceived important relationships. But, there is no guarantee that the training would achieve the changes thought to be necessary by the writer. The question remains: are we trying to change the key leaders' behaviour or will Lewin's approach bring about change within the group itself? What we see here may be an improvement on the functional approach of behaviour modification. However, it does not give any clear hope that change can be brokered more easily through the group or their putative leaders.

This brings us to a third approach to change: the Open Systems school. Here, the focus of the management of change is the organization and its context. The theory considers the organization as being made up of various subsystems, which relate to different elements and functions within the business. However, as the title suggests, its proponents accept that other influencing factors lie outside the organization. This move away from the organization as closed model to the organization as open, whilst seeming a realistic step in acknowledging that individuals have a life outside of work, is a move away from change as a manageable process. Perceptions based on life outside work may well be equally influential on individuals' attitudes to their work and present the manager of change with a challenge: how can you manage things over which you have no direct control? Further, the headings given to the subsystems involved may themselves be difficult to accept uncritically. An early proponent of subsystems lays them out as follows:

The organizational goals and values subsystems
The technical subsystem
The psychosocial subsystem
The managerial subsystem.

(Miller, 1967)

From the point of view of analysis, it may well be that an observer or researcher finds it convenient to define subsystems in this way. The headings may well coincide with distinct and definable procedures or processes, which are predictive and mechanical in the way they operate. However, for the individual worker and manager such subsystems may be part of a seamless experience, which is assimilated subconsciously and not viewed as the discrete elements featured in the list. Only the outside observer seeking to make sense of a complex reality uses them to interpret the significance of what is going on within the organization. Finally, it could be said that the subsystem way of thinking risks seeing the organization as mechanically as did the tradition of structural functionalism. As we will see later in the book, the significance of organizational symbols and their manipulation by managers derives from a literature whose roots lie in social anthropology (Mead, 1934). The ideas derived from the study of tribes and the concepts and the rationalities that hold them together has been a rich source of ideas for explaining culture and its formation in organizations (Hofstede, 1980, 1991). It is less clear how the interpretation of such symbols can be managed in any planned or predictive way as part of the management of change.

It will be useful at this point to reflect that, throughout the literature underwriting the management of change, the three disciplines of psychology, sociology and social anthropology sit uneasily together. Definitions derived from one discipline sometimes sit uneasily with claims made uncritically in another research context. Throughout our work we will attempt to identify just where contributions derive their theoretical validity and how far they are applicable in a contributions that fail to clarify the basis of their underpinning theoretical assumptions.

PLANNED INTERVENTIONS AND THE MANAGEMENT OF CHANGE

We have already referred to the tradition of interventional change in organizations described as Organizational Development. It is a movement which approaches the management of change with a series of tools and techniques, whose application can be viewed as a replicable, reliable means of effecting such change. Its definitions are sometimes stated simply and directly. Here is one example:

Planned organizational change is a deliberate attempt to modify the functioning of the total organization or one of its major parts in order to bring about improved effectiveness. The persons attempting to bring about this change will be referred to as

35

consultants and the organization being changed will be referred to as the client system. Planned change efforts can focus on individual, group, or organization behaviour.

(Harvey and Brown, 1992, 57 from *An experiential approach to organizational development*, 4th edn. Reprinted with kind permission of Pearson Education)

It would be fair to point out that the agenda that underwrites change interventions is often very instrumental: those who promote it expect an improvement in effectiveness that is often assumed to be commensurate with the more efficient achievement of the organization's objectives. This is not necessarily a repeat of the rationale behind the Hawthorne experiments in which the ease of the individual workers was thought to lead to their improving productivity. This definition places the organizational objectives as the primary gauge of success, howsoever achieved. Further, for ease of identification, the people on whom these interventions will be exercised are yet another system – a client system. We are not offered any reason why this corporate concept is used of individuals or groups of people comprising the body in which change is sought.

However, often the assumptions underpinning the practice of such managed interventions suggests the willing involvement of these clients in some way:

empowering employees to act

creating openness in communications

facilitating ownership of the change process and its outcomes

the promotion of a culture of collaboration

the promotion of continuous learning.

(Hurley *et al.*, 1992)

The underlying assumption of this list seems to rest on assimilation by individuals whose involvement is required to make the change successful. As with so much of the optimistic and positive literature, the feasibility of these objectives is not questioned. Such descriptors as 'the culture of collaboration' and 'continuous learning' lie unchallenged at the heart of such assertions. In both cases, as we shall see, there is much to be discussed about the feasibility of approaching these objectives as if they are a unitary task. What we shall see suggests that such challenges, though they may be undertaken within an organizational context, will necessarily involve different working groups with different functions whose members are equally diverse in their responses to change.

Interestingly, if we examine the claims of Kurt Lewin's work, we are confronted with what seems like a group-based initiative. Sensitivity or T-groups encourage members to be frank about their beliefs and taken-for-granted assumptions. In one sense we could argue here that an attempt is being made for emergent change in that the facilitators of such a programme can have no firm idea of what exactly will be divulged. They must, therefore, respond to the contributions of the group. In fairness the messages may be mixed. Not all working experience is positive and most people given a chance to unburden themselves freely may be only too pleased of an opportunity to divest themselves of views, which are as likely to be negative as they are positive. This first stage of Lewin's three steps is called 'unfreezing' and fits well with the idea of individuals divulging their beliefs about themselves, their jobs, their work and the organization.

Lewin's force field analysis has about it a logic that is compelling: it may well be that there are as many forces in favour of change as there are against it. The purpose of the facilitators, therefore, is to identify where such forces lie in the perceptions of the individuals who join the groups. The messages will be both positive and negative and, as more groups are worked with, the same messages may be heard from different individuals. A similar process takes place in any sales cycle when the negotiator probes during the initial stages to discover what the prospect's needs are and what are their expected standards for future engagement. In the latter example, at the end of this questioning phase the negotiator needs to make a decision: can the need be satisfied, can the expected standards be met? If not, the negotiation does not continue and the negotiator withdraws. However, in the case of Lewin's change process, there is no suggestion that facilitators withdraw should they find the opinion of participant workers inimical to all idea of change.

THE ENDURING PROBLEM OF RESISTANCE

The problem of resistance, therefore, lies at the heart of most change programmes, but it is especially critical where planned or imposed change is envisaged. After the open phase of consultation, this places the burden of proving the benefits arising from the change very firmly on the shoulders of the change agents. So far, there is no guarantee that participants in the groups will believe such assurances. Indeed, the second stage described as 'moving' is vague about what the facilitators do to overcome resistance. Most individuals prefer working life to proceed according to accustomed norms. Changing the norms brings disruption, to say the least, and there is no guarantee that the vision of the future will find favour with those on whom it is to be imposed.

When we get to the third stage of Lewin's steps we encounter the word 'refreezing to the new level'. We should consider what exactly is involved in this refreezing process. As we will see later in the book, the term 'reframing' is frequently used of this and other transition management programmes. It returns us to the theories surrounding learning and how individuals derive their beliefs and patterns of behaviour during initial socialization. If these behaviours and beliefs are to be changed, then the question of intervention at the individual/group level becomes important. In other words the traditional descriptor of 'the way we do things round here' has to be changed (Deal and Kennedy, 1982), and most often training seems the most direct intervention.

One famous example often quoted was the transformation of British Airways from publicly owned megalith into privately owned lean and risk-averse, entrepreneurial, customer-focused miracle. The stories of how this transformation took place are often repeated by those who were closely involved (Georgiades, 1990). The programme for all employees was called Putting People First and was conducted by an outside consultant with the frequent attendance of Colin Marshall, the then Chief Executive. A participant describes the feelings evinced by this experience:

> There was a match between the message and the delivery. You can't get away with saying putting people first is important, if in the process of delivering the message you don't put people first. Employees were sent personal invitations, thousands were flown

in from around the world and a strong effort was made to prepare tasteful meals and treat everyone with respect. Grade differences became irrelevant during PPF, as managers and staff members were treated equally and interacted freely. Moreover, a senior director came to conclude every single PPF session with a question-and-answer session. Colin Marshall himself frequently attended these closing sessions, answering employee concerns in a manner most thought to be extraordinarily frank.

(Jick and Peiperl, 2003, 33)

However, the attitudinal sessions were complemented by training sessions:

About the time PPF concluded in 1985, BA launched a program for managers only, called, appropriately, Managing People First (MPF). A five-day residential program for 25 managers at a time, MPF stressed the importance of, among other topics, trust, leadership, vision and feedback.

(Jick and Peiperl, 2003, 33)

The problem with any planned change will always be that it has been planned and therefore managers who have initiated the change largely define the expected outcomes beforehand. Consultants are often engaged to facilitate change and such change, again, will have preset objectives, often focusing not just on long-term objectives but the short-term behaviours as well. Top-down change raises two critical questions for the individuals on whom it is visited: 'can I do this?' and 'do I want to do this?' There is, therefore, an underlying issue of competence and commitment – does the individual have the aptitude to undertake the newly prescribed and expected behaviours? Does the individual feel committed to the change and comfortable with the new way of doing things? More importantly, for those evaluating the success of the programme, will individuals divulge such concerns at the time of the change programme or is their need for employment more critical than the risk of voicing opposition?

As we shall see when we come to look at the n-step approaches to change, they have about them a predictive quality that commend them to those managers and consultants who want to implement change in a planned way. Collins summarizes the common characteristics of such programmatic approaches as:

A rational analysis of organizational change
A sequential approach to the planning and management of change
A generally up-beat and prescriptive tone.

(1998, 84)

This analytical approach to change (see Figure 2.3) assumes a set of factors and then seeks to assess the evidence for the factors themselves. All these approaches work from an assumption of change as a movement from State A to State C via transition State B. State A is often considered as a steady state, followed by State B, the transition stage of change, followed finally by State C, the steady state resuming at the new 'level'. It is not difficult to see the similarity between this idea of change and the earlier models we were offered of

Case Analysis Form

Name ....

I.   Problems
    A. Macro
       1. ....
       2. ....
    B. Micro
       1. ....
       2. ....

II. Causes
       1. ....
       2. ....
       3. ....

III. Systems Affected
       1. Structural ....
       2. Psychological ....
       3. Technical ....
       4. Managerial ....
       5. Goals ....

IV. Alternatives
       1. ....
       2. ....
       3. ....
       4. ....
       5. ....

V.   Recommendations
       1. ....
       2. ....
       3. ....

Figure 2.3 *Example of a Case Analysis Form*
Source: Harvey and Brown (1992, 1994)

both incremental and punctuated equilibrium changes. A prior state is replaced by a subsequent state and the intermediate period of flux needs to be managed in a proactive way.

But not all change is as identifiable in its stages as these models seem to suggest. Some changes are more gradual and it is therefore more difficult for the observer or researcher to see exactly when a transition has been made. The change from childhood to adolescence is a case in point: at which point is the individual going through this kind of organic change a child and when exactly is he or she an adolescent? We could take some physiological indicators as a gauge of this transition. However, experience suggests that these are only one set of indicators. The change between adolescence and adulthood is even more fraught with difficulty. When exactly does adulthood take effect for the individual? Again, there may be physiological indicators, or psychological indicators, and these can be set and measured by an outside observer. What of the internal experience of those undergoing the transition? Some individuals find the transition between the three stages a very stressful time, others take it in their stride. For some there is, say, a definite change in the register of the voice, which makes singing impossible while the transition is going on. For others the transition is a gradual and uninterrupted process during which singing is possible throughout with just a gradual drop in the register of the voice.

But throughout this change, howsoever conceived or conceptualized, there lies the ever-likely possibility that resistance will rear its head. Individuals and groups do not have to concede compliance. The human being is capable of complying in terms of behaviours while withholding commitment long term. As we shall see in the following chapters, there are two different approaches to the basis of resistance: for those who espouse the belief that the employer–employee relationship is inherently exploitative, then resistance is an expected outcome of imposed change at work. However, there are others who will accept resistance as a concomitant of change, but suggest that this is a temporary aberration which can be managed (Nadler, 1993).

This example of organic growth stages relates better to the third type of change that we referred to: continuous change. It also relates to the second type of organizational change referred to: emergent change. It is to this type of change that we will now turn.

EMERGENT CHANGE AND THE MANAGEMENT OF CHANGE

Our previous paragraph has drawn attention to the need for a different approach to change, which allows for difference and acknowledges that organisms respond to stimuli in their environment and therefore are affected by forces over which they have no control. Such factors are like any other stimuli: they are arbitrary and often unavoidable and mostly the organism can only react to them.

When human beings are the subjects of such outside intervention, then their interpretive faculty comes into play and they will impute meaning to what they experience according to their expectancies. This in turn may challenge their basic assumptions or taken-for-granted beliefs about jobs, work, managers, career, organization and other significant factors and affect the way they evaluate their experience of change (Schein, 1985). The literature on culture will place us once again, as we shall see, in that interface between the personal and corporate that we referred to earlier. Some proponents of the management of culture would have us believe that this is just another element in the pattern of factors to be managed during change. However, when we ask how basic assumptions are acquired, we may be looking at a less predictable path than some writers on change would suggest.

If basic assumptions are internalized beliefs, then at some point they have been derived from a world around about. As individuals we gain our ability to speak by learned categories (Greene, 1986). We must then use those categories to communicate and if necessary modify what we seek to change in the world about us. But, individuals belong to many communities: family, tribal, institutional and work. The open approach to organizations allows us to accept that this phenomenon of people working together to achieve common goals may be dependent on coordinated efforts and unitary commitment, but still allows individual perception and interpretation of whatever activity is involved. For those who accepted the open model of organization, the planned approach to change attracted increasing questioning throughout the years when top-down change programmes became increasingly popular. Researchers began to express increasing doubt about the ability of planned change schemas to take account of human complexity during enforced change at work (Wilson, 1992; Dawson, 1994).

One name in particular is associated with this movement to take into account the environment or context within which change takes place and that is Andrew Pettigrew. For Pettigrew the emphasis should be on:

> The interconnectedness of change over time.
> How the context of change shapes and is shaped by action.
> The multi-causal and non-linear nature of change.

> (Pettigrew, 1990)

The first point he makes is fundamental to continuous change: the perception of time itself is subjective. Perceptions of time lie with the individual and, the longer the memory, the more likely that different perceptions are employed to interpret an experience. Indeed, this long-term group memory is sometimes used to indicate the likely basis of corporately held beliefs. There are those who suggest that historical threats to the organization or group are likely to be part of what is taught to joining members and so form part of organizational culture (Schein, 1990). Examples of such taught behaviour predominate, for example, in environments where worker associations or unions seek to defend their own interpretation of work experience (Gall, 2003).

So, returning to the porous or open boundary approach to organization we can observe that individuals are as likely to be influenced from outside the organization as they are by experience from within. Human beings experience modification of their basic assumptions from the experience of diverse influences and they in turn will seek to influence others both within and outside the organization. Such a nexus of relationships would be difficult to control or manage in a way that would guarantee consensus of meaning or values.

Finally, Pettigrew alerts us to the multi-faceted nature of change influencers and the complexity of their interchange, which makes it difficult for the researcher to assert with confidence that a single set of causes can influence one or more effects. Most individuals will recognize, for example, that, however skilful the persuader may be, the object of his or her efforts may be quite amenable or could be unyielding. Motivational levels are not determined and could well be dependent on comparative factors (Genus, 1998). For some writers this complexity merely drives the prospective manager of change into employing as many expertises as are required (Clarke, 1994). Knowledge of inside complexity is a prerequisite, suggesting that it may be difficult for outsiders to venture in unaided (McCalman and Paton, 1992).

41

The idea of the organization as having porous boundaries allows us to be more realistic in assessing the influences that affect growth, change and development. Particularly where industrial sectors are concerned, comparison between competitors can be a potent driver for awareness of trends and tendencies in, say, customer demand and the initial responses that may engender. Reading accounts of this approach to change seems much more comprehensive in its inclusion of context and content:

> The model depicted in the preceding chapters arises from studying firms in four sectors of the UK economy, namely: automobile manufacture, book publishing, merchant banking and life assurance. The result of that investigation has been the identification of a pattern of activity which arises from observable differences in the way higher performing firms, in given periods, managed change from their lower performing counterparts. The higher and lesser performing firms contrasted sharply in the way they: assessed their environment, led change, linked strategic and operational change, managed their human resources and the degree to which they achieved coherence in the management of the change process.
>
> (Pettigrew and Whipp, 1991)

There is a readily expressed awareness of the significance of context and the connection it must have with the content of the organization. The corporate expression of that in the above summary, however, alerts us to the danger of what some writers speak of as reification or personification (Hyman, 1975; Collins, 1998, 151). It may seem pedantic to point out that firms have no brain and therefore cannot make the kind of decisions implied in the quotation. In reality we have a fragmented focus of different managers and groups of managers who make assessments and then follow through in strategic decision-making (Coopey and Hartley, 1991). This then leads us to the transformational manager or leader whose vision inspires others in the organization to see things differently and then to behave differently to effect the required change.

One such example from the early 1980s is the Jaguar Car Company, which was taken out of the British Motor Corporation and led by John Egan. His experience of turning the company round is well recorded. The then new-to-the-company practice of Quality Circles was implemented in a series of programmes similar to the example of British Airways that we saw above:

> Management leadership is seen as vital. As one senior manager said, 'Categorically it is our key people issue in 1987 to 1988.' As part of this, extra recruitment of foremen was under way in order to take the ratio from the then 1:35 to 1:22. All new foremen were sent on a full-time, off-the-job training programme for six months. And a shorter version was designed for the existing stock of supervisors: 'The emphasis will be to change them from being progress-changers into fully-fledged managers accountable for budgets and even for training and developing their own employees.' (Manufacturing Manager, Jaguar)
>
> (Storey, 1992, 60)

Once again the programme included training and the emphasis was on changing supervisor behaviour – imposing management tasks like budgeting and training their staff. Interestingly, both here and in other brownfield sites the success in imposing Quality Circles was less than 100 per cent and in some cases 45 per cent failed to adapt to the new ways of working. In the case of a greenfield site, however, Nissan was able to achieve total success from the outset (Wickens, 1987), reinforcing the belief that individual competence and commitment is a prerequisite to success in the management of change.

We could well identify such management of change as being focused outside-in: the competition challenges the survival of custom and practice in manufacturing and the response leads to an assessment of current systems and people and their need to increase knowledge, enhance skills and consolidate the experience needed to support the new way of improving productivity to achieve new targets. Pettigrew admits that the process may not be as rational as some summaries suggest:

> Competition and the management of strategic change do not emerge therefore as an entirely rational process. On the contrary, the ability of an enterprise to compete relies heavily on: first the capacity of the firm to identify and understand the competitive forces involved; and second, the competence of the business to mobilise and manage the resources necessary for the chosen competitive response through time.
>
> (Pettigrew and Whipp, 1991)

All that we have seen so far should remind us of the points that were made earlier: the aptitude of an historical workforce. The success of continuous change therefore rests on the ability of individuals to embrace new ways of doing things at the core competencies of their jobs and possibly extra duties relating to more managerial responsibilities as described in the excerpt on Jaguar. It also depends on the willingness of individuals to accept that challenge and willingly embark on the training programmes designed to provide the means of filling the gap between what is current practice and what is the desired goal of senior managers for other staff to accomplish. This willingness lies at the heart of the second part of our title 'changing managers'.

EMERGENT CHANGE AND CHANGING MANAGERS

What individuals feel about proposed change becomes more prominent in the investigation of the content of emergent change. During the 1980s engaging hearts and minds was deliberately embarked upon in several well-known initiatives. Some commentators see these as an attempt to include individual commitment in the aim of activities which take place as the background to change. Others regard them as integral to everyday practice for enlightened managers in modern industrial practice. Early on came the Employee Involvement initiative, which gave General Electric prominence under a proactive CEO, Jack Welsh (Pascale and Athos, 1982). Getting individuals to take ownership of company processes as if they were their own was seen as one way of gaining commitment to company targets. Strategic integration became essential to the employer who wanted individual workers to know not just how, but why he or she was being asked to do things differently as well (Marchington and Parker, 1990, 282ff.). The new practice of shared communication was not just downward, but upward, too. Those who know 'what works round here' could much better address problem-solving and consequent change at the work face.

43

It would be fair to say that this movement was preceded by a number of years of work in the Human Relations school, in which worker involvement in solving problems or serious threats to work enabled workers to apply their minds jointly to feasible options for the future. The long-wall coal-mining method has gone down in the annals of good personnel practice as the one sure way of getting those on the ground to take responsibility for what would previously have been a management decision, often involving closure (Trist and Bamford, 1968; Revans, 1980). Another initiative to involve individuals in attempts at redesigning their jobs was Task Participation, along with consultation and representative participation (Marchington and Parker, 1990, 284). Here the emphasis is on the competence and experience which alone enable the practitioners to assess what sort of change will be feasible and practicable.

Hand in hand with this went the attempt to influence and involve workers by perhaps using some form of share option or profit-related pay. Privatization programmes sometimes offered a prime opportunity for managers to gain more commitment by linking effort to reward in a way that might seem to offer a link between productivity and the deferred reward of longer-term investment for workers (Pendleton and Winterton, 1993; Wilkinson, 1995). However, the results were not always as clear-cut as proponents suggested they would be, as workers discovered that their efforts were not always related to the performance of share prices – market factors outside their control could sometimes be a more critical factor in how much reward was yielded (Dunn *et al.*, 1991; Fletcher, 1993).

At the heart of change brought about by management intervention there lies the question of whether individuals want to embark on a newly imposed way of working or not. Training focuses on behaviours and the underpinning knowledge required to support it. However, training may not by itself change underlying attitudes. A good example will be customer care initiatives. There has been a series of attempts to rationalize the way phones are answered in some organizations. The gauge of whether training has been done successfully is often demonstrated by the same format delivered by all staff members answering the telephone: 'Hello, this is _____ at ABC; how can I help you?' Similar training initiatives sometimes characterize the passengers as they board or leave an aircraft. A smile and greeting is pitched at all individuals passing the member of staff on duty at the door as passengers (customers) enter or leave.

In general customers can usually tell whether the greeting is genuine or not. But, for managers enforcing a new set of behaviours towards customers, testing whether the message was genuine or not is almost impossible. One of the early attempts to challenge the optimistic assertions of Human Resource Management contained a chapter addressing precisely this subject:

> The majority of staff interviewed by the author, especially the front-line staff in direct contact with the customers, are unhappy about being told to put a smile on for customers. They claim that they are sometimes reprimanded by their supervisors for not smiling, a point which one supervisor's comments confirm: 'We are able detect when a check-out operator is not smiling or even when she is putting on a false smile. We call her into a room and have a chat with her.' This task is not always easy, especially when customers have problems, which cannot be appeased with a smile. As one store manager

explained: 'They (the operators) are told to smile all the time and if the customer has a particular problem then they should try and get them through the check-out and contact a supervisor or a manager to deal with it.' One check-out operator indicated that she had got the message: 'We are given customer care training when we join the company and as an on-going thing. We are told to smile all the time and the customer is always right.' Nonetheless, responses for the majority of operators interviewed suggest that their job is becoming more difficult because the attempt to increase the level of service offered by the store is directly associated with the increase in the number of difficult customers they have to deal with.

(Ogbonna, 1992)

This change of attitude is necessarily difficult for those who are not disposed to demonstrate the required displays of behaviour or initiate forced performances with customers or colleagues. Attempts to transform office staff into call-centre operators or sales executives necessarily run the risk of meeting an aptitude barrier, which individuals may be unable or unwilling to overcome.

Professional staff are expected to assimilate an identity which reinforces knowledge of the subject, decisiveness and adherence to the conventions governing their relations with clients or colleagues. For them, therefore, change into different behaviours may be equally uncongenial. Some authors refer to these expected behaviours as archetypes and have charted the effect of required change on such professionals as engineers in the public sector who are required to adopt and adapt to a more entrepreneurial management style:

The move to job redesign deepened the scope and significance of (this) challenge to professional autonomy. . . . Professional engineering skill is being turned into a rule-based technique. This is like the AA experience . . . where the recovery man comes and basically has a check-list. Is the battery faulty? Is it the spark-plugs? If there is a real problem he loads the car up and takes it away. We can deskill what was done by clever people.

(Carter and Mueller, 2002, 1342)

One popular movement that might seem to address this question of emergence is the Learning Organization (Senge, 1990). The realism of learning as a proactive response to change became an important part of the optimistic assertions of some management change experts. The assumption lying behind this made sense from one point of view, at least: that, during the stage of transition, everybody has a positive opportunity to reassess what they know about themselves and their work and respond to new skills and, perhaps, rewards. As we shall see when we look at stepped approaches to change, there are some who would see the initial resistance to change as an opportunity for support, as threat to status, control and knowledge of the old job are gradually supported by retraining and re-establishment into the required level of competence and commitment (Nadler, 1993). Proponents of this view see great benefits for individuals caught up in undesired change:

Learning organizations themselves may be a form of leverage on the complex system of human endeavours. Building learning organizations involves developing people who

45

learn to see as systems thinkers see, who develop their own personal mastery, and who learn how to surface and restructure mental models, collaboratively. Given the influence of organizations in today's world, this may be one of the most powerful steps toward helping us 'rewrite the code' altering not just what we think but our predominant ways of thinking. In this sense, learning organizations may be a tool not just for the evolution of organizations, but for the evolution of intelligence.

(Senge, 1990, 367)

We may question how far reframing, if that is what is being referred to, can extend from individual to group and then into the organization itself. We might accept that this is possible if we reformulate policies, procedures and plans in the new way, and promulgate and reinforce them for old and new members of staff alike. We may accept that this process would be better if accepted by the working group and entered into fully, as examples above imply can happen. However, experience would suggest that even those involved will move on or leave and then the re-educative process will need to begin all over again. A new formulation of competencies becomes eventually the old way of doing things. Individuals may have found the change experience stimulating and may have responded in a way that reveals new ways of thinking as suggested. But the claim that this constitutes a Learning Organization would be difficult to substantiate. What people learn at work belongs to them as individuals; however, whether this is transferred to the working group is harder to identify. The literature on tacit knowledge suggests that this is not always shared with others. Furthermore, for some workers there might be a benefit in not divulging such knowledge to other members of staff, still less members of management (McKinlay, 2002; Proctor and Mueller, 2000). Indeed, for some writers the new way of working can become the means of establishing the same hegemony of work using different parameters of control (Taylor and Bain, 2003).

Some writers seem confident that this new world of change can be an opportunity to involve individual workers in a constant reassessment of what is needed to re-establish efficiency and effectiveness in response to outside competitive threat:

Management in organizations today is largely people management. If people are the important asset, effectiveness is related to:

- how managers perceive the individual
- how people relate to one another
- how we get maximum contribution
- how we go about changing from a situation which is seen to be ineffective to one that ensures high standards of performance.

(Paton and McCalman, 2000, 145)

What seems to lie at the heart of claims made in favour of emergent change is an acceptance that individual perception is central to success. In this regard we have moved significantly from structural functionalism into the interpretive part of Burrell and Morgan's paradigm – the actor side of the structure–actor debate now comes into its own. As we do so we have to allow that individuals interpret their own experience based on their own expectancies, however caused, and such reflexiveness is not open to immediate inspection by others, still less can it be managed. In later chapters we will attempt to examine the ways in which individuals make sense of this sometimes confusing experience of change. We will, however, question how far this learning process can be construed as common learning, group learning, still less organizational learning.

There is one other point that we will make here, which will continue to challenge proponents of emergent change: if the process of acceptance of change is to be the prime purpose of such change, then at what point will change be committed to and implemented? Will it be when a majority of like-minded and accepting individuals have assimilated the need for change and acted upon it? Will it be when the budget for the change programme runs out and there is no other choice but to make an executive decision to proceed without consensus? At what stage will further resistance no longer be tolerated? It would seem that there may come a time when the top-down, imposed model of change would be the only option.

As we shall see, the question of resistance is the crucial one. Its basis may be pragmatic or it may be principle. But the way in which it is overcome will be critical in assuring those involved that the change continues to be bottom-up and emergent rather than a sudden shift into top-down and imposed. Most change experts accept participation in decision-making during change as the desirable management style to adopt. It usually passes over the problem of the turkeys voting for Christmas:

> The danger of the purely learning approach to change is that managers [and others] may actually recognise the need for change, yet still refuse to 'learn' because they understand perfectly well the implication for their power and status. Resistance to change may not be 'stupid' but based on a very shrewd appreciation of the personal consequences.
>
> (McNulty and Whipp, 1994, 130)

DISCUSSION QUESTIONS

Here are some questions you may find useful to consider as the basis for a formulated answer, either in an assignment, essay or examination question. You may like to draw up a framework of main points, which you think would support your answer.

1   Explain what is meant by the term 'planned change'. Discuss the main implications of the planned approach for managers of change.

Our first chapter suggested that essay and examination questions often contain at least one hostage to fortune in either a quotation or a word or phrase offered uncritically. You may want to examine this question for such material.

It seems here that we will need to answer two parts, which run from the definitional first section to the more pragmatic second part. First, the phrase 'planned change' may merit some further detailing in your answer. What sort of change might be considered a 'planned change'? Going back over the chapter and reading some of the references more fully may give you some guidance as to different types of planned change.

In one sense you could say that any sort of change, including emergent change, would have to be planned. It would be difficult to arrange even a brain-storming meeting or a sensitivity group without some pre-planning.

This could lead you on to clarify your answer into 'programmed change'. How far would 'programmed' be a clearer word to qualify the type of change you want to comment on?

Following on from this you might look at what sort of programmes might be envisaged. This could give you an opportunity to examine the types of change we discussed earlier: functional change, or systemic change – changing something simple, like a procedure at work (answering the phone, say) or changing a process from paper-based to computer-based. Then you could look at more complex change in which it will be necessary to get workers involved. Behavioural changes may need a programme of training to support them. Finally you might look at deeper changes in which types of work are changed radically, perhaps over a longer period of time. A current example might be the change from counter work in a bank to call-centre working, for example.

The aspect all three examples have in common would be the assumption that the change is business-driven or that the senior managers have decided that this change shall take place in principle, even if the exact detail of its implementation is left to the workers subject to the change to work out.

This last point could lead you into the second part of your question. If we accept the process of change as similar to solving a problem and making decisions, then the question of involving others now comes to the fore. We have already seen the kind of schema offered as a typical example of such a programme of change (Collins, 1998, 83). What we now need to do is discuss how these steps might themselves include the participants and how this might be managed.

The implications may be similar to the classic steps of management as defined by Fayol (1949). However, the way in which individual members of staff are involved in that becomes the question to be addressed. Implementing a programme can be a function of a directive style of management by managers themselves, once, say, all are agreed on the steps themselves. Alternatively, the style alighted on may be more delegational and therefore involve workers in monitoring and reviewing the implementation for themselves.

What seems to underpin this question is the assumption of the mandatory nature of change whose programme in principle is already determined by significant others, such as senior managers. The discretionary part of the change is the way in which it is implemented. The traditional way of regarding appropriate management style has always depended on the competence and commitment of the participants themselves (McGregor, 1960). Choosing the appropriate way, therefore, would be a function of judgement and assessment of those subject to the change.

A similar question might be:

2   Explain what you understand by the bottom-up approach to change. How would a manager of change ensure that the principles underlying such change were observed in practice?

I think you might adopt a similar approach to this answer as we described in the preceding question. The difficult and taxing part is delineating what the principles of emergent change actually are. If you are stuck you might like to reread Burnes (2000, 294ff.). But be critical about the claims made in some of the recipes offered by the authors quoted. We will look in more detail at such apparently simple suggestions in the chapter on n-step change.

Finally, here is a question which is effectively a combination of the two previously offered:

3   Describe the difference between top-down and bottom-up approaches to the management of change. Use examples to illustrate when each would be more appropriate in effecting organizational change.

The first part of this question should be a simple examination of top-down and bottom-up change and the significance of each in both principle and practice. The second part is more difficult to answer, however. Throughout this chapter we have offered examples of authors who feature accounts of change programmes and their alleged benefits. It will be difficult to ascertain from most accounts how far they were top-down or bottom-up. In actual fact there are often elements of both in any programme of change.

However, the question asks when each would be appropriate and here you might need to clarify your response carefully. In general terms you will want to note, perhaps, that the types of change we noted above may offer the first indication of which type might be most appropriate. However, involvement in any change might be more desirable than straight imposition – even if such involvement requires more time and, therefore, resource.

There is a balance between top-down and bottom-up, which will require careful thought by managers. How far is involvement possible and which stages may be affected by competence and commitment? Once again the style of management may necessarily be affected. But, overall, if learning organization theory is to be believed, then the more involvement of those affected in the elements of change, the more fruitful the experience may be to all concerned. Such involvement could turn a threat or challenge into an opportunity, as the changing perceptions of managing change would indeed be achieved through changing managers. However, the change of perceptions would be self-induced rather than managed by external agents.

REFERENCES AND FURTHER READING

Allen, V. and Van der Vliert, E. *Role transitions: explorations and explanations.* New York: Plenum, 1984.

Balnaves, M. and Caputi, P. Corporate constructs: to what extent are personal constructs personal? *International Journal of Personal Construct Psychology*, 1993: 119–138.

Belbin, M. *Managing teams: why they succeed or fail.* Oxford: Butterworth Heinemann, 1980.

Blyton, P. and Turnbull, P. *Reassessing human resource management.* London: Sage, 1992.

Burnes, B. *Managing change: a strategic approach to organizational dynamics*. London: *Financial Times*/Prentice Hall, 2000.

Carter, C. and Mueller, F. The 'long march' of the management modernizers: ritual, rhetoric and rationality. *Human Relations*, 2002, *55* (11): 1325–1354.

Clarke, K. *The essence of change*. London: Prentice Hall, 1994.

Collins, D. *Organizational change: sociological perspectives*. London and New York: Routledge, 1998.

Coopey, J. and Hartley, J. Reconsidering organizational commitment. *Human Resource Management Journal*, 1991, *1* (3): 18–32.

Dawson, P. *Organizational change: a processual approach*. London: Paul Chapman Publishing, 1994.

Deal, T.E. and Kennedy, A.A. *Corporate cultures: the rights and rituals of corporate life*. Reading, MA: Addison Wesley, 1982.

Drucker, P.F. *Managing for the future*. London: Butterworth-Heinemann, 1992.

Dunn, S., Richardson, R. and Dewe, P. The impact of employee share ownership on worker attitudes: a longitudinal case study. *Human Resource Management Journal*, 1991, *1* (3): 1–17.

Fayol, H. *General and industrial management*, trans. P. Straw. London: Pitman, 1949.

Fletcher, C. *Appraisal*. London: IPM, 1993.

Gall, G. *Union organizing: campaigning for trade union recognition*. London: Routledge, 2003.

Genus, A. *The management of change: perspective and practice*. London: International Thompson, 1998.

Georgiades, N. A strategic future for personnel. *Personnel Management*, 1990 (February).

Gersick, C.J.G. Revolutionary change theories: a multi-level exploration of the punctuated equilibrium paradigm. *Academy of Management Review*, 1991, *16* (1): 10–36.

Greene, J. *Language understanding: a cognitive approach*. Buckingham: Open University Press, 1986.

Hamel, G. and Prahaled, C.K. *Competing for the future*. Boston, MA: Harvard University Press, 1994.

Hammer, M. and Champy, J. *Reengineering the corporation*. London: Nicholas Brealey Publishing, 1995.

Harvey, D.F. and Brown, D.R. *An experiential approach to organization development*. Englewood Cliffs, NJ: Prentice Hall International, 1992.

Hofstede, G. *Culture's consequences*. Beverley Hills, CA: Sage, 1980.

Hofstede, G. *Cultures and organization*. Maidenhead: McGraw Hill, 1991.

Hurley, R.F., Church, A.H., Burke, W.W. and Van Eynde, D.F. Tension, change and values in OD. *OD Practitioner*, 1992, *29*: 1–5.

Hyman, R. *Industrial relations: a Marxist introduction*. London: Macmillan, 1975.

Jick, T.D. and Peiperl, M.A. *Managing change: cases and concepts*. 2nd edn, Boston, MD: McGraw/Irwin, 2003.

Leigh, A. and Walters, M. *Effective change: twenty ways to make it happen*. London: CIPD, 1998.

Lewin, K. Frontiers in group dynamics. *Human Relations*, 1947, *1*: 5–41.

McCalman, J. and Paton, R.A. *Change management: a guide to effective implementation*. London: Paul Chapman Publishing, 1992.

McGregor, D. *Human side of enterprise*. New York: McGraw Hill, 1960.

McKinlay, A. The limits of knowledge. *New Technology, Work and Employment*, 2002 (July), *17* (2): 76–88.

McNulty, T. and Whipp, R. Market-driven change in professional services: problems and processes. *Journal of Management Studies*, 1994, *31* (6):829–845.

Marchington, M. and Parker, P. *Changing patterns of employee relationships*. Hemel Hempstead: Harvester Wheatsheaf, 1990.

Mead, G.H. *Mind, self and society*. Chicago, IL: University of Chicago Press, 1934.

Miller, D. and Friesen, P.H. *Organizations: a quantum view*. Englewood Cliffs, NJ: Prentice Hall, 1984.

Miller, E. *Systems of organization*. London: Tavistock, 1967.

Nadler, D.A. Concepts for the management of strategic choice, in C. Mabey and B. Mayon-White (eds) *Managing change*. London: Open University/Paul Chapman Publishing, 1993.

Ogbonna, G. Organizational culture and human resource management: dilemmas and contradictions, in P. Blyton and P. Turnbull (eds) *Reassessing human resource management*. London: Sage, 1992.

Pascale, R.T. and Athos, A.G. *The art of Japanese management*. Harmondsworth: Penguin, 1982.

Paton, R.A. and McCalman, J. *Change management: a guide to effective implementation*. London: Sage, 2000.

Pendleton, A. and Winterton, J. (eds) *Public enterprise in transition: industrial relations in state and privatized corporations*. London: Routledge, 1993.

Pettigrew, A.M. *Training and HRM in small–medium size enterprizes: a critical review of the literature and a model for further research*. London: HMSO, 1990.

Pettigrew, A.M. and Whipp, R. *Managing change for competitive success*. Oxford: Blackwell, 1991.

Proctor, S. and Mueller, F. *Teamworking*. Basingstoke: Macmillan Business, 2000.

Revans, R.W. *Action learning*. London: Blond & Briggs, 1980.

Schank, R. and Abelson, R. *Scripts, plans and knowledge*. Hillsdale, NJ: Erlbaum, 1977.

Schein, E.H. *Organizational culture and leadership*. San Francisco, CA: Jossey Bass, 1985.

Schein, E.H. Organizational culture. *American Psychologist*, 1990, *45* (2): 109–119.

Senge, P.M. *The fifth discipline: the art and practice of the learning organization*. London: Century Business, 1990.

Skinner, B.F. *About behaviourism*. New York: Knopf, 1974.

Storey, J. *Developments in the arrangement of human resources: an analytical review*. Oxford: Blackwell, 1992.

Taylor, P. and Bain, P. *Call center organizing in adversity, c: campaigning for trade union recognition*. London: Routledge, 2003.

Trist, E.L. and Bamford, K.W. The professional facilitation of planned change in organizations. *Reviews, Abstracts and Working Groups*, 1968: 111–120.

Tushman, M.L. and Romanelli, E. Organizational evolution: a metamorphosis model of convergence and reorientation, in L.L. Cummings and B.M. Staw (eds) *Research on organizational behavior*. Greenwich, CT: JAI Press, 1985, *7*, pp. 171–222.

Wickens, P. *The road to Nissan*. London: Macmillan, 1987.

Wilkinson, A. Re-examining quality management. *Review of Employment Topics*, 1995, *3* (1): 187–211.

Wilson, D.C. *A strategy of change*. London: Routledge, 1992.

Chapter 3

Managing systems
Open or closed?

TOPIC HEADINGS

- Organization as system
- Systems-thinking approach to change
- Managing resistance to change
- Issues arising from change
- Systematic approaches to change

INTRODUCTION

We have looked briefly at the different approaches to the management of change: top-down, imposed change and bottom-up, emergent change. We have looked at some of the examples offered in which different types of change were featured and different claims made about their success. We have also touched on the underlying debates which govern the field of the management of change: how the structure–actor debate has polarized the tendency to see systems or people as the focus of change and how the idea of organization itself can be conceived of as open or closed. The challenge for all students of the management of change is to identify exactly what claims underlie the sometimes general assertions made about the principles and practice of the management of organizational change.

In order to consolidate what we have looked at so far, we will offer some examples of these claims and examine the assumptions, which may or may not be acknowledged by their authors:

> Managers today face risk situations unlike those of the past and in an era of accelerating change, management's degree of excellence results from its ability to cope with these changes. Organizations either become more adaptive, flexible and anticipative, or they become rigid and stagnant, reacting to change after the fact, often when it is too late. Seldom can management decisions be based solely on the extrapolation of historic

experience. Many decisions are unique, innovative and risky, involving new products and new areas of opportunity. Putting a new product or a new process into production is a major business decision.

Because an organization exists in a changing environment, it must have the capacity to adapt. At Sun Microsystems (a fast-growing computer maker) for example, company executives have outlined a bold strategy to lead a revolution in the computer industry by offering industry-wide standards for hardware and software. In response to criticism, Sun CEO, Scott McNealy responds, 'I guess that's what happens when you're trying to change a whole industry.' Because high tech firms are moving faster on the experience curve, the consequences of being slow to respond to change are most severe in that business.

(Harvey and Brown, 1992, 39 from *An experiential approach to organizational development*, 4th edn. Reprinted with kind permission of Pearson Education)

Here are some questions to consider:

1   How supportable is the first sentence by evidence?
2   Can descriptors such as 'anticipative' or 'stagnant' be attributed to organizations?
3   How far could one business change a whole industry?
4   What do you understand by the phrase 'experience curve'?
5   What assumptions may be being made about those who are slow to respond?

As we have seen in the previous chapter, the claims made about organizational change sometimes seamlessly pass over assumptions about managers, workers and the ways in which they work together to achieve successful results.

In the first place, the journalistic claims often found in popular management texts, that change is greater now than it was in the past, are impossible to substantiate. There may be some surface validity to claims that technological change appears to have accelerated in some sectors and that, as in this example, computers are an obvious driver of such increasing change. However, the changes which presaged the Industrial Revolution may well have seemed to come as suddenly and have impacted as significantly on ordinary people in a similarly surprising way. Unfortunately, there is no way of making accurate comparisons. The reason for this will include our inability to assess what individuals find surprising and how they interpret that surprise. So, even in this first question we have cut across the debate on structure versus actor: structures, be they the ways processes are organized or the ways individuals work, are always liable to be threatened by the need for change. However, the actor side of the argument reinforces the need to acknowledge that the responses to such change lie with the individuals themselves: they may find the experience exhilarating or profoundly depressing. In most cases commentators cannot assume that the response of individuals will be uniform.

We mentioned personification or reification in the previous chapter. We noted that it is the tendency to give inanimate objects attributes which belong to human beings. To assert that an organization decides to sack people or develop new products masks the fact that the organization has no brain or critical functions of itself to accomplish either of these tasks. So, it cannot be responsible for decisions that are the prerogative of the human actors. We would be more correct in describing those actors as a group of managers, say the Board, or an individual, say the CEO. Part of this lapse into personification is the tendency to apply human characteristics to an organization. So, we describe the organization as lazy or slow. Alternatively, we may describe it as quick-witted or responsive. It may be that this seems unduly pedantic. However, the risk of masking cause–effect linkage in this way may obscure the precise dynamics of the event being described.

The third of our questions offers the one clear link between assertions of significant change agency and the claims made for leadership in a sector or industry. The standards for hardware and software referred to in the second paragraph may indeed be testable and measurable. In that sense we could agree that such claims for innovation could at least be validated. However, how far such a change by one company could be said to change an industry would be difficult to establish. Similar claims have been made for such innovative examples as the Model T Ford. However, it could be argued that this car did not cause other Model T cars to be produced by competitors, but rather that it triggered competitors to come up with better vehicles, which outstripped the Model T. Standards are therefore comparative, not absolute, and, while they may offer a target initially, they will often be exceeded thereafter.

This brings us to the fourth question. What exactly is an 'experience curve'? It could be said that experience is the consolidation of knowledge and skill whose focus is the individual. Individuals working together may well pass on such experience to those they work with. They do this either deliberately, by training say, or through sharing closely in a working environment. As we noted at the end of the previous chapter, there is a tendency in popular management books to impute or imply that such experience can belong to the organization. Sometimes such a phenomenon is described as a learning organization (Senge, 1990). Such learning may indeed be captured in procedures, policies or training manuals, so that others may assimilate and learn from it too. However, while the individual and group may be the base of such learning and experience, there is no guarantee that the organization will capture that newly found knowledge or skill. Indeed, the discussion on managing knowledge and tacit learning should alert us to the fact that individuals can learn at work and deliberately not divulge what they have learned to the organization that employs them. In situations where the expertise of workers exceeds that of their managers there may be no mechanism for requiring knowledge workers to download their expertise in the way suggested (McKinlay, 2000; Willmott, 2000).

The excellence literature gave prominence to the idea that excellent organizations exhibit characteristics that exceed the opposition or competitors (Peters and Waterman, 1982). Their people are faster, more responsive, more flexible and, if necessary, more entrepreneurial. They will take risks more readily and are very enthusiastic about pioneering successful products and services ahead of the general run of operators. The assumption that innovation comes from clear-thinking, open and courageous individuals may neglect other factors, which can be significant in whether change is sponsored successfully or not. Increasing evidence suggests that those on greenfield sites may well be better at achieving high standards and fresh approaches than their colleagues on brownfield sites (Wickens, 1987; Storey, 1995). So, for example, the question of investment in new equipment and premises may often be significant for those seeking to initiate change on traditional sites. A

55

fresh start may well enable managers to select those who are more compliant and accepting of new ways of conducting and transacting a traditional business.

In this chapter we will look at systems thinking and organizational change. As we do so we will offer opportunities to read some of the claims made by both writers and practitioners of the management of change. As we shall see, the claims made by successful practitioners sometimes overlook the theoretical assumptions that underlie the assertions being made and may therefore make their uncritical adoption uncertain in its outcome.

ORGANIZATION AS SYSTEM

If we recall the types of change debate in the previous chapter, we will remember that one of the models referred to was that of punctuated equilibrium. We acknowledged that the idea of a mechanical system lends itself to illustrating how that type of change takes place. What we are invited to see is a series of cause–effect relationships, which allow us to analyse what is going on in an organization. One approach that typifies this is the Congruence Model of Organizational Behaviour (Nadler and Tushman, 1979). The authors offer a framework comprising inputs, transformation processes and outputs (see Figure 3.1).

This three-fold model can be found in a similar format in other general accounts of organizations described as input preceding process, which generates output. In this example the headings are further subdivided. First, the Input phase. Here the authors offer three factors:

■ Environment
■ Resources
■ History.

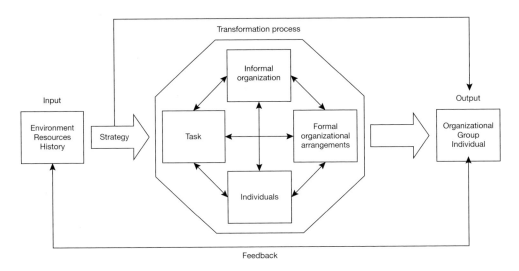

Figure 3.1 *Congruence model*
Source: Nadler and Tushman (1979)

The three factors listed are each sufficiently general to allow a range of separate elements within each one. So, environment could include, say, industry factors, market forces, societal influences and so on. Whatever is thought to be significant might be included here. Similar comments could be made about resources. We could include physical resources, financial resources and human resources – factors that might have been included under the headings of capital, land and labour in traditional accounts of the socio-economic factors underwriting work and organization. Finally, there is the summary heading of history, which may itself be a particular view or account of what has occurred in the past and the significance it has for present and future. Together these are schematic headings. They are not predictive or specific elements required by the work process.

The second heading of Transformation Process includes the four organizational components, which interact to form that process which lies at the centre of organizational activity:

■   Task
■   Individuals
■   Formal organizational arrangements
■   Informal organization.

The components themselves have about them a narrative that commends them to an observer of activities within a work organization. Individuals are often to be found engaged in routine, functional tasks. They rely on and generate formal organizational arrangements to support their activities in a consistent way. However, not everything they do is formulaic – there are variances which the observer might notice and question. The answer would be that these fall into the fourth category of informal organization.

The diagram itself is similar to the internal triggers for change outlined by Leavitt (1965) (see Figure 3.2).

Here the traditional elements of task and people remain the same and we might see similarities between the formal organizational arrangement and administrative structure. However, technology replaces the informal organization. What this suggests is that these schematic illustrations of what comprises organizational activity include whatever the authors delineate as being significant rather than an essential set of components such as we might expect to find in a mechanistic account of a planned system.

Furthermore, the arrows in Figure 3.1 indicating relationships between the components are double-ended and all four components interact between and within each other. This

Figure 3.2 *Leavitt's diamond*

suggests either constant interaction or even sporadic randomness. It also makes it difficult to suggest where the dynamics of the diagram begin and, if we want to intervene to institute change, whereabouts we would make such an intervention. Nadler gives the following account:

> For example, if we look at the type of work to be done (task) and the nature of the people available to do the work (individuals) we could make a statement about the congruence between the two by seeing whether the demands of the work are consistent with the skills and abilities of the individuals. At the same time we would compare the rewards that the work provides to the needs and desires of the individuals. By looking at these factors, we would be able to assess how congruent the nature of the task was with the nature of the individuals in the system. In fact, we could look at the question of the congruence among all the components, or in terms of all six of the possible relationships among them. The basic hypothesis of the model is therefore that organizations will be most effective when their major components are congruent with each other. To the extent that organizations face problems of effectiveness due to management and organizational factors, these problems will stem from poor fit, or lack of congruence, among organizational components.
>
> (Nadler, 1993, 87)

It would be fair to say that the extension of the original components of task and people into the area of competence and reward is not one that would have been evident from the original diagram. The question of 'fit' or congruence, which the author raises, while being important, is not self-evident from the diagram. The components themselves act as a catch-all into which different elements can be sorted by the observer or researcher. In some organizations, for example, it would be difficult to define factors as either formal or informal among the various and varying systems that comprise an organization.

In some accounts the final component of Outputs includes the following five elements:

- Goal achievement
- Resource utilization
- Adaptation
- Group performance
- Individual behaviour and affect.

Here, we are offered observable outcomes of organizational activity. However, it could be said that activities like resource utilization and adaptation could be as much part of the process as they are of output. Similarly, the group performance and individual behaviours may be a source of conflict as much as they are of cooperation.

For Nadler, then, the list of criteria for the successful management of change is as follows:

1   The organization is moved from the current state to the future state.
2   The functioning of the organization in the future state meets expectations, i.e. it works as planned.

3   The transition is accomplished without undue cost to the organization.
4   The transition is accomplished without undue cost to individual organizational members.

(Nadler, 1993, 89)

What is offered here is a statement of aspirations, which in its final three parts acknowledges that perceptions will play a major part in the assessment of the success of the change. We might also reflect that the trade-off between individuals and the wider group may well be as much a cause of contention and dissatisfaction as it is of cooperation.

THE SYSTEMS THINKING APPROACH

If we want to move away from the mechanistic models and look more holistically at the change process, then the model of organization that we adopt might focus on the open model. What lies inside this definition of organization is not so much a set of interacting components, which interact in the manner, say, of the parts of an internal combustion engine. It is the elements that are critical in conceiving of the concept of organization in the first place. This minimum set of assumptions is laid out by one writer as follows:

- Interdependency
- Synergy
- Boundary
- Binding ideology.

(Brown, 1995)

What differs here from the mechanistic approach is the acceptance of little or no assumption of structure and organization. While traditional bureaucracies have about them the suggestion of a large body of people assembled on one site and organized in a stratified, command and control manner, these assumptions could equally well apply to the lighter, smaller and dispersed organizations supported in more modern configurations. Home workers or internet companies could be included under these minimal assumptions.

It would, for example, be difficult to conceive of an organization whose members had no *interdependency*. *Synergy*, too, is a concept which suggests the sum total of value added being dependent on joint effort and the consequently enhanced outcome of the result.

More challenging are the last two factors mentioned. *Boundary* here is much more in line with the open systems model in which boundaries are porous rather than definitional. Individuals and their thoughts and feelings are influenced by factors outside the operational sphere of their work, so they draw on the diverse values which affect their everyday lives.

The term *binding ideology* differs from the traditional view of organizational objectives, in that it is enough to offer a working consensus without requiring a total commitment to a set of values or beliefs that are comprehensive or exclusive in their application.

If we look at a model of change in such an open system, then we might be presented with a process which seems very similar to those offered by the more mechanical model. There might still be inputs, processes and outputs. But this time their content would be subtly different (see Figure 3.3).

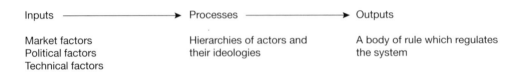

Inputs ⟶ Processes ⟶ Outputs

Market factors Political factors Technical factors	Hierarchies of actors and their ideologies	A body of rule which regulates the system

Figure 3.3 *An input-process-output model of Dunlop's system of industrial relations*
Source: Dunlop (1958) in Collins (1998, 147)

What is different here is the fact that the outcome is not the product or service, which the organization is committed to producing, but a continuous devolving of necessary regulation sufficient to enable the actors to generate what they need in order to succeed.

This model allows us to consider the organization less as an assemblage of parts, each one of which may be replaced or repositioned in a systemic change process. Rather, this holistic view allows the idea of organic change in which the process of change is self-generating – much closer to the emergent idea of change that we considered in the previous chapter. It sits more easily with the idea of continuous change rather than the punctuated change model.

At first sight this model offers a realistic format for envisaging organic change within the different individuals working together in an organization. They evolve their own consensus as they assess the strengths, weaknesses, opportunities and threats that face them as a group. They recognize and respond to the optimum outcome for survival and growth. Like Darwin's origin of species, this fits well with the idea of the survival of the fittest.

There is one problem that might cause us to question just how valid this model is as an account of organic or emergent change: the question of irreconcilable difference between members. Change models often assume a rationality whose logic will be apparent to all right-minded individuals. As such everyone will eventually reach agreement on what is the best outcome for them. To assess whether this belief is justified or not, we will need to examine that sometimes ignored element of change experience involving human beings: resistance.

MANAGING RESISTANCE TO CHANGE

For those who see changing systems effectively as the key to managing change, the rationale behind strategy is to define clearly the required state and then plan the change from state A (the existing situation) to state B (the new situation). The transition state is sometimes referred to as state C. Many commentators feel that this middle stage is not particularly well thought through, which may account for its being the least successful (Tushman, 1977; Salancik and Pfeffer, 1977). Nadler (1993) offers a threefold summary of the critical factors underlying change programmes, which are not always addressed in the way he suggests they ought to be in order to gain the commitment of those caught up in them.

For Nadler, the resistance to change is triggered by loss of security and a reduction in the worker's sense of autonomy and self-control. Familiarity with working procedures brings with it competence and repetition, allowing roles and functions to be exercised with a minimum of concentration. Mastery of functional complexity is dependent on the individual internalizing working systems which are then reinforced over a long-term period of acceptance and commitment to performance.

Interrupting this pattern of normal working will often mean loss of control for the individual worker. No one wants to be seen struggling with a new system or having to ask for assistance as they try to overcome the teething problems of a new system, especially if all this takes place in front of clients or customers. Nadler's point here is that managers of change too often think of change as, say, the simple move from a paper-based system into a fully computerized system. To the designers of the system, its ease of operation will be obvious. To those attempting to master the new skills, it may seem disastrous. They may have felt that it would have been much better to stick with the old system, which everybody knew so well.

The third problem that Nadler identified was power. Changes are rarely neutral. They affect the position of expertise, perhaps, that jobholders are used to exercising. Technological change often makes things easier, ostensibly, but can also destroy the mystique of previously well-preserved knowledge held in a few significant hands. Deskilling may mean ease of operation to some, but can mean loss of status for those in whose hands a skill or craft was held. Not surprisingly, resistance could be expected from such highly skilled groups.

For Nadler, the answer required closer attention to managing the detail involved in the transition stage C. He lays out the three problem areas identified and then offers the outcomes that managers of change need to address (see Figure 3.4).

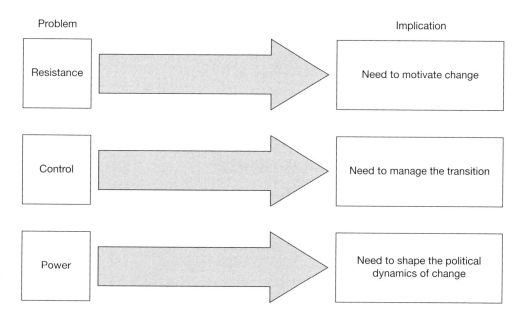

Figure 3.4 *Problems of change and implications for change management*
Source: Nadler (1993, 92). From Mabey, C. and Mayon-White, B. (eds) Managing change, *1993. Reprinted with kind permission of Paul Chapman and Open University*

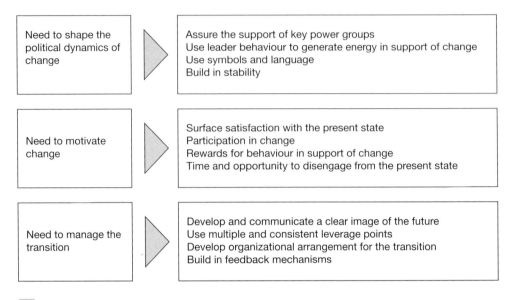

Figure 3.5 *Implications for change management and related action steps*
Source: Nadler (1993, 97). From Mabey, C. and Mayon-White, B. (eds) Managing
change, *1993. Reprinted with kind permission of Paul Chapman and Open University*

The action steps for each of the three stages can then be further drawn out (see Figure 3.5).

We see here that there are elements that coincide with the practice of traditional OD consultants. Its proponents would likewise encourage us to develop and communicate a clear image of the future (Beckhard and Harris, 1977). They would encourage us to support people through the change by training (Porter *et al.*, 1975) and involve them in the change process (Selznick, 1948). Symbols and language have a resonance with social anthropology literature and arise frequently as part of change strategy (Pfeffer, 1981). All in all, then, we could assert that we have a traditional formulation of support policies to overcome temporary resistance to the management of change.

RESISTING MANAGEMENT AND CHANGE

Nadler and the practitioners of OD suggest that careful management can overcome the occasional disturbance of an otherwise steady-state working life. Normal service can be resumed as soon as possible, if managers are thoughtful, supportive and planned in their approach. However, we should distinguish the temporary resistance envisaged by Nadler to the more radical resistance which informs the beliefs of radical structuralists. If we accept as a basic assumption that all employer–employee relationships are basically exploitative, then no amount of planned intervention will alleviate the belief that the enforced change to working conditions is inherently alienating in that, in this example, it deprives workers of pride in achievement and ownership of their craft or skill.

So, too, the perspective of Radical Humanism offers a different view of working relations as constructed between individuals and thereafter containing frameworks of power

(Clegg, 1989). The Foucauldian insight into power/knowledge relations offers a different perspective on work and those who would seek to control others to gain that power (Foucault, 1977). Just as the tools of production are held by the owners and their managers, so the construction of key relationships leaves little discretion for the powerless to assert their independence or deconstruct assumptions of dominance that can come to govern the employer–employee relationship (Fox, 1985, 32). Early examples of industrial control demonstrate the inability of the worker to exert his or her own independence. Successful progression in a career is defined in terms of compliance with predictive behaviours as defined by the owners and their agents, the managers (Savage, 1998).

In this view modern managers have control over the workplace through even more pervasive technologies. The computer can track and monitor as comprehensively as Jeremy Bentham's panopticon did in Victorian prisons. The autonomy and apparent freedom, then, are only skin-deep (McKinlay and Starkey, 1998); the analysis of effort through accountancy techniques can be equally effective in the exercise of power (Hoskin and Foucault, 1998) and even the kindly and supportive technologies employed by Human Resource Managers can be just as controlling as was Taylorism in the realm of production at the beginning of the twentieth century.

Returning to the Sociology of Regulation and Radical Change (Burrell and Morgan, 1979, 18), there is a difference between the axes of Regulation and Radical Change, which may lead to a different interpretation of what is transacted at work and how change and change management are to be viewed (see Box 3.1).

What this suggests is that the interpretation of change depends on the basic assumptions held by those who seek to manage it and those who undergo it. Actors always interpret what happens to them in their lives. However, their views may also be governed by an ethicality that makes it unlikely that they will accept change uncritically (Townley, 1994, 166).

What this deeper agenda of radicalism should alert the managers of change to is the fact that the structure–actor debate projects us into the realm of subjective interpretation. Ascertaining what basic assumptions are held to be immutable by individuals involved in change and transition will be the gauge of whether their responses can be modified by

BOX 3.1 REGULATION VERSUS RADICAL CHANGE

Regulation	Radical change
Status quo	Radical change
Consensus	Modes of domination
Solidarity	Emancipation
Actuality	Potentiality
Social order	Structural conflict
Need satisfaction	Deprivation
Social integration and cohesion	Contradiction

Source: Burrell and Morgan (1979, 18)

adroit and supportive management systems or whether resistance and alienation is more fundamental to their basic beliefs about themselves, their work and their future (Randall, 2001). We will examine the impact of enforced change on individuals and the differences that such basic assumptions are likely to trigger in more detail in subsequent chapters of this book.

SUMMARY ISSUES ARISING

We have so far looked at the underlying issues of structure versus actor and the open versus closed view of organizations. We are here touching on a tradition which has developed over the twentieth century, following the different historical practices and theoretic understanding of managers and academics alike. Reading the research and accounts of change written by those directly involved is important as they provide our only link with evidence of what was included in the change itself, what were the intentions of those managing the change and what were the responses of those who participated. As we read these accounts they will give rise to the question of who wrote them, why they drew them up in the way they did and what has been omitted from the account or just not been addressed directly.

Before we examine some of the examples offered by practitioners and researchers and analyse the theoretical assumptions and practical evidence, we will attempt to summarize the issues. Stickland (1998) offers a list of emerging themes, which can be used to both review those issues and identify the debates.

Emerging themes of change

- *Role and position of observer relative to change phenomenon*

Without revisiting the debate on whether it is possible to write unbiased accounts of any kind, we can at least ask about the role and position of the observer who writes an account of a change event and the attempt to manage it. This is not merely because all writers will have a tendency to portray their own role in a favourable light. Contributors are sometimes unaware of other significant factors affecting change. They may also have their own basic assumptions of what underlies the change or transition they report.

Sometimes individuals may be unaware that they are making any assumptions about the nature of change, the nature of the organization, or the implication of the intervention being made in terms of the theory of motivation. It will require the reader to identify such assumptions and consider how far that may affect the conclusions drawn by the writer about the outcome of the change programme.

- *The multi-level nature of change and the interconnected levels of analysis*

We have already commented in previous chapters on the different research literatures that might apply to change. We can accept that individual responses lie at the heart of organizational change, while noting that research and writing are rarely able to identify the full range of responses from all those involved in a change programme. So, some form of selectivity is necessary as part of an evaluation of change.

People working in teams may be drawn from a single discipline or multi-disciplinary groups. Capturing team responses is equally difficult for the researcher and also difficult to compare between and within groups. The impact of change programmes affects teams as variously as it affects individuals. Lewin's original work might be offered as an example of working teams and their discussions facilitated by an observer. However, the number of groups involved may then leave no alternative to the use of many facilitators. They themselves may well have had an effect on the groups they worked with, again making comparison difficult.

The level of the organization is the most difficult to address. Whose voice is taken to represent the agglomeration of individuals and teams who joined in the change programme? The writers who draw on this level may often have no alternative than to speak to senior change promoters and the CEO him- or herself. How typical are they of the varied opinions held by those who work for them? The literature of change management is replete with confident assertions of successful gurus or hero-managers. As evidence they need to be treated with care (Huczynski, 1993; Collins, 1998).

- *Historical time as the continuum upon which change may or may not be said to occur*

Few research projects are in place before change programmes are put in place. Not many more are in place during the change intervention itself. Most research is conducted shortly afterwards and therefore lacks the longitudinal dimension which might give that longer-term view of change programmes and the varying responses that individuals have over time.

A further question underlies Stickland's point here: change takes place over a period and is itself open-ended. Individuals involved have their own perceptions that may date back over a long career or may be compared with similar experience elsewhere. Even simple stepped or incremental change had antecedents that may predate employment. Taking actors into account here, the affect of change in the past may be critical to interpretation of present change. Such long-term memory is difficult for researchers to access with any accuracy or reliability (Schein, 1990; Isabella, 1990).

- *The dialectic of change and stability and the tension this generates*

The point being addressed here would seem to follow logically from the previous point and moves away from the more traditional stepped approach of before, during and after perspective on change. If we were to use Burrell and Morgan's lists of Regulation and Radical Change above, then we might suggest that the tension between, say, status quo and radical change is a spectrum within which different groups compete for ascendancy.

An understanding of change based on flux and variance makes it difficult to measure outcomes and conduct evaluation exercises. Voices of individuals and group reflections become impressionistic and base lines for comparison are necessarily arbitrary. At their most extreme such change events would preclude meaningful validation, becoming the basis for individual deconstruction and emancipation (Lyotard, 1979; Willmott, 1992), but almost impossible for the researcher to access, and even more so for the manager of change to predict.

- *The teleology of change and the extent to which a given change is regarded as purposeful or purposeless*

This point revisits a discussion which recurs throughout the study of the management of change. How do individuals perceive the stated aims of change – its teleology? Are there hidden agendas, which participant groups or individuals perceive as operating within the change programme (such as an opportunity for management to reduce headcount). This raises the question: how often are accounts of change written by the survivors rather than those who have become casualties to the effects of change?

Then we might ask whose purpose is being served? Again, we come to the heart of interpretation: it depends on the basic assumptions held by those who make the judgement of what has been valuable and useful as an outcome of the change programme or intervention. The contestants of change are various, so too are their perceptions. The evaluation made by participants may reinforce views held about other groups. Surprise at outcomes and events may confirm or disconfirm individual basic beliefs. How sense is made of unexpected events depends on whether basic beliefs are modified or retained (Louis, 1980a, b).

■   *The deterministic and non-linear qualities of change*

What changes and what remains the same during change may well appear relatively simple to assess for those whose focus is structural. The before–after list will reveal the gap between what will remain after the change and what will be replaced or simply disappear. Proponents of punctuated equilibrium will assert that the system will generate energy to move towards a state of balance (Dunlop, 1958).

However, those whose focus is the actor side of the debate will perhaps have more of a voluntaristic view of change. This may make perception within individuals and groups the key factor in the assessment of change. We have considered the immediate impact that enforced change may have on basic assumptions about self, job, work, career and the organization. But perhaps the perceptions that evaluate change are longer-term and unconnected with previous experience. The porous model of organizational boundaries may find individuals entering an experience from very different expectancies. Outsiders or incomers with different previous experience of change events can give a different perspective on change events. Such peer-group insights may be instrumental in bringing about modification in group perceptions (Nicholson and West, 1988; Isabella, 1990).

■   *The degree and extent of a given change and how this is described or labelled*

Stickland's final point alerts us to a further proviso: if change is continuous, then it is also open-ended. No one can say when it is completed or where exactly it will seem unusual or unexpected to its participants. Individuals perceive not just as a single experience, but also as an ongoing assessment of what they reflect on as being valid or important.

Second, who labels or describes the change? There may well be a formal process in which official change-agents define and promulgate change programmes in the manner of popular literature (Peters, 1991; Hamel and Prahaled, 1994). Threats become opportunities and, when the going gets tough, the tough get going. But participants themselves may also have labelled and described what they perceive the intentions of the change agents are really about. Which description or label is believed by which participants? For managers and researchers alike the answer is not easy to establish.

66

Students of any discipline can only acquire skill and expertise by practice. In this they join the community of those who spend their time involved in the management of change, either as practitioners or researchers. In the next section of this chapter we will attempt to provide a selection of examples written by both and allow the reader to use his or her critical faculties to decide what are the underlying assumptions the writers present.

PRACTICAL EXAMPLES

The traditional OD approach to the management of change involves positive interventions by managers and change agents. In this sense change is a top-down initiative. The following account may illustrate this:

> The staff were all anxious. The ailing UK retail concern had been bought from its American parent by a new British board. Did the change disguise an asset-stripping programme? Could the new team turn the ship around?
>
> For years the company, which was rich in assets and people had been poor on results and profits. The new management's main concern was to win staff support and gain commitment to a new strategy. To assess part of the problem an attitude survey was conducted amongst the 20,000 employees who nearly all replied. Their message was clear:
>
> ■ Fear existed at all levels
> ■ Management meant 'I tell, you do'
> ■ Customers were seen as a threat
> ■ Communications were generally poor
> ■ Bureaucracy was rife.
>
> Management were treated like clerks, being conditioned to handle systems, procedures, stock and property. People were to be manipulated and disciplined. Creativity and initiative had neither been expected nor rewarded. The survey results indicated a heartfelt cry from all staff to return pride and confidence in working for Woolworths. Fundamental perceptions had to be changed about what it meant to manage people. The behaviour of a great many people had to be modified.
>
> To get action the top management decided to send a signal across the company: management means doing things right, leadership means doing the right things. All 1,200 managers were to be given training spread over three years. The first year would emphasise leadership and the team; the second leadership and the customer; the third leadership and the business. The aim was to revitalise leadership skills, sharpen awareness of customers and improve managers' perception of the entire business, not just their own part of it.
>
> As a result of the trials the stores' management structure and how they looked inside were changed. There was more emphasis on personal responsibility, more scope for the development of teams and freer, more open communication. The overall results of Woolworths Holdings, bolstered by strategic takeovers, improved for a £6 million profit in 1982 to a spectacular £115 million in 1986–7.
>
> (Leigh and Walters, 1998, 111)

Consider some questions based on the passage you have just read:

1   What role did the writers fulfil in the company?
2   What conclusions were drawn from the results of the survey?
3   Comment on top management's 'signal across the company'.
4   How far can training change attitudes?
5   What evidence is there that the training brought about the improvement in profits between 1982 and 1987?

We have mentioned already the likelihood that accounts of change in organizations are written by either top managers or the change agents, some of whom may be outsiders brought in by the company. They may very well be accurate in the details and accounts that they present. However, we could ask whether there might not be other voices and different perspectives from members of staff and those who underwent the training.

The conclusions focused on alleged attitude changes required by the company. It would be difficult to know how to induce pride and confidence and use it as a training objective directly. One of the challenges that companies face is how to change perceptions. We will see in the next chapter that, while there may be a link between basic assumptions and what is referred to as culture, there is no guaranteed link between training and the outcome of perception change as an objective of any change strategy in itself.

The idea of top management signals is an interesting one. Symbol and significance are often attested as being an indicator of cultural change. The content of this message is a statement which would be difficult to validate in practice. How far could an observer assess whether what a manager was doing at any particular moment was the right thing or just doing things right? Is doing things right wrong in itself? How would a manager identify the difference between the one and the other in any case? Training messages as a vehicle of strategic intentions are difficult both to promote and consolidate. Clear guidance and examples would be needed to enable managers to distinguish between these different types or styles of management and who would be responsible for delineating where distinctions lay exactly.

Our fourth question is a general observation. It lies at the heart of training interventions: modifying behaviours can be validated, changing attitudes is much more difficult to attest. If we take the topics offered in the three-year training courses, we might also ask how far the team, customer and business can be separated in the way suggested. In the retail sector much of a store's business is the customer and getting the staff team to work together for the customer's benefit cannot be easily separated from that key objective.

Our fifth question is a classic and engages all trainers on the question of evaluation. Validating training most often focuses on the observable behaviours required of trainees. Evaluating training focuses on the effect the training had on change of results in the business. The writers are clearly implying that the up-turn in profits is linked to the training in which the company invested. What evidence is there for this assertion? This question is not intended as a criticism of the writers: there may indeed by some causal connection between the training programme and the up-turn in profits. However, identifying where those links occur is the difficult challenge. A simple example would be the case of a sales trainee who undergoes a negotiation training course and then experiences an increase in sales. Ostensibly, the training has worked as intended. However, the sales might be nothing to do with the training received, but just a fortunate surge in demand unrelated to the newly developed competence.

What we have read here would be a good example of the traditional OD approach to the management of change. Indeed its proponents sometimes offer core values, which underpin the validity of their work:

> Belief that the needs and aspirations of human beings provide the prime reasons for the existence of organisations within society.
>
> Change agents believe that organisational prioritisation is a legitimate part of organizational culture.
>
> Change agents are committed to increased organisational effectiveness.
>
> OD places a high value on the democratisation of organisations through power equalisation.
>
> (French and Bell, 1973)

There is a clear expression here of a desire to address the aspirations of the individuals within the organization, a belief that changing structures is linked to changing the culture, a commitment to organizational objectives and yet a commitment to democratization within the organization, too.

If we look for evidence of emergent change in organizations, the audit trail is much more difficult to establish. Again, those involved are not often the voices heard in the accounts. However, we may find a different approach underlying the accounts, whoever writes them. Andrew Pettigrew is well known for his work in ICI and one of the individuals who emerged at a senior level in that company is John Harvey Jones. Getting people involved in the process of change is a vital part of continuous change and individuals coming to terms with a changing environment. Harvey Jones explains this approach:

> I remember when I was appointed as deputy chairman responsible for the Wilton site in the late 1960s. The site had been characterised by almost total lack of cohesion in the management team and as a result we had lost all ability as a group to influence our work force. There was a common feeling prevalent at the time that the site was really run by the shop stewards. They were a tightly knit team who were absolutely clear about their aims. The problem was clear for all of us to see. The objective was not in doubt but we had always failed on the tactics for the simple reason that the managers did not feel that they owned theirs. I remember chairing my first meeting of the works managers who were the key management representatives on the site. They were all friends of long standing and I had worked with or for most of them at one time or another. As I took the chair one of them said, 'Well, John, we're glad you've come, things will be alright now. Just tell us what to do and we'll do it.'
>
> I remember replying, 'No, that's absolutely wrong, if I tell you what to do I know you won't do it because you never have in the past, so I don't see why you should start

now. We're going to decide what to do together and I think enough of you all to know that if you have actually taken part in the decision and if you share the responsibility for it, you are going to be dedicated to it and share the responsibility for making sure it doesn't fail.' From that day on things got better. We spent hours discussing the tactics until we were sure that we could live with them and at no time, no matter what the pressures, did any of the team let the others down. I had succeeded in transferring the 'ownership.'

(Harvey Jones, 1988, 73)

As we review the content of the author's logic here we can identify the principles that are espoused by some OD practitioners:

Five clear values
Empowering employees to act
Creating openness in communication
Facilitating ownership of change
Promoting a culture of collaboration
Promoting continuous learning.

(Hurley *et al.*, 1992)

It would be fair to note that the empowerment in this example is for the management team. The hidden agenda of greater control over the workplace in the face of well-established union management is also apparent here. However, it would be a good example of what the proponents of emergence sometimes refer to as a climate receptive to change which, according to some writers, is dependent on:

Extent to which key players gather and assess information on the organization's behalf
Degree to which such information is integrated into business operations
Extent to which environment's pressures are recognized
Structural and cultural characteristics of the organization.

(Pettigrew and Whipp, 1991)

Certainly the first three conditions are apparent in Harvey Jones' account. However, it does suggest that what emerges is a strategy for action that may be as much a top-down strategy as it is a release of democratic resurgence among the wider workforce.

Listening to the voices of those affected by enforced change at work sometimes offers very different accounts from those written by the change agents themselves. Not everyone is depressed at the outcome of such change and sometimes the result at a personal level can seem to an outside observer a very positive advantage in personal prospects and development opportunity. One such manager in a pharmaceutical company relates his own feelings:

I took over 4 people and now I have a staff of 21. I am in the managerial ranks so overall I feel very positive. At a personal level I feel I have done very well. Having gone through all that I have, it's up to me from therein on. I think it was at the takeover by _____ and I was asking myself whether I should stay or not. And I thought, 'I am going to make this work. I will become more marketable.' You have to have an attitude to your career – one of stability. People are less willing today to wait for things to happen. They are more proactive now. Loyalty cannot exist to the same extent. Companies don't matter anymore. This happened quite recently when a friend of mine working for a local firm was told, 'You're no longer required.' And I said to him, 'Don't take it personally, it's not you.' You can have this loyalty but it takes a blow and then you never trust again. But for the individual the result is you will have clearer goals about what you want to achieve.

(Randall, 2001, 167)

Here we can observe the different assessment that even a successful individual puts on the outcome of enforced change at work. Ostensibly such an individual might be thought to be satisfied with the personal success now achieved in career and job. However, the reservations expressed might take even colleagues by surprise. If the rewards of change are not evaluated as the company might expect, the cost to loyalty and trust may be significant when a change programme is implemented.

One movement in the management of change, which has proved quite popular, has been the Learning Organization. Its author, Peter Senge, has offered extensive examples of change and the way in which its stages reinforce each other. He offers a simple illustration in terms of filling a vessel with water (see Figure 3.6).

What question does this raise about the author's assumptions about change?

Senge offers another example of a similar cause-effect cycle. He calls this a vicious circle (see Figure 3.7).

What might happen to break this cycle?

In an earlier part of this chapter we looked at systemic change. Cause–effect relationships that occur in a predictive way may encourage the belief in the observer that there is a system of some dynamic involved in some iterative processes. In justice to him, Senge acknowledges that pure accelerating growth or decline rarely continues unchecked, either

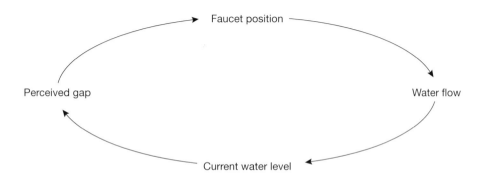

Figure 3.6 *The structure underlying actions*
Source: Senge (1990, 77)

71

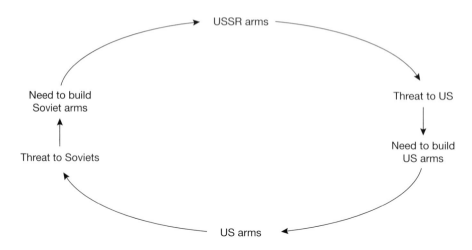

Figure 3.7 *Structures that underlie complex situations*
Source: Senge (1990, 75)

because reinforcing processes rarely occur in isolation, or because eventually limits are reached to stop, divert or even reverse the process (Senge, 1990, 83).

However, it would be fair to note that such a schema suggests an example of punctuated equilibrium, which we discussed earlier, rather than continuous change. What the model does not address is the possibility of change of mind – something that quite clearly occurred to the contestants in the arms race in the early 1990s. That change of mind may mean that individuals change their basic assumptions in ways that we will examine more closely in the next chapter. Finally, we should mention the possibility of resistance or alienation to the process, which brings about its cessation.

In Chapter 6 we will be looking at stepped approaches to change in several different examples. At this point it may be worth examining the sort of framework consultants who get involved in change management might use as a guide to assessing an organization. This one goes back to the early 1980s and would have been used by partners working for McKinsey, one of whom, Peters and Waterman (1982), is well known for his contribution to the excellence literature, which surfaced at about the same time:

McKinsey Seven-S Framework
Strategy
Structure
Systems
Style
Staff
Skills
Shared values.

(Burnes, 2000)

Consider the following questions:

1 What do the words in the list have in common?
2 Is there an internal logical structure in the list?
3 What do you understand by the word 'style'?
4 What do you understand by the phrase 'shared values'?
5 How would you use this list as a manager of change?

At first sight the list of words seems a somewhat arbitrary selection. The first three are redolent of a structural functionalist view of organization. Indeed, Chandler (1962) offers them as the basis of thinking about strategy and the part that it plays in setting up an organization. In that sense, then, it can be seen as the plan that governs the aims and objectives of the organization, dictating the structure of its implementation: how many departments, how many levels and the lines of reporting and authority leading to the top of the organization. As to systems, we can see them as the software that supports the organization, be it IT, finance, HR or production – each will have its policy, procedure and plans which define what is done, why it is done in the way it is and the budgetary factors which constrain or enable the different parts to interact successfully within the larger group.

There are some authors who regard this approach to thinking about organizations as 'undersocialized', in that it assumes compliance from the individuals working within the structure and is a somewhat cerebral approach to defining the organization (Collins, 1998, 82–99).

So, the four further factors that appear on the list beg the question: how did they come to find a place there? For Burnes (2000), the answer is that Peters and Waterman derived them from research into excellent organizations, and offered them in their book *In search of excellence* as typifying the significant factors governing success.

We may notice that the clarion call of Human Resource Management, which emerged at about the same time, was often 'people are our most important resource'. So we can accept that the previous lack of mention is at least redressed towards the actor in the balance between the dimensions of the structure–actor debate. Indeed, if we view the individual as being the basis of the competences available to the organization in fulfilling its objectives, then we would see a close link with the heading 'skills'.

The remaining words require closer examination. First, 'style'. If we are looking at performative or behavioural factors, then the word could apply to individuals performing in a similar way either within the job functions themselves or in the way in which they relate to other people, staff or customers. Here we would be getting closer to the factors of culture that are thought to inhere in common behaviours which characterize national cultures or groups (Hofstede, 1980, 1991). However, as we come to consider the final heading 'shared values', we are looking at another interpretation of the word 'culture': something the organization is; the perceptions of the individuals in the group (Schein, 1985). Reviewing more of the many contributions made to this discussion in the succeeding years, as we will do in the next chapter, will demonstrate that the fault-line that runs through the

73

subject of the management of change remains as firmly fixed as ever between personal and corporate perception.

What we see here, then, is an amalgam of a traditional OD list complemented by factors which emerged at the opening of what has become a long-running debate about the significance of culture in the management of change and whether there are any entry points for the agents of change to intervene and affect the way individuals think and feel about themselves, their work, their careers or the organization in which they work. For some authors these four 'soft Ss' open the way to 'oversocialized' accounts of management of change (Collins, 1998, 100–127). However, the complexity that they emphasize remains the context for continued study of organizational change and attempts to manage it.

DISCUSSION QUESTIONS

1   Critically evaluate the Congruence Model of organizational behaviour. Does it illustrate a closed or open view of organization?

First, you may want to sketch out the model from Nadler and Tushman (1979) (see Figure 3.1, p. 56). Then, you may want to explain the background of the diagram, which is laid out as input–process–output. Does this schema suggest a cause–effect model and would it suggest to you a mechanistic view of organization?

You may then want to consider each part of the model in turn, examining the elements included by the authors. So, at first sight, the Input section includes in broad terms what might be described as the context of the organization. Is the list inclusive? Could we add other elements? Do the three elements mentioned correlate or interact in some way, or are they just general headings to be used to consider critical factors affecting organization in the opinion of the authors?

If the strategy arrow is dependent on the Input box, how far do the three factors enable us to assess whether the strategy is adequate or not?

Then you might move to the Transformation Process. Again, do you accept the four factors included here? How do they relate to each other, exactly? What do the double-headed arrows connote? Is this an example of subsystems interacting together? Is this part of the schema as closed as the diagram seems to suggest?

Finally, we have the Output box. We might have expected to find the contents including the products or services, customer care and customer satisfaction elements. However, here we are simply presented with the constituent groups: organizational, group, individual. Is this a summary of the different levels in an organization? It could be argued that these are part of the input or process. Perhaps the output of each group jointly adds up to the total output of the organization, in the classic configuration of management by objectives (Drucker, 1986).

We might conclude that there are elements of open theory demonstrated, particularly in the input box. However, how the authors see these three factors working together is not explained in detail. The Transformation Process looks mechanical in its diagrammatic portrayal. However, on closer inspection, it is scarcely iterative and, it could be argued, not closed either. This brings us to the final part of outcomes, which is even less clear in its meaning.

The Feedback loop seems to suggest that the whole diagram feeds back in on itself. But, how exactly do organizations affect their environment, resources and history? At first sight it might look like an example of punctuated equilibrium. But then the Feedback loop suggests that it is continuous change. In fact the contents of the model and the connections between them are a jumble of different elements, which are diagrammatic and generally descriptive, rather than specific cause–effect elements in a mechanistic system.

2   Discuss the factors included in the McKinsey Seven-S Framework. Explain how it illustrates the undersocialized/oversocialized debate.

First, you may want to sketch out the list of factors and explain how they were derived historically. You can mention that the first three factors are part of a traditional view of OD as laid out by Chandler (1962). Then you can mention the excellence literature and the contribution of Peters and Waterman, *In search of excellence* (1982), and the generation of the last four factors as significant, according to the writers, in identifying excellent companies.

The undersocialized approach would seem to coincide with the structural view of the organization. Here the rationale of what makes an organization effective depends on strategy first: decide what it is you want to achieve – you being the owner/directors. Then set up the structure of departments to support the different roles and function required, including the appropriate number of management levels to control and organize the numbers needed to do the work on a 1:8 span of control ratio. Finally, include the supportive systems needed to connect these different departments, be they facilitative, like IT, or informational, like HR.

The move into the actor side of the debate focuses on the emergent beliefs fostered by Human Resource Management in the 1980s. In this view, people are the organization's most important resource. They exhibit the competence and commitment to delight the customer.

You will want to examine the four factors in detail. How far are they separate? Do they overlap? Are they presented in a significant sequence or is the list random? Is the list exhaustive or merely what the authors thought at the time was significant?

You might wish to consider why some commentators think that these four factors could lead into an oversocialized model? For example, how far are the four soft factors controllable, testable and measurable – objective, in that sense? Or are they subjective – dependent on customer perception and in any case hard to manage or control, let alone change?

Finally, you might discuss how significant is the fact that this list was drawn up by consultants. How might it help management consultants/change agents to effect change in an organization? Could it be used as a checklist? Is it for guidance only? Can the change agent ever pay too much attention to the soft Ss or is the list aspirational rather than definitive, so causing some to believe that it is oversocialized?

For both questions the answers will be a matter of opinion. However, any examiner would seek a logical answer well supported by clear definitions and illustrated by examples.

REFERENCES AND FURTHER READING

Beckhard, R. and Harris, R. *Organizational transitions: managing complex change*. Reading, MA: Addison Wesley, 1977.

Brown, A. *Organizational culture*. London: Pitman, 1995.

Burnes, B. *Managing change: a strategic approach to organizational dynamics*. London: *Financial Times*/Prentice Hall, 2000.

Burrell, G. and Morgan, G. S*ociological paradigms and organizational analysis*. London: Heinemann, 1979.

Chandler, A.D. *Strategy and structure: chapters in the history of the American Industrial Enterprise*. Cambridge, MA: MIT Press, 1962.

Clegg, S. *Frameworks of power*. London: Sage, 1989.

Collins, D. *Organizational change: sociological perspectives*. London: Routledge, 1998.

Drucker, P.F. *The frontiers of management*. London: Heinemann, 1986.

Dunlop, J.T. *Industrial relations systems*. Carbondale, IL: Southern University Press, 1958.

Foucault, M. *Discipline and punish: the birth of the prison*. Harmondsworth: Penguin, 1977.

Fox, A. *Man management*. London: Hutchinson, 1985.

French, W.L. and Bell, C.H. *Organization development*. Englewood Cliffs, NJ: Prentice Hall, 1973.

Hackman, J.R and Lawler, E.E. Employee relations and job characteristics. *Journal of Applied Psychology*, 1971, *55*: 259–286.

Hamel, G. and Prahaled, C.K. *Competing for the future*. Boston, MA: Harvard Business School Press, 1994.

Harvey, D.F. and Brown, D.F. *An experiential approach to organizational development*. Englewood Cliffs, NJ: Prentice Hall, 1992.

Harvey Jones, J. *Making it happen*. London: Collins, 1988.

Hofstede, G. *Cultures consequences*. Beverley Hills: Sage, 1980.

Hofstede, G. *Cultures and organization*. Maidenhead: McGraw Hill, 1991.

Hoskin, K. and Foucault, M. Examining accounts and accounting for management: investment understandings of 'the Economic', in A. McKinlay and K. Starkey (eds) *Management and organization theory*. London: Sage, 1998: 93–110.

Huczynski, A. *Management gurus: what makes them and how to become one*. London: Routledge, 1993.

Hurley, R.F., Church, A.H., Burke, W.W. and Van Eynde, D.F. Tension, change and values in OD. *OD Practitioner*, 1992, *29*: 1–5.

Isabella, L.A. Evolving interpretations as a change unfolds: how managers construe key organizational events. *Academy of Management Journal*, 1990, *33* (1): 7–41.

Lawler, L. and Hackman, J. Behavior in organizations. Porter, New York: McGraw Hill.

Leavitt, H.J. Applied organizational change in industry: structural, technological and humanistic approaches, in J.G. March (ed.) *Handbook of organizations*. Chicago: Rand McNally, 1965.

Leigh, A. and Walters, M. *Effective change: twenty ways to make it happen*. London: CIPD, 1998.

Lewin, K. Frontiers in group dynamics. *Human Relations*, 1947, *1*: 5–41.

Louis, M.R. Surprise and sense making: what newcomers experience in entering unfamiliar organizational settings. *Administrative Science Quarterly*, 1980a, *25*: 226–251.

Louis, M.R. Career transitions: varieties and commonalities. *Academy of Management Review*, 1980b, *5*: 329–340.

Lyotard, J.F. *The post-modern condition: a report on knowledge*. Minneapolis, MN: University of Minnesota Press, 1979.

Mabey, C. and Mayon-White, B. (eds) *Managing change*. London: Paul Chapman and Open University, 1993.

McKinlay, A. The bearable lightness of control: organizational reflexivity and the politics of knowledge management, in C. Prichard, R. Hull, M. Churner and H. Wilmott (eds) *Managing Knowledge*. Macmillan Business: Hampshire, 2000.

McKinlay, A. and Starkey, K. *Foucault, Management and organization theory: from panopticon to technologies of self*. London: Sage, 1998.

Nadler, D.A. Concepts for the management of strategic change, in M.L. Tushman and W.L. More (eds) *Readings in the management of innovation*. New York: Ballinger, 1988.

Nadler, D.A. Concepts for the management of strategic change, in C. Mabey and B. Mayon-White (eds) *Managing change*. London: Paul Chapman and Open University, 1993.

Nadler, D.A. and Tushman, M.L. A congruence model for diagnosing organizational behaviour, in D. Kolb, I. Rubin and J. McIntyre (eds) *Organizational psychology: a book of readings*. Englewood Cliffs, NJ: Prentice Hall, 1979.

Nicholson, N. and West, M. *Managerial job change: men and women in transition*. Cambridge: Cambridge University, 1988.

Peters, T. *Thriving on chaos*. London: Pan, 1991.

Peters, T. and Waterman, R.H. *In search of excellence*. New York: Harper Row, 1982.

Pettigrew, A. and Whipp, R. *Managing change for competitive success*. Oxford: Blackwell, 1991.

Pfeffer, J. *Power in organizations*. Cambridge, MA: Pitman, 1981.

Porter, L.W., Lawler, E.E. and Hackman, J.R. *Behavior in organization*. New York: McGraw Hill, 1995.

Randall, J.A. *Enforced change at work, the reconstruction of basic assumptions and its influence on attribution, self-sufficiency and the psychological contract*. Unpublished Ph.D. thesis, University of St Andrews, 2001.

Salancik, G.R. Commitment and control of organisational behaviour and belief, in B.M. Staw and G.R. Salancik (eds) *New directions in organisational behaviour*. Chicago, IL: St Clair Press, 1977.

Salancik, G. and Pfeffer, J. An examination of need satisfaction models of job attitudes. *Administrative Science Quarterly*, 1977, *22*: 427–456.

77

Savage, M. Discipline, surveillance and the career: employment on the Great Western Railway 1833–1914, in A. McKinlay and K. Starkey (eds) *Foucault, management and organizational theory*. London: Sage, 1998.

Schein, E.H. *Organizational culture and leadership*. San Francisco, CA: Jossey Bass, 1985.

Schein, E.H. Organizational culture. *American Psychologist*, 1990, *45* (2): 109–119.

Selznick, P. Foundations of the theory of organization. *American Sociological Review*, 1948, *13*: 25–35.

Senge, P. *The fifth discipline: the art and practice of the learning organization*. London: Century Business, 1990.

Storey, J. *Human resource management: a critical text*. London: Routledge, 1995.

Stickland, F. *The dynamics of change*. London: Routledge, 1998.

Townley, B. *Reframing HRM*. London: Sage, 1994.

Tushman, M. Special boundary roles in the innovation process. *Administrative Science Quarterly*, 1977, *22*: 587–605.

Wickens, P. *The road to Nissan*. London: Macmillan, 1987.

Willmott, H. Postmodernism and excellence: the differentiation of economy and culture. *Journal of Organizational Change*, 1992, *5* (1): 58–68.

Willmott, H. From knowledge to learning, in C. Prichard, R. Hull, M. Chumer and H.W. Wilmott (eds) *Managing knowledge*. Hampshire: Macmillan Business, 2000.

Chapter 4

Individuals and change

Manageable or not?

TOPIC HEADINGS

- Individual learning: theory and practice
- Schemas, frames and scripts
- Motivational theory and HRM links
- Enforced change and basic assumptions
- Basic assumptions and reframing

INTRODUCTION

When we speak of changing organizations our theory finds its context in the assumption that a group of people responds to enforced change at work in a corporate way and sometimes presupposes that there will be a consensus that change agents should work for in the larger group. Common sense suggests that in fact change initiatives, though planned for centrally, are implemented at group and individual levels. Indeed, behaviours must be based at the level of the individual, as it is individuals who learn about and respond to their environment. Their behaviours may then be coordinated into group endeavours and the groups brought together to cooperate with a larger body of people.

The problem that we have in decoding popular accounts of corporate change is that the writers may conflate the process of change at the different levels of individual, group and organization learning into one seamless series of events. That is exactly how it may seem to those who have come through a series of changes when they look back and summarize what has taken place. Such accounts often start from the conclusions and then draw up recommendations for the reader to implement should a similar change event be implemented again. Here is a typical example, which we can examine in detail to establish what assumptions are being made by the writers about change and how it impacts on individuals, groups and organizations:

Tony Blair once said that trying to get the public sector to change its ways had left him with scars on his back. But the government's strategy for modernising Britain's public services has left many public servants feeling equally scarred.

The relentless emphasis on change has led to widespread complaints of initiative overload. Many police officers, teachers and other public sector employees who had started their working lives with hopes of making things better for their fellow citizens have become jaded as they grapple with centrally imposed targets and initiatives. But the findings of research we have been conducting for the CIPD and the Cabinet Office's Centre for Management and Policy Studies show that some public-sector organisations have found the key to successful change. We have been looking at how six public-sector bodies have tackled the challenge of modernisation. Although they are each very different, these organisations have achieved a real focus on results and have released the latent capabilities of their people.

Our report, entitled Delivering Public Services, suggests that it's time to move the debate about public services away from the resourcing problems that have so far dominated it. Instead of focusing on the three 'resource Es' — economy, efficiency and effectiveness — we need to start considering how to energise, enable and empower employees. It is these people Es that make a difference to the quality of public services.

(Vere and Beaton, *People Management*, 6 March 2003. Reprinted with kind permission of Personnel Publications and the respective authors)

Consider the following questions:

1   Why do change initiatives lead to overload?
2   What seems to be the main complaint underlying this dissatisfaction?
3   What is the alleged key to success in the organisations cited in the article?
4   What sort of resourcing problems might be referred to here?
5   How might they link with the three 'resource Es'?
6   How might the 'people Es' make a difference?

The complaint about overload is commonly made in the accounts of public sector change initiatives (Bate, 2000; Jackson, 2001; Hood, 1998). Writers often assume that the volume of change initiatives alone causes dissatisfaction. Perhaps it would be fairer to ask what might underlie such discontent. It could be argued that radical change makes demands on those who are required to perform in very different ways to those they have become accustomed to. Change initiatives are, in this scenario, a harbinger of change requirement in work behaviour. But why should such change on its own trigger such a response? Are we assuming that changing work practice will always be resisted because it requires unaccustomed behaviours? This does not always need to be the case, surely? Some change to work practices might be welcomed, say, where individuals felt they were being relieved of bureaucratic burdens or clearly inappropriate or unworkable behaviours.

A second assumption frequently made is that imposed targets will be a source of discontent to workers (Huxham and Vangen, 2000; Pollitt, 2001). We can understand that imposed targets or targets for targets' sake may well be resisted where individuals feel they are being asked to work harder without recompense or where they feel that such targets do not make them either more efficient or more effective. But is consistency of performance always viewed as a management intrusion or a spy in the cab?

The challenge to those requiring change of others is indeed resource. Making bricks without straw will always be seen as making the job harder, i.e. not giving workers the tools they need to achieve higher or more consistent standards. We might ask where such resource is lacking and what comparators there may be for evaluating lack of resource. Perception is an important factor here. However, if resource is thought to be lacking, whose opinion is taken be valid about where the lack lies? Demands for increased efficiency may be perceived as being unrealistic without the training and support to enable individuals to deliver it.

Finally, we are presented with a new set of basic assumptions, which may or may not be feasible and which are accepted uncritically by the writers. It seems that an assumption is being made that the worker will be committed to work, which he or she was previously inconsistent at or disinclined to do efficiently or effectively, because the rhetoric has changed from directive to facilitative. What guarantee is there that uncongenial work will be more readily accepted because a different management style is introduced?

What should interest us as students of the management of change is the actual content of change programmes. What actually took place as a result of the programme of change? Was it a different working procedure, a different management style or a different way of thinking about the work? We come back to the distinction, which we have seen earlier, that behaviours and attitudes are usually both involved for those expected to change what they do at work. However, it may be difficult for us to assess how these two critical elements interlink with each other for the individuals concerned.

We will let the article speak for itself to see whether we will be any further enlightened about the content of the change programmes themselves:

> A starting point for most of the organisations was to create an energising goal to provide a focal point for the change process and to paint a picture of the future. At Selly Park Technology College in Birmingham, for instance, staff led by head teacher Wendy Davies established a single-minded focus on improving its educational results. By contrast, the aim of the National Blood Service was to define the core values that would govern attitudes to the organisation's stakeholders: donors, patients, the health service and employees themselves.
>
> Their ability to achieve this goal depended on the visible commitment and active engagement of those at the top. This involved listening properly to their people – a time-consuming but highly rewarding activity. For example, Peter Hampson, chief constable of West Mercia Constabulary, met all 3,200 employees over several months in groups of 20. This approach paid off, giving Hampson a better understanding of the issues that concerned the organisation. The evident integrity of the leaders also helped to forge a bond of trust between them and their staff.
>
> The importance of the leader's role cannot be overstated. The management teams that we studied helped to set the direction by personally initiating and often leading the

81

goal-setting process. They created the right climate for change by putting in place processes or giving others the opportunity to tackle organisation-wide problems. They modelled the future by demonstrating the organisation's values in their own behaviour, actively engaging in programmes to improve services and showing others the way forward. And lastly they were generous in recognising what others had achieved and in rewarding success.

Also important was the organisations' willingness to confront the issue of senior management competence – to ensure that the right people were in place for the future. Those individuals who did not feel that they had the skills, motivation or interest to go in a new direction were given chances to move sideways into new positions or leave the organisation. Many people took these opportunities willingly, because they did not feel committed to or equipped for the new set-up.

(Vere and Beaton, 2003, 37)

Again, consider some questions arising from this passage:

1 What difference can you identify between the approaches of the Selly Park Technology College and the National Blood Service?
2 Leader behaviour is often thought to be critical in such change programmes. What comment would you make on the chief constable's approach to this?
3 How can a leader model the future in his or her own behaviour?
4 What is the effect of moving on current leaders who are deemed uncommitted to change?
5 What is the distinction between those who were not committed and those who did not feel equipped?
6 What would be the effect on others of the suggested redeployment of senior managers?

The aims and objectives on which a change programme is based may, wittingly or unwittingly, set people on a particular path, which then absorbs all available energy and effort. In the case of Selly Park Technology College we might want to find out more about the exact content of what was involved in 'improving its educational results'. It might be pass rates of its students, or numbers of graduates placed in employment or any of the internal factors by which efficiency can be measured. Certainly such measures might well be quantified and if necessary made the subject of targets for individuals – staff and students alike. We might enquire whose idea it was to use this as the focus of the programme: the head teacher or a consensus among the staff. Did it involve the students? At this point we are looking at the difference between a top-down approach or the more emergent change strategies of the bottom-up approach. The article is unspecific on this point.

By contrast, we can look at the National Blood Service, where a different approach was embarked on. Core values of stakeholders are nothing new. Indeed, they were laid out in the early literature of the proponents of Human Resource Management in the early 1980s (Beer *et al.*, 1984; Fombrun, 1984). However, the writers seem to assume that there can be coherence between the expectancies of the stakeholders, which may make it difficult for all of them to be satisfied in the way that each group hopes. The article does not tell us what the change agents hoped to achieve by surveying all the stakeholders. We can only assume that it was intended to enable them to review how far they were able to fulfil individual expectancies and where the new initiatives might be seen as contradictory.

Our second and third questions revolve around leader behaviour. As we shall see when we review the n-step approaches in Chapter 6, most to-do lists for change leaders involve at least one element about leader behaviour. There has been no lack of commentators prepared to assert that leadership behaviour is critical both to the formation of strong cultures and the management of change (Schein, 1985; Van Maanen, 1978; Legge, 1995). What is difficult for the researcher to discover is exactly how significant any particular leader behaviour may be. The significance of leader behaviour is in part a function of the perceptions of the led and therefore we would have to allow that what the 3,200 employees thought of this intervention by their chief would be the gauge of its success. We may note here how easy it is for writers to assume that the events would give the leader 'an understanding of the issues that concerned the organization'. It might indeed give the leader some random thoughts from those brave enough to speak up. However, what the organization thought, felt or believed could well be more difficult to discover.

Similarly, we might question how leaders can model the future of the organization. Chief Constables are rarely to be found arresting malefactors or warning speeding motorists. So, apart from using the opportunity of the groups to preach a different message, it would be hard to attest that leader behaviours could be demonstrated that easily or transfer to the workplace in very simple or demonstrable ways.

Finally, we come to an aspect of change that is not often dealt with as directly as it is here: what is to be done about those who will obstruct change if left in place? We should note here that a distinction is being made whose significance it is easy to lose. First, the issue of competence: how do we assess whether individuals have the potential or aptitude for change? The answer may be as difficult as finding out whether human beings have either at any stage in their career. As we know, testing is often suggested as a route for finding out about recruits and trainees. However, it would be difficult to visit such tests on incumbent managers and difficult to find appropriate tests that are both valid and reliable (Toplis *et al.*, 1987). If we focus on interest and motivation, then the task is even more difficult. Individuals do not often divulge their opposition to the proponents of change, especially if those proponents are themselves more senior in the organization. Finally, brokering a deal in which individual change refusers are moved elsewhere or removed completely could leave the organization with large redundancy costs and arguably fewer people with the necessary skills and experience to carry the organization forward during the transition.

What the article has revealed so far, then, is the difficulty of identifying where change could best be started, who should initiate change and what happens to those who have neither competence nor commitment for the change. For individuals there is a clear choice to be made if they can identify the distinction between competence and commitment and its significance to the change required by the organization. For the organization, that is, the agents of the change, there is the decision about what to do with those who do not wish to go along with the change, for whatever reason. What we do know is that those left behind may be aggrieved at the loss of their erstwhile work colleagues and less inclined to cooperate with change programmes (Hallier and Lyon, 1996). So, the risk of instituting change is always high.

At this point we can usefully look at the three people Es laid out in the article. The six organizations we studied all faced their own particular challenges and confronted them in different ways. But, by following common themes, they emerged from their efforts to release the potential of their people by energizing, enabling and empowering them.

Energizing

- Creating an energizing goal to crystallize commitment.
- Leading from the front by showing integrity and establishing trust.

Enabling

- Invigorating the top team by strengthening its leadership capability.
- Building a culture of empowerment by opening the door to ideas.
- Working with the community to forge understanding and clarify expectations.

Empowering

- Forging teams by releasing energy and making things happen.
- Aligning HR processes and practices to improve capabilities.
- Navigating change by seizing opportunities and adapting rapidly.

(Vere and Beaton, 2003, 36)

Of the eight bullet points, we have been offered examples of leader behaviour being used to derive new ideas from the groups involved in the example of West Mercia Police. The National Blood Service has sought to elicit the views of all stakeholders and therefore could be said to have worked with the community to forge understanding and clarify expectations. The empowering factors have not been explored in any detail and it is to these that the article turns in its final part:

> As well as energising and leading the modernisation programme, senior managers also looked to establish a culture of empowerment by developing the organisation's capacity to take on individuals' ideas and bring them to fruition. At the National Blood Service, for example, focus groups were established across the organisation, breaking down functional boundaries and working progressively on core ideas, business problems and value change analysis. Here again, one of the keys to success was that senior managers listened to the focus groups' ideas and acted upon them.
>
> In all six organisations, HR had a crucial part to play in building capability and then helping to release it. Our findings reinforce the conclusions of previous research by John

Purcell at the University of Bath into how HR practices can improve organisational performance ('Groundforce,' PM, 27 June 2002). In the context of change, one of the critical questions is the impact on the 'psychological contract' with employees. When people believe that their employer has dashed their expectations about work and future career opportunities, they feel less committed to their organisation and their job satisfaction will sometimes fall as well. In the six organisations, the recognition that change would affect the psychological contract meant that HR policies and processes had to be reviewed to support the new climate and help to rebuild the contract. The clearest examples of this were the emphasis on new skills and behaviour for the future and the opportunity for employees to learn and develop these skills.

(Vere and Beaton, 2003, 37–38)

Consider the following questions:

1   How far are focus groups an emergent strategy?
2   What should managers do if focus group suggestions are impracticable?
3   What exactly is a psychological contract?
4   How can HR affect the psychological contract?
5   In which part of the psychological contract do new skills and behaviour fit?

The use of focus groups has become popular for all those seeking to discover consensus from consumer or public opinion groups. Such opportunities for discussion would certainly be a primary means for eliciting thoughts, feelings and opinions in any emergent strategy and can be found in the early practice of Lewin (1947). The problem comes when focus groups come up with solutions which managers find impossible or too impractical to implement. This can be for practical reasons, like lack of funds to support training, or for political reasons, such as that other stakeholders would find the suggestions unacceptable. Perhaps the key factor here is that open communication is not just an opening gambit, but should be the basis of ongoing feedback between managers and user-groups. As we shall see the idea of phases rather than stages allows the continuation of such discussion so that any modification of initial ideas is fed back to those who first made the suggestions while the programme of change is still being implemented (Bullock and Batten, 1985). We will consider such phases in more detail in Chapter 6.

Psychological contract is an idea that emerged during the 1980s. Indeed, one of its proponents has kept alive the debate about its existence over the intervening years (Rousseau, 1995, 1998; Guest, 1998). The original idea arose from the suggestion that individuals carry a set of expectations about their job and the conditions under which they carry it out. Some writers have suggested that it contains two elements: transactional and relational (MacNeil, 1985). The first category is equivalent to the contract or conditions of employment that might be found in any contract of exchange: effort and time in return for monetary reward. The second part of the contract contains the more personal affective aspects of trust and loyalty, based perhaps on an expectancy that there will be ongoing support for career, training and development.

With this in mind, if we now address the fourth question, we can see that HR can affect the contract in as much as they can alter the terms and conditions contained in the contract. Reinforcing good behaviour and the avoidance of bad behaviour would be part of the approach to affecting how individuals feel about change and its effect on that part of the contract. However, the relational part of the contract would be more difficult to influence directly. Lack of trust or loss of loyalty would be a function of basic assumptions in the individuals concerned. How each worker interprets the impact of change will affect the outcome of meaning and value imputed to enforced change at work, as we shall see later (Randall, 2001).

The answer to the final question, then, lies in the transactional part of the contract: HR might be writing up new behaviours, procedures, terms and conditions in the contract. However, we cannot determine how these changes will affect loyalty and trust in the relational part of the psychological contract.

The final part of the article illustrates the points that we have been making about the psychological contract:

The Court Service took a number of steps to reconnect its HR policies and systems to the reshaped organisation. These included making better use of its competency framework, forecasting the future shape of the workforce and ensuring that the appraisal process fully recognised people's contributions.

The best example of the connection of the HR function to the business has been the work done so far by the e-HR strategy team at the Inland Revenue. Here the development of an e-HR strategy has been used to identify the key changes needed in HR systems and processes to support the future requirements of the organisation. It has developed a new strategy in four areas to mitigate the risks posed by the organisation's increasing use of information technology: enhancing management and leadership capability, developing the right skills and knowledge, building a flexible workforce and taking forward strategic workforce planning.

One of the most striking characteristics of the case-study organisations has been their capacity to navigate through turbulence caused by the need to improve how they deliver their services. They have demonstrated not only the ability to put together well-planned strategies but also a degree of flexibility and optimism. As a result, they have been able to seize chances to pursue their own agendas for improving delivery. This contrasts with many organisations' negative reactions to new initiatives – especially those that have been imposed on them from the outside.

The organisations that we studied have seen such initiatives as a chance to achieve their long-term goals – bearing in mind that they had put a lot of effort into crystallising what those goals were. For example, at West Mercia Constabulary both the police service and the police authority took a positive view of the new requirements to bid to the Home Office for new resources to develop their services. They saw this as a means to achieve better results, rather than a constraint on local accountability.

Such a positive approach is typical of these organisations. It has been injected into their life blood through the methods that we have described in a way that is truly energising, really enables change and readily empowers people to make a difference. Maybe these three Es really are here to stay.

(Vere and Beaton, 2003, 38)

We might conclude this review by remarking that the basis of the claims made in the final paragraph has not been established in detail. As always, empowerment is a difficult concept to define in the way it frees individuals to exercise decision making in their own lives and over the processes for which they have responsibility. Budgets and resources are usually finite for any group of people. As such, individuals usually have to compete for a share in these. How much each gets can be the result of determination, negotiation, political manoeuvring or personal influence. This social aspect of resource allocation reminds us that the individual is rarely at liberty to determine investment in people and systems. Constraint means less opportunity to choose than might be desired and therefore a less empowered situation. In other words, a less than feasible resource may be all that is available.

Similarly, functional flexibility, while much lauded in the theoretical presentation of HRM (Guest, 1989), has some constraints in how far it can be exercised. Individuals have a finite ability to respond to opportunity offered by systemic change. Potential and aptitude play their part in affecting final outcomes and responses to new opportunities at work. Change programmes rarely acknowledge this constraint on developing the new competencies required in the changed organization.

All in all, then, both the individual and the organization have limits, which may restrict the options available to the agents of change. We can accept that the secret of management is to deploy the right person in the right place at the right time. We can accept that there will be a need to vary management style according to the need of the team at the time (McGregor, 1960). However, the ease with which some claims are made for achieving radical change in a democratic or consensual style sometimes overlooks the constraints of both individual competence and organization resource. Similarly, turning threat into opportunity is the desirable outcome that all organizations strive for. However, the gauge of success is not just reinterpreting a set of perceived external constraints on individuals, but also adjudging how far the internal agents are able to respond to the demands being made on them.

In this chapter, then, we need to examine how individuals learn, how their group experience affects their learning and how far these different perceptions facilitate change and its acceptance.

INDIVIDUAL LEARNING: THEORY AND PRACTICE

How individuals learn has been the subject of research as long as individuals have been involved in finding out how to develop and control other people. Various techniques have surfaced and resurfaced about how to enable individuals to learn, from the highly directive to the more facilitative. Sometimes the only difference between either technique may be the amount of time available to complete the programme successfully.

Learning is a prerequisite for successful human survival and development. It enables individuals to assimilate the world around them and to interact with other people in a way that gives them reasonable control over the inputs that they make to their environment and the people they live with. The inductive process of learning allows the individual to assess the environment and make sense of it for him or herself. What goes on around one becomes the subject of observation, reflection, and then the attempt to intervene, perhaps, in a pragmatic way. Some theorists see this as a cycle of learning (Kolb et al., 1971) in which intervention becomes the trigger for yet another cycle of learning. But for those who wish to induce the learning process in others, the question of how to initiate this process is dependent on how it is believed individuals learn.

Popular works on psychology frequently cite the examples of researchers who have investigated how animals learn and extrapolated their findings to apply the theoretical outcomes to human learning. Most readers of such work will have heard of the Russian psychologist, Pavlov, who in the early twentieth century conducted experiments on dogs, which are sometimes referred to as 'classic conditioning' (Arnold et al., 1991, 153). Anticipation of feeding time signalled by a bell triggered the animals to salivate at the sound even when feeding did not always follow, thereby indicating that learning is possible in animals given the reinforcement of causal connections linked to a sequence of predictive events.

In the field of human psychology such an approach would be described as behaviourism and is often associated with the name of B.F. Skinner (1974), who described the same technique when applied to humans as 'operant conditioning'. The descriptors of stimulus–response are well known to those who have read the many experiments surrounding the application of the theory to practice. The process is sometimes referred to as 'antecedent–behaviour–consequence'. The antecedents refer to the stimuli or conditions provided by the experimenter, which trigger the required performance and are rewarded with the required consequent behaviour in the subject.

It is this final stage that is often referred to as 'reinforcement'. In other words, the reward, which the subject of the experiment requires, is the final determinant of the continued behaviour required by the instructor. Reinforcement will become apparent from time to time in several of the top-down approaches to change. Its inclusion reminds us that the underlying theory is based on an assumption that required behaviour can be managed, provided a pathway of expected reward is put in place by the manager. Most teachers will be aware that reinforcement may be positive or negative. It may be based on pleasure or on pain. Both carrot and stick may govern the outcome and different mixes of both may provide a strategy for coping with different operant responses.

SCHEMAS, FRAMES AND SCRIPTS

Of course, direct response to simple need satisfaction is easy to illustrate and usually straightforward to put in place both for the trainers of animals and humans. Most hungry organisms will respond to food and learn to associate it with preset signals. But there are many more complex processes, which humans are required to internalize, that might make it difficult to continue using operant condition in such a simple format. For the learner there has to be a logical sequence of operations, tasks or concepts, which together enable entry into logic or system. Making sense of and controlling events in a predictive set of performances therefore requires the instructor first to break down the content of the learning into connected events, each of which can be assimilated by the learner.

How individuals make sense of reality has been the subject of much research in cognitive psychology. Understanding the descriptors of a world which must be entered into in an ordered way requires concepts and the words which represent them. Those who wish to enter a new realm of learning replicate the deep questioning of early childhood. There are ideas and concepts, which need to be sorted into an order of connectedness that enable stability and cause–effect relationships to be derivable from apparent randomness or disorder. This ordering requires a system of dependencies between different but related aspects of reality, sometimes referred to as a hierarchy of knowledge. For an example of this see Figure 4.1.

Placing words in a hierarchy of relationships enables the learner to identify not just classes of animal, but also their attributes and behaviours The categories themselves can be enhanced by expert knowledge or further descriptors, but basically they will remain in place to allow identification and then representation. For instance the concept 'gold' may be represented in the following three ways:

Yellow glittery stuff
Precious yellow non-rusting malleable ductile metal
Atomic number 79.

(Roth and Frisby, 1986, 72)

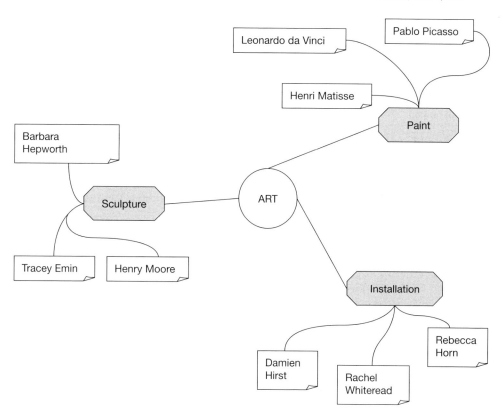

Figure 4.1 *A schematic summary of conceptual categories*
Source: Adapted from Rosch (1975)

Sometimes trainers refer to such hierarchies as underpinning knowledge: it makes it easier for individual learners to understand a process by being able to identify its constituent parts. Thereafter they can both control a process using practised skill and so understand how a system works in the way that it does.

As we move into the more complex sequences involved in complex processes we can examine how individuals learn, say, to conduct themselves within a social setting. If we suppose that a visiting friend had never been to a restaurant, then enabling them to make sense of the experience and conduct themselves properly would require that they learn a sequence of behaviours expected by those who run the restaurant. The visitor would need to learn not just the categories of people and things he or she will encounter, but also a series of steps that would be necessary to get service without causing confusion, misunderstanding or embarrassment. See, for example, the restaurant script in Box 4.1.

The point made by those who have developed this approach to constructed knowledge is that communication requires both speaker and listener to be cognizant of the appropriate script applying to a common situation (Schank and Abelson, 1977). However, once the script is learned and practised it becomes transferable into other similar situations. Such descriptors can assist individuals to assess their own interventions into complex negotiational interactions where they need to identify other behaviours and respond appropriately themselves. Such a schema was developed by Bales (1950) and used to train individuals with developmental problems (see Box 4.2).

The way of teaching processes can now become the method by which individuals recall ways of doing everyday, complex tasks. Routine and practice become the reinforcing factors that enable the individual to internalize the steps required to achieve the objective by rehearsing key tasks or steps in a preset sequence. However, the downside of this technique may also be that failure in the system may leave the operant struggling to find a solution to a variation in the learned schema. This would require further training in problem-solving schemas (Cohen *et al.*, 1986).

As we have seen, mechanical systems usually have a design or dynamic that allows those seeking to control them to both learn the steps and learn to solve any problems occurring as a result of breakdown in the system. This allows those seeking to make sense of problem-solving to use a similar structured approach to analyse the required steps to solution. When these steps are analysed, they can be listed into what some researchers refer to as well-defined problems:

> In well-defined problems the solver is provided with four different sorts of information:
> Information about the initial state of the problem.
> Information about the goal state.
> Information about legal operators (things you are allowed to do in solving the problem).
> Information about operator restrictions (factors that govern or constrain the application of operators).
>
> (Kahney, 1986, 19)

As we discussed in our example of the aircraft passenger left with an unconscious pilot, the task of finding out what the legal operators and operator restrictions are could be

BOX 4.1 RESTAURANT SCRIPT

Name: Restaurant

Props		Roles	
	Tables		Customer
	Menu		Waiter/waitress
	Food		Cook
	Bill		Cashier
	Money		Owner
	Tip		

Entry conditions		Result	
	Customer is hungry		Customer has less money
	Customer has money		Owner has more money
			Customer is not hungry

Scene 1   **Entering**

Customer enters restaurant

Customer looks for table

Customer decides where to sit

Customer goes to table

Customer sits down

Scene 2   **Ordering**

Waitress brings menu

Customer reads menu

Customer decides on food

Waitress gives food order to cook

Scene 3   **Eating**

Cook gives food to waitress

Waitress brings food to customer

Customer eats food

Scene 4   **Exiting**

Customer asks for bill

Waitress gives bill to customer

Customer gives tip to waitress

Customer goes to cashier

Customer gives money to cashier

Customer leaves restaurant

Source: Greene (1986, 38)

BOX 4.2 THE BALES CATEGORIES

1. Shows solidarity, raises other's status, gives help reward
2. Shows tension release, jokes, laughs, shows satisfaction
3. Agrees shows passive acceptance, understands, concurs, complies
4. Gives suggestion, direction, implying autonomy for the other
5. Gives opinion, evaluation, analysis, expresses feeling, wish
6. Gives orientation, information, repeats, clarifies, confirms
7. Asks for orientation, information, repetition, confirmation
8. Asks for opinion, evaluation, analysis, expression of feeling
9. Asks for suggestion, direction, possible ways of action
10. Disagrees, shows passive rejection, formality, withholds help
11. Shows tension, asks for help, withdraws out of field
12. Shows antagonism, deflates other's status, defends or asserts self

Source: Argyle (1967, 67)

achieved by judicious trial and error inputs to the control system. Indeed, research supports the view that those who become masters at such problem-solving games as chess have long-term memory of stored patterns, which are memory representations of legitimate, meaningful board positions categorized in terms of clusters of pieces attacking or defending each other (de Groot, 1975).

Ways of structuring information and learning in the schematic way suggested can account for language acquisition, representation, memory and problem-solving. They can also facilitate structured learning programmes and validational exercises (with or without reinforcement). However, they are not as useful in coping with non-systemic problems or problems not based on such structured systems of operation. Among such non-predictive areas must feature the problem of why people work or achieve or aspire to grow, develop, acquire or perform in any sector in which they engage. Learning then becomes dependent on the aspiration of the individual.

MOTIVATIONAL THEORY

As we have commented earlier, the move away from Taylorism in the early twentieth century was influenced by the findings of Elton Mayo during the Hawthorne experiments. The thought that the experimenters' changes to the workers' environment could bring about increases in productivity confirmed a belief in some managers that motivation could be the missing link that managers had been seeking between constant supervision and the internalization of company performance targets.

Students of business and management studies seem to remember readily the names of Maslow and Herzberg, while remembering little of the theoretical implication of their results apart from such generalized conclusions as the hierarchy of needs and hygiene factors.

They may be aware of X and Y theories of management as proposed by McGregor (1960), but, apart from the myth that people work for money so that the more they are paid the harder they work, there may be no further insight into exactly what different theories of motivation are suggesting for managers and agents of change.

Certainly, it would be fair to say that intrinsic motivation is connected to the physiological needs laid out by Maslow (1943). But even these bring us no closer to the reality of a complex and diffuse field than do Pavlov's experiments with dogs. In both cases there is a basic assumption that the connection between motivation and work is instant reward. The cause–effect connection adduced here does not address the factors of satisfied need: that individuals would stop working once hunger had been relieved and that a level of expectancy in monetary terms would suggest a cut-off point for effort which, once reached, would see a cessation of further effort.

So, the question of why people continue to strive for long-term goals, sometimes deferring immediate gratification to do so, is critical to the goals they set themselves and the outcomes they seek in choosing one career path rather than another. There will always be the pragmatic factors of no other choice or no further aspiration. But, that apart, the desire to develop, grow and move on does need to be addressed by the individual and those seeking to gain continued commitment from individuals at work, especially through extended periods of disruption and change.

Researchers have identified need fulfilment (McClelland, 1961), where specific areas of need such as power, affiliation or achievement are identified as crucial to decisions made by individuals. This desire to isolate and assess particular drivers of motivation has been complemented by a more subjective acceptance that motivation is a function of expectancy (Vroom, 1964). In this assessment we are offered three conditions:

> Employees perceived that they possessed the necessary skills to do their jobs at least adequately (expectancy).
>
> Employees perceived that if they performed their jobs well, or at least adequately, they would be rewarded (instrumentality).
>
> Employees found the rewards offered for successful job performance attractive (valence).
>
> (Arnold, 1991, 178)

There are a number of assumptions being made here, but we can see the beginnings of what was to become a search for a cognitive calculus, in which individuals put together a calculation that time and effort combine in any occupation to give a reward. As individuals compare the effort and time required in one occupation, they may consider that there are other options available that would give a higher reward elsewhere or offer a similar reward for fewer efforts or less time (Farrell and Rusbult, 1981; Rusbult and Farrell, 1983).

The final comprehensive expression of motivation connected with productivity lies in the theory of Human Resource Management as offered by its early proponents (Beer *et al.*, 1984; Fombrun, 1984). The links between HRM policies, HR outcomes and organizational outcomes are illustrated diagrammatically in Table 4.1.

93

Table 4.1 Links between HR policies and organizational outcomes

HRM policies	HR outcomes	Organizational outcomes
Organization/Job design		High job performance
Management of change	Strategic integration	High problem-solving
Recruitment selection/socialization	Commitment	Innovation
Appraisal, training development	Flexibility/adaptability	High cost-effectiveness
Reward systems		
Communication	Quality	Low turnover
		Low absence
		Low grievances

Source: Guest (1989, 21)

Here, we can see the assumptions drawn about the conflation of HR activities with individual commitment and organizational outcomes. Guest has continued to attempt to test this model, but has so far failed to support the links in the way that the diagram suggests (2001). This is largely because the key idea of employee satisfaction is itself a diffuse concept and is nowhere found to be correlated to productivity. However, the link between productivity and financial results is supported, thus reminding us that managerialism may well achieve the required outcomes of financial effectiveness without necessarily achieving the motivational outcome of employee/job satisfaction. Least supported of all is the concept of organizational commitment. Individual commitment may be focused on the job, work, career or manager. But no combination of these will link predictively with the elusive goal of organizational commitment (Coopey and Hartley, 1991).

INDIVIDUAL LEARNING THEORY AND CHANGE

When we consider the preceding theories of how and why individuals learn it should come as no surprise to find that change programmes should access the level of individual learning from a similar standpoint as learning *ab initio*. If children learn by training and that training is a structured programme of frames, schemas and scripts, then reframing or offering new schemas and scripts ought to be a feasible strategy available to the change agent for adults, too.

We have already examined change theorists whose views would concur with this approach. One such is Nadler (1993), who sees the onset of change as challenging the status, power and control which routine functions have given their operators. Naturally enough, such individuals may resent losing what they see as their expertise before peers and clients alike. New systems will find them struggling to appear professional in the face of unaccustomed procedures, perhaps based on different technologies. The emphasis in this strategy will be support, training, assistance and helplines during the initial period to allow the individuals to become fully familiar with the new technologies and procedure. In this account resistance to change can be considered as a temporary phenomenon, so that after a period of adjustment to the new requirements normal service will be resumed as soon as possible.

More deep-rooted opposition to change may arise from conditions of work which the individual feels are unsuitable or unfitting to their own beliefs about what is correct behaviour and what is not. This can occur whether such change takes place at the outset of a career (Fournier, 1998) or when professional status is threatened by newly imposed managerialist practices (Carter and Mueller, 2002). This raises the question of individual self-perception and the role of competing rationalities in institutional change (Townley, 2002). This is an area that remains to be examined as the traditional hegemonies of professions are eroded by technologies or assaulted by political or technological interventions. Assumptions about self, job, career and perceptions within and outside the organization then become germane in the lives of those subjected to enforced change at work.

BASIC ASSUMPTIONS AND ENFORCED CHANGE

If we accept that basic beliefs or taken-for-granted assumptions lie at the heart of professional identity, then it would be fair to ask how these are acquired. For some commentators the answer would seem to be part of the culture into which they have been inducted (Schein, 1990). It is suggested here that experience of external threat to the organization may have caused the group to draw conclusions about expectancies in the future – people who are perceived to be a threat, or those who are natural allies. There are similar claims made about significant leader behaviour affecting expectancies of working groups (Isabella, 1990). The question of managed change then becomes the subject of reframing expectancies and allowing strong leaders to reformulate what is accepted and taken for granted under the new work regime.

Whether this reframing occurs as easily as its proponents suggest is a matter that invites further scrutiny. And, as it happens, enforced change is an opportunity for researchers to examine basic assumptions that have been challenged during enforced change and whether new and required ways of perceiving new work procedures have been accepted or not. Some research has attempted to examine how individuals interpret change events that occur in working life (McKinlay, 2004; English-Lueck et al., 2004), for interpretation itself assumes that individuals adjudge such events using criteria to evaluate the outcome. In this sense, then, enforced change requires individuals to confront what may initially be regarded as uncongenial and reassess whether taken-for-granted assumptions are to be defended and reinforced, modified or perhaps even abandoned.

For most individuals, the challenge to previously accepted beliefs would engender some element of surprise, pleasant or otherwise. The threat to expected conditions experienced at work at least raises the question of why previously accepted arrangements are subject to arbitrary intervention. We can observe this surprise in such research as cognitive dissonance (Festinger, 1957) or side-bets (Becker, 1964). There is a strong tradition among some commentators that, following disruption of work processes, there will be a process of assimilation by the individual workers involved in change. We may be asking people to adjust to new roles (Allen and Van der Vliert, 1984), but, whatever the basis of the change, for most writers assimilation is assumed. For some it is a question of training interventions (Lewin,

95

1947), for others a stepped approach in which initial resistance is eventually overtaken by acceptance (Nicholson and West, 1988; Isabella, 1990).

However, more recently, evidence supported the view that such assimilation could not be taken for granted. The redundancies of the 1980s, for example, affected not just those who lost their jobs, but also those who were left behind. Job security as a previously held basic assumption was now questioned by those remaining at work (Hallier and Lyon, 1996). But the question remains to be answered: have the survivors accepted the new reality of risk and uncertainty or are they aggrieved that their previously assumed rights to employment have demonstrably been withdrawn? Finding out whether expectancies have been modified and basic beliefs reconstructed lies at the heart of the challenge to researchers to examine reframing in more detail.

BASIC ASSUMPTION AND REFRAMING

If we are to examine how individuals change their basic assumptions, then the focus of our research needs to be what surprised them or not about the way in which change was instituted and whether they have modified their basic beliefs and assumptions or not. This focus on surprise and sense-making has allowed different researchers access to what could be regarded as a personal crossroads between past belief and future expectancy (Louis, 1980; Brown, 2000; Weick, 1999). One such piece of research has attempted to do just that (Randall, 2001).

Initially, a group of managers in three organizations were interviewed and the opening questions about what surprised them during the enforced change was put to them. For many there were the predictable responses of anger and frustration that their loyalty and industry on behalf of the organization had been repaid by unacceptable threat and possible loss of employment. However, for none of them did this threatened loss occur. The proponents of assimilation would expect that such individuals would get used to the new regime in time and settle back gratefully into a life of continued employment, less self-assured about the future, perhaps, but resigned to change as normal and part of a more turbulent employment situation.

However, such eventual acceptance and compliance was not always the final outcome. For many there was a withdrawal of goodwill and a desire for redundancy and opt-out. For others there was an acceptance but continued grievance. For both groups, then, there was a continued belief that loyalty and trust as evidenced by their long service and good conduct should merit a reward in terms of job security and continued career opportunity even though new terms and conditions had been regretfully accepted.

For others there was what appeared to be success as a result of change, in that promotion and opportunity for them personally accompanied the change. But this apparent reward from the new work regime did not always guarantee a resumption of trust and loyalty. In one case a younger manager's department had increased from 4 to 21 staff. His final summary illustrates the review that he made of his career and those of others:

> You have to have an attitude towards your career – one of stability. People are less willing today to wait for things to happen. They are more proactive now. Loyalty?

I don't think it can exist to the same extent. Companies don't matter any more. This happened quite recently where a friend of mine working for a local firm was told, 'you are no longer required.' And I said to him, 'Don't take it personally. It's not you.' You can have this loyalty but it takes a blow and then you never trust again. But for the individual the result is you will have clearer goals about what you want to achieve.

(Randall, 2001, 135)

Younger members of staff are less likely to hold traditional beliefs about their career and its dependence on the traditional long-term loyalty and trust. Basic assumptions for them may be much more instrumental and pragmatic. The engagement with the world of work offers them an opportunity to gain experience and to become more employable. One senior female manager expressed it thus:

It's all about achievement and effort. You have got to deliver. Make sure you do what you say you will do. Confront change and don't shy away from it. Ability may determine how far you will get but attitude is far more important: you must be positive and enthusiastic. The thing is there are not the same chances that there were when I started and these days there is not so much opportunity for promotion. So, you have to concentrate on lateral development. The only thing you have to fear is failure to deliver. You have to be seen to be a producer of solutions and a problem solver.

(Randall, 2001, 145)

For some there was a radical rethink of what they were doing with their lives, not just at work but personally. Such a fundamental reappraisal might include self-employment or acceptance of a consultancy contract within the existing organization. But always there were conclusions drawn about the significance of work and the organization's part in mediating meaning. The tone of some contributions became at times prescriptive, even encouraging:

Ask what you want. Keep your expectation of organizations down. But keep hope alive in your heart. Look at why you are still there. Be honest with yourself. You must be getting something out of it – now what is it? And if you're not getting anything out of it then move on. I have a client who still works there. It's a harsh environment and no hostages are taken. But don't look back to the good old days and the way things were. The past is irrelevant. Look at what you want. Look at why you are doing things. You need a new psychological contract. If it's not enough then you need to change. Make a conscious choice.

(Randall, 2001, 148)

For organizations the rhetoric of Human Resource Management as a cohesive philosophy of staff commitment has finally come apart for many individuals who have suffered enforced change at work. Basic assumptions about work are therefore likely to be more personal, instrumental and pragmatic. The relational elements mentioned by the proponents of the psychological contract are much less likely to be credited with any value. Like genetically modified foods, these individuals are immune to the blandishments that once underwrote the world of work – of continued employment for those who were loyal and hard-working.

97

So, behaviour modification, training and T-groups, followed by reinforcement and reward for new behaviours, may seem to work well at the level of surface validity (Skinner, 1974). We may well identify perceptual blocks, emotional blocks, cultural blocks and environmental blocks and deal with them in a direct and proactive way (Carnall, 1999, 77ff.). We may well address change programmes in a structured way, altering tasks and responsibilities, rewriting procedures and policies to reinforce it and establishing appropriate support (Child, 1984). However, underlying the best planned interventions may be a growing perception by those on the receiving end of change that the time has come to reconstruct the basic assumptions governing work and life, thus appearing to comply with the changes, but making sure to derive experience that makes you more employable elsewhere.

SAME SONG OR NEW TUNE?

How far people have absorbed new ways of looking at problems is significant if we are to adjudge whether change has embedded itself or not. Workers may have a different perception, but how far do those who manage change or become the agents of change internally share that change of perception? Each month *People Management*, the magazine of the Chartered Institute of Personnel and Development, publishes articles from practitioners, consultants and academics alike, many of them advising on successful strategies for change in organizations. The following excerpt is not untypical of the tenor of the content of many contributions:

> Many surveys have shown that good people management influences performance. It would be odd if it didn't. What we don't know is how it influences performance. This is the so-called black-box problem, where the way that inputs (people) are transformed into outputs (performance) is hidden from view. When we consider excellent firms that have enjoyed a long-term competitive advantage, it's often hard to find out why they are so good. This gives them the great advantage of making it hard for competitors to copy them.
>
> Three years ago the CIPD asked us to get inside twelve organizations to analyse how they managed to link people management to performance. Our research report is published this month.
>
> We conducted extensive interviews with managers and employee representatives at all levels, collected performance data in specific areas of these organizations and developed an attitude survey, which we used with employees in the first year and again in the second. We were able to compare the results with national averages.
>
> To help answer our core question we developed the people and performance model. Better performance, we argue, comes about when people are stimulated to do their job better: becoming better at looking after customers, better at solving problems and better at working with colleagues. This is discretionary behaviour in the sense that employees give and can take away co-operation and effort and 'go the extra mile' once they have met minimum standards of performance. We know from a large body of previous research on organizational citizenship behaviour that someone who likes their job, feels motivated and is committed to their organization is much more likely to display discretionary behaviour.

So, what triggers these positive attitudes? We believe that good companies need able people and will seek to develop their abilities. They will find ways to motivate people to use their skills and give them the chance to help make their team, section and company better. In other words organizations that support their employees by developing effective policies based on ability, motivation and opportunity will create higher levels of organizational commitment, motivation and job satisfaction.

(Purcell *et al.*, *People Management*, 15 May 2003. Reprinted with kind permission of Personnel Publications and the respective authors)

Consider the following questions:

1   What assumptions are the authors making about the link between input and output?
2   What assumptions lie behind the methods chosen for the research?
3   What comment would you make about the elements chosen for the model?
4   Who identifies 'the extra mile'?
5   How do HR policies motivate individuals at work?

The first question raises a debate that has endured for at least 15 years in the UK at least. We have seen it laid out above in Guest (1989), in which the HR policies are linked to the four outcomes of Strategic Integration, Flexibility, Quality and Commitment, which in turn feed into the organization's objectives. As we have discussed, there is no guarantee that these links exist in the way illustrated and increasing dissatisfaction with the assumption that prescriptive HR practice could guarantee their continued linkage.

On the surface the extent and depth of the research chosen would seem to satisfy the need for validity and reliability. However, we might question how far representatives can be expected to convey what must be essentially individual perceptions and the question arises as to with which national averages these results were compared.

There do seem to be a number of assumptions about the work priorities of any job. At the end of most supply chains there is a consumer. Effectiveness is finally measured by the beliefs of those consumers. How could their opinions be embodied in this research? What sort of problems are individuals expected to solve and who assesses when they have succeeded? Perhaps problems are solved without any indication or record being made. And how many problems are part of doing the job itself? Finally, some people do not work with others directly. How can we gauge their working better with colleagues?

The last question brings us to the perennial discussion of the link between HR practices and motivation. Do individuals work better because they are in receipt of good HR practices? Unless we withdraw the practices for a while and compare results or have a control group not in receipt of the practices, how can we tell? It may be that newly introduced practices do bring a downturn in the incidence of accidents, say. However, after a while that novelty of training may cease to have an impact and our efforts to achieve safety will need to start all over again.

Managing and implementing change is a complex challenge. Behavioural change may well be easy to introduce, support by training, monitor and reinforce at work. However, the

99

long-term impact on underlying basic assumptions may make those of HR-led manageri-alism more difficult to achieve thereafter.

DISCUSSION QUESTIONS

You might like to examine two questions which consolidate some of the points discussed in this chapter:

1   The steps in a problem-solving model of change are sometimes listed as follows:
    ■ Problem awareness
    ■ Problem identification
    ■ Information gathering
    ■ Solution generation
    ■ Solution evaluation
    ■ Decision
    ■ Implementation
    ■ Review.

    How far can an individual schema for problem solving transfer into a guide for the management of change? Cite examples or evidence to support your answer.

The source of the question can be found in Collins (1998, 83). He deals with it in his chapter on undersocialized models of change. You may want to offer an explanation of what this term means and how the author distinguishes such change from oversocialized models.

You may then want to examine the different types of change we looked at in Chapter 2. We looked at incremental change, punctuated equilibrium and continuous change. We noted that the first two types of change might find their context in examples of mechanical or systemic change. The problem-solving schema offered seems to suggest that there is an underlying rationality, which can be uncovered by judicious probing by the problem solver.

You may want to add in an example to illustrate how this kind of problem-solving would work. The example of the aeroplane passenger with the unconscious pilot could be used here: experimenting with the controls of the plane would enable the untutored passenger to discover what sort of inputs produce different results to the aeroplane's flight. You might then also add in the possible advice to be received through the radio transmitter. Putting together the inductive knowledge discovered by trial and error, the passenger could accept advice from the control tower to join the right flight path and achieve a successful landing.

The assumption behind this sort of example, as of punctuated equilibrium itself, is that the system has an inherent design which can be discovered and that the knowledge thus acquired can then be used to exercise control and implement successful change in the system.

What sort of problems might confound such a simple problem-solving model? Well, the third type of change – continuous – would be more complex and not so open to predic-tive intervention even if there was an internal system involved. External factors, sometimes referred to as context, are often mentioned here (Pettigrew, 1992). Organic change and environmental factors also need to be considered. If we extend our previous example we can demonstrate this. For the potential pilot, learning the plane's systems is open to discovery of the system over which control must be exercised. However, weather is the context or environment of flight. Working out the effect of cross-wind on flight performance is a specific knowledge not easy to acquire without instruction from an expert and much practice to master in the landing phase of flight. So, too, in business: efficiency factors may be manageable in a systematic way. However, two factors gauge effectiveness: the customer and the competition. Over neither of these has the potential manager any direct control or more than marginal influence.

The management of change takes place more often in a complex set of circumstances. Some of it may be functional and systemic. Such factors may well be open to the problem-solving schema offered in the question. However, more complex configurations may require prior expertise or defy direct intervention in the simple way suggested.

2   In his article 'Concepts for the management of strategic change' David Nadler delineates the problems of resistance, control and power. How does he suggest these be managed during organizational change? How helpful do you find his concept of equilibrium in explaining the processes of change?

You may want to explain the context of Nadler's background assumptions to change. He explains his views as based on the effect of change on individual expertise and competence. Individuals used to procedures and systems to do with their jobs have obviously grown used to the knowledge and skills which underpin the job functions. Experience has consolidated these competences and allowed the individuals to internalize them so that much less effort is required in their exercise.

Changing systems or procedures for individuals evidently brings disruption to this seamless and well-practised operation of human–system interaction. Nadler goes on to outline the loss of control and of status that may be consequent on such an imposed change. Not surprisingly such change is resisted. Nadler's position is that such change needs to offer support to the individuals whose expertise is about to be dispersed by change. There must be some sort of positive promotion of the benefits of the proposed change. There must be supportive training to enable individuals to come to the requisite levels of knowledge and skill in the new system and there must be extended available help while individuals settle into the assimilative stage of being familiar with and confident in the use of new systems.

Nadler does not engage with deeper-seated change. Such change might mean deskilling or even loss of professional status. The perception of change as, for example, requiring more effort for less reward or as an extension of managerial supervision and control may well be resisted for philosophical or moral reasons. Turkeys are unlikely to vote for Christmas. Workers, too, are always likely to see through explanations which gloss over the realities of perceived freedom and autonomy being replaced by greater managerial constraint.

The second part of the answer will require you to examine the term 'equilibrium'. You may want to address the context in which the term is used: normally 'punctuated equilibrium'. The context of this term is usually a mechanistic model of the organization. This sort of model is often illustrated diagrammatically as a closed series of cause–effect relationships. It suggests that the model is systemic; therefore it has a design inherent in it, which is capable of intervention by managers of change. As we have seen, this model does not easily accept the context or environment and the influence these may have on the system.

Finally, the term equilibrium itself suggests the intervention made into the system to get it to operate at a different performance level. The equilibrium is the new level that it will settle at once the intervention is complete. So, for example, pulling the control yolk towards the pilot will cause an aeroplane to climb. Once the climb is completed it can be pushed forward to regain straight and level flight. Equilibrium of the flight surfaces of the plane will now resettle at the new height. The example here is once again mechanical. The system is closed and balanced – it was designed that way. It will indeed rebalance. However, as a model it may not transfer into more complex fields of less predictable environments and actors. So, once again the phrase 'equilibrium' is more likely to apply to structural, closed models.

In short, then, you may feel that Nadler's model may find its context in functional change, where the need for new competence is accepted by individuals and supported by the company in training and support while new competence is acquired. However, it does not so easily account for overcoming resistance to change where change is perceived as a threat to traditional craft and skill, nor does it offer change strategies where change is complex or continuous. In such cases there may be a limit to the kind of change that traditional training can achieve and sustain.

REFERENCES AND FURTHER READING

Allen, V. and Van der Vliert, E. *Role transitions: explorations and explanations*. New York: Plenum, 1984.

Argyle, M. *The psychology of interpersonal behaviour*. London: Penguin, 1967.

Arnold, J., Robertson, I.T. and Cooper, C.L. *Work psychology: understanding human behaviour in the workplace*. London: Pitman, 1991.

Bales, R.F. Interaction process analysis. Reading, MA: Addison-Wesley, 1950.

Bate, P. Changing the culture of a hospital: from hierarchy to networked community. *Public Administration*, 2000, *78* (3): 485–512.

Becker, H. Personal change in adult life. *Sociometry*, 1964, *27*: 40–53.

Beer, M., Spector, B., Lawrence, P.R., Quinn Mills, D. and Walton, R.E. *Managing human assets*. New York: Free Press, 1984.

Brown, A.D. Making sense of inquiry sense making. *Journal of Management Studies*, 2000, *37* (1): 45–75.

Bullock, R.J. and Batten, D. It's just a phase we're going through: a review and synthesis of OD phase analysis. *Group & Organization Studies*, 1985, *10*: 383–412.

Carnall, C.A. *Managing change in organizations*. London: *Financial Times*/Prentice Hall, 1999.

Carter, C. and Mueller, F. (2002) The 'long march' of the management modernizers: ritual, rhetoric and rationality. *Human Relations*, 2002, *55* (11): 1325–1354.

Child, J. *Organization*. Cambridge: Harper & Row, 1984.

Cohen, G., Kiss, G. and Le Voi, M. *Memory: current issues*. Buckingham: The Open University, 1986.

Collins, D. *Organizational change*. London: Routledge, 1998.

Coopey, J. and Hartley, J. Reconsidering organizational commitment. *Human Resource Management Journal*, 1991, *1* (3): 18–32.

de Groot, A.D. Perception and memory versus thought: some old ideas and recent findings, in B. Kleinmuntz (ed.) *Problem solving: research, method and theory*. New York: Krieger Publishing Co., 1975.

English-Lueck, J.A., Darrah, C.N. and Saveri, A. Trusting strangers: work relationships in four high-tech communities, in K. Starkey, S. Tempest and A. McKinlay (eds) *How organizations learn*. London: Thomson, 2004, pp. 423–438.

Farrell, D. and Rusbult, D.A. Exchange variables as predictors of job satisfaction, job commitment and turnover. *Organisational Behaviour and Human Behaviour*, 1981, *29*: 78–95.

Festinger, L. *A theory of cognitive dissonance*. New York: Harper Row, 1957.

Fombrun, C.J., Tichy, N.M. and Devanna, M.A. *Strategic human resource management*. New York: Wiley, 1984.

Fournier, V. Stories of development and exploitation: militant voices in an enterprise culture. *Organization*, 1998, *5* (1): 55–80.

Greene, J. *Language understanding: a cognitive approach*. Buckingham: The Open University, 1986.

Guest, D.E. Personnel and HRM: can you tell the difference? *Personnel Management*, 1989 (January): 48–51.

Guest, D.E. Leadership/culture/strategy in P. Blyton and P. Turnbull (eds) *Reassessing human resource management*. London: Sage, 1992.

Guest, D.E. Is the psychological contract worth taking seriously? *Journal of Organizational Behaviour*, 1998, *19*: 649–664.

Guest, D.E. Human resource management: when research confronts theory. *International Journal of Human Resource Management*, 2001, *12* (7): 1092–1106.

Hallier, J. and Lyon, P. Job insecurity and employee commitment: managers' reactions to the threat and outcomes of redundancy selection. *British Journal of Management*, 1996, *7*: 107–123.

Herzberg, F. *Motivation to work*. New York: Wiley, 1957.

Hood, C. *The art of the state: culture, rhetoric and public management*. Oxford: Oxford University Press, 1998.

Huxham, C. and Vangen, S. Ambiguity, complexity and dynamics in the membership of collaboration. *Human Relations*, 2000, *53* (6): 771–806.

Isabella, L.A. Evolving interpretations as a change unfolds: how managers construe key organizational events. *Academy of Management Journal*, 1990, *33* (1): 7–41.

Jackson, P.M. Public sector added value: can bureaucracy deliver? *Public Administration*, 2001, *79* (1): 73–88.

Kahney, H. *Problem solving: current issues*. Buckingham: The Open University, 1986.

Kolb, D.A., Rubin, I.M. and McIntyre, J.M. *Organizational psychology: an experiential approach*. Englewood Cliffs, NJ: Prentice Hall, 1971.

Legge, K. HRM: rhetoric, reality and hidden agendas, in J. Storey (ed.) *New perspectives in HRM*. London: Routledge, 1995.

Lewin, K. Frontiers in group dynamics. *Human Relations*, 1947, *1*: 5–41.

Louis, M.R. Surprise and sense making: what newcomers experience in entering unfamiliar organizational settings. *Administrative Quarterly*, 1980, *25*: 226–251.

McClelland, D.C. *The achieving society*. New York: Free Press, 1961.

McGregor, D. *Human side of enterprise*. New York: McGraw Hill, 1960.

McKinlay, A. Smart workers, dumb organizations, in K. Starkey, S. Tempest and A. McKinlay (eds) *How organizations learn: managing the search for knowledge*. London: Thomson, 2004, pp. 406–422.

MacNeil, I.R. Relational contract: what we know and do not know. *Wisconsin Law Review*, 1985: 483–585.

Maslow, A.H. *Motivation and personality*. New York: Harper, 1954.

Nadler, D.A. Concepts for the management of strategic change, in C. Mabey and B. Mayon-White (eds) *Managing change*. London: The Open University/Paul Chapman Publishing, 1993.

Nicholson, N. and West, M. *Managerial job change: men and women in transition*. Cambridge: Cambridge University Press, 1988.

Pettigrew, A.M. *Shaping strategic change*. London: Sage, 1992.

Pollitt, C. Clarifying convergence: striking similarities and durable differences in management reform. *Public Management Review*, 2001, *3* (4): 1–22.

Purcell, J., Kinnie, N. and Hutchinson, S. Open minded. *People Management*, 2003, 9 (10): 31–33.

Randall, J.A. *Enforced change at work: the reconstruction of basic assumptions and its influence on attribution, self-sufficiency and the psychological contract*. Unpublished Ph.D. thesis, University of St Andrews, 2001.

Rosch, E. Cognitive representations in semantic categories. *Journal of Experimental Psychology*, 1975, *104* (3): 192–233.

Roth, I. and Frisby, J.P. *Perception and representation: a cognitive approach*. Buckingham: The Open University, 1986.

Rousseau, D.M. *Psychological contracts in organisations: undertaking written and unwritten agreements*. Thousand Oaks, CA: Sage, 1995.

Rousseau, D.M. The problem of the psychological contract considered. *Journal of Organizational Behaviour*, 1998, *19*: 665–671.

Rusbult, C.E. and Farrell, D. A longitudinal test of the investment model: the impact of job satisfaction, job commitment and turnover of variations in rewards, costs, alternatives and investment. *Journal of Applied Psychology*, 1983, *68*: 429–438.

Schank, R. and Abelson, R. *Scripts, plans and knowledge*. Hillsdale, NJ: Erlbaum, 1977.

Schein, E.H. *Organizational culture and leadership*. San Francisco, CA: Jossey Bass, 1985.

Schein, E.H. Organizational culture. *American Psychologist*, 1990, *45* (2): 109–119.

Skinner, B.F. *About behaviourism*. Knopf: New York, 1974.

Toplis, J., Dulewicz, V. and Fletcher, C. *Psychological testing: a manager's guide*. London: IPM, 1987.

Townley, B. Managing with modernity. *Organization*, 2002, 9 (4): 549–573.

Van Maanen, J. People processing: strategies of organizational socialization. *Organizational Dynamics*, 1978, 7 (1): 18–36.

Vere, D. and Beaton, L. Three-point turn. *People Management*, 2003, 9 (5): 36–38.

Vroom, V.H. *Work and motivation*. New York: Wiley, 1964.

Weick, K. Theory construction as disciplined reflexivity: tradeoffs in the 90s. *Academy of Management Review*, 1999, *24*: 797–806.

Chapter 5

Cultural transformation
Behaviours or perception?

TOPIC HEADINGS

- Culture as a working concept
- Culture and Human Resource Management
- Formation of cultures/national cultural typing
- Culture as metaphor/metaphors for culture
- Managing cultural transformation

INTRODUCTION

The concept of culture is one that pervades not only academic literature on the management of change, but also the many popular attempts to describe processes of change as they have occurred at work. There is an assumption that everyone will know what is meant by the term and be committed to the need to change whatever sort of culture is being described. Unfortunately, the various descriptions themselves require closer examination to discover whether what is described bears any relation to any other narrative in which a similar term is used. Different uses of the term and lack of definition bedevil the study of culture.

In this first part of a chapter featuring the term we will attempt to examine some of the ways in which culture is described and assumed by different writers. Each of the passages will be allowed to speak for itself. We will then invite some reflection on some of the questions raised by the passage quoted. Academics, consultants or managers within organizations often write narratives about the management of change. They are often anecdotal, but also contain or assume theoretical underpinnings which are not always clearly expressed or readily acknowledged. In each example we will attempt to discover what the underpinning assumptions are and whether the writer offers evidence to suggest that these assumptions have been addressed during the account of change at work.

The first passage comes from a body of literature we have referred to already and is described as OD in practice:

Reinventing the corporate culture

Proctor & Gamble, once considered very slow and cumbersome, is pushing authority down, speeding up decisions, and becoming more responsive to its customers. P & G is reinventing its corporate culture and undergoing a radical restructuring under new chairman, Edwin Artzt. In the process, P & G is inventing the packaged goods industry for the year 2000 and beyond. But can a large and bureaucratic organization make these radical changes without totally destroying the culture that made it great?

Traditional values

P & G has been known as a corporation with traditional, old-fashioned values. The organizational man in the grey flannel suit feels right at home and hierarchy and tradition reign – drinking at lunch, wearing light coloured socks, or red suspenders is discouraged. Middle managers rarely made key decisions and the decision process often travelled through several management layers. But, as John G. Smale, former CEO commented, 'You can't be old fashioned and be successful in the markets in which we compete.'

A new vision

In the first two years of restructuring, Proctor & Gamble has reorganized its marketing, sales, manufacturing and distribution. Driving the reorganization is the long-term vision to become the market leader in each of P & G's 39 product categories.

As part of the reorganization, CEO Edwin Artzt is changing the vaunted brand management system. Only one of every three new brand hires ever makes it through the four-year process to become a brand manager, a position responsible for every part of their brand's marketing, advertising and development. But Proctor & Gamble's brand managers were so focused on one single product that they often lost sight of the total market.

This led to the creation of the category manager position who has total profit and loss responsibility for the entire product line. The category manager has the authority to make quick decisions, which attempt to create small stand-alone businesses within the corporation.

Edwin Artzt, CEO and leader of the change, who spends 60 to 70 percent of his time on the road says, 'I give everyone the opportunity for input, and – consensus or no consensus – off we go.' He has earned the nickname 'the prince of darkness' because he comes in, makes changes and moves to the next problem. Artzt's goal is for a new management structure, a fresh global approach, an enduring corporate culture and a commitment to the long-term.

(Harvey and Brown, 1992, 92 from *An experiential approach to organizational development*, 4th edn. Reprinted with kind permission of Pearson Education)

Consider the following questions:

1 What sort of change is being considered here?
2 Are these structural changes or people changes?
3 What impact will these changes have on brand managers?
4 How would you describe the CEO's management style?
5 What sort of cultural change is being embarked on here?

At first reading, the passage seems to be referring to style or image. The man in the grey flannel suit seems to be a comment on the image the company gives out. But management layers and decision-making seem to relate to structural issues within the organization. Clearly, the vision mentioned in the second paragraph relates to a target, which the new CEO has set to become the market leader in each of the product categories the company competes in. So far, then, we could say that a number of different factors have been raised, but their relationship has not been established.

The key change appears to affect the role of the brand manager. Already a demanding position which has a high drop-out rate of one in three hires, the scope of this job is both demanding and exposes those who exercise it to immediate scrutiny. It seems that the new job description will include more responsibility for all functions pertaining to the product. In these times we might hear this described as empowerment. The individuals concerned in this job need to make the decisions on budgets for marketing and all associated costs to project the company into the top position. We can, therefore, see a link emerging, though not expressly stated, between freeing up these key performers and allowing them to take full responsibility unfettered by bureaucratic constraints. So, personal changes in job responsibility to enable organizational targets to be achieved in turn require that decision-making be freed from layers, which perhaps impeded it in the past. Perhaps these are the emerging causal links envisaged in the changes described.

In a sense, then, we are looking at areas of structural change related indirectly in the article to personal change. The individuals who undertake the newly created positions of brand manager now need to be competent and committed to the responsibilities required of them and given the freedom to make decisions without reference to time-wasting hierarchical decision makers.

Interestingly, the narrative does not focus on those currently doing the job and how they feel about this newly imposed extension of their responsibilities. We might want to evaluate such a change by examining what sort of support is being offered to those about to be engulfed by such a change and whether it affects the one in three drop-out advantageously or not. The article does not elaborate on this aspect.

Reference is made in the narrative to the CEO's style indirectly. He says of himself that he seeks some element of consensus, but that, once a decision is made, it is then a closed matter. His nickname seems to suggest that he is as ruthless as he is decisive. There is a suggestion that insiders mistrust or dislike the import of the changes embarked upon. We can see the CEO's goal of a new management structure and its link to the fresh global approach mentioned, which is in turn a commitment to the long-term target of being the first in the market in all 29 of their products. Less clear to us is the statement about 'an enduring corporate culture'. How exactly would such a change be achieved through the changes in brand managers' responsibilities, which we have just read about? Perhaps the assumption here is that culture is a series of performances, which are to be changed in individuals and facilitated by structural changes to decision-making for the newly appointed managers.

As we remarked earlier, writers frequently offer theoretical explanations to complement their narratives about change and its management. In this case we have such an explanation as follows:

Cultural resistance to change

Changing a corporate culture is not easy. Culture emerges out of the shared behaviours of organization members and working relationships, which have developed over time. Consequently, it takes time for the cultural transformation to take effect.

A culture can also prevent a company from remaining competitive or adapting to a changing environment. People Express, Inc built its early success on an unusual and highly decentralised form of management in which every employee was an owner-manager. Employees were encouraged and even required to perform different functions, such as a pilot also working as a ticket agent. The result was the employees tended not to get bored and learned other aspects of the business. This type of happy disorganisation worked well when the company was small but it became chaos and created substantial problems for a billion-dollar-a-year company. When People was warned about their management practices being inappropriate, the company would respond with the statement: 'This philosophy is what made us great. We're not going to change.' The company president, Donald C. Burr, still held on to this culture up to the point that People, suffering heavy losses was forced to sell out to its arch rival, Texas Air.

People Express demonstrates the importance of culture to successfully implement a strategy is critical. 'OD as practice' illustrates this difficulty at Proctor & Gamble.

(Harvey and Brown, 1992, 92 from *An experiential approach to organizational development*, 4th edn. Reprinted with kind permission of Pearson Education)

Consider the following questions:

1 What do you understand is the definition of culture from the first paragraph?
2 What sort of management is being described in People Express?
3 Why are individuals committed to this culture?
4 What assumptions does the writer make about the consequences of this commitment?
5 Has the writer successfully demonstrated the link between culture and strategy?

At first sight, the writer seems to be emphasizing the performance side of culture. It is the way that individual workers behave that demonstrates a culture in this narrative. If we follow this line of argument to its source we might expect to find such behaviours set up in early working life (Van Maanen, 1978). Socialization may include training, or the example of more experienced work colleagues, to reinforce similar behaviours that then characterize the culture to the outside observer. But, if this is true, then we might expect that retraining can effect a change in this kind of culture. As we shall see, however, such direct approaches to change at work are not always successful in their application.

The account now refers to what we might describe as functional flexibility. Designated roles overlap and one person is expected to fulfil more than one function at any one time. Smaller organizations may often find a need to employ staff that have diverse competencies and are happy to use them as required by the client need. The writer follows with the assumption that this motivates staff and ensures that they do not get bored without citing any evidence that this is the case. However, it is also referred to as 'happy disorganization'. The assumption here is that the motivated staff are actually operating less than efficiently due to this proliferation of their duties. Again, no evidence of this is cited in the account.

The account suggests that, as the company grows, such behaviours become the cause of inefficiency and therefore ineffectiveness as well. The assumption seems to be that growth means change is necessary and that these happy staff are now obstructing the company's development by retaining what has now become inappropriate behaviour. Again, no evidence is offered nor examples given of how this may be the case. If a pilot happily checking tickets is causing obstruction due to an increase in the number of passengers, say, then it would be fair to ask whose responsibility it is to make a management decision to separate the functions and put another member of staff on board to relieve the pilot of that duty.

The final assumption made by the writer is that the intransigence of the staff in retaining these happy practices has brought about the demise of the company. Again, no evidence or example is offered of how this connection is made. Ineffectiveness in the face of more efficient operation by competitors may be the fault of inflexible working practices. However, it may be nothing to do with such practices at all.

What we see here is not untypical of uncritical accounts of culture, loose in definition and lacking rigour in the causal connections alleged in the narrative offered. As we shall see in further examples, the reader needs to question the assumptions made in accounts of culture and attempt to evaluate its significance during change.

Our previous account featured a traditional view of change as part of Organizational Development. More modern accounts can be compared and contrasted with that approach and the following is a current account from the magazine of the Chartered Institute of Personnel and Development, *People Management*. The feature is headed 'Empowerment' and gives an account of the National Blood Service, which as part of the National Health Service was reorganized in 1993 into three zones instead of 15 regions 'to introduce greater efficiency and economy into the service'. More recently, the zone idea has been abandoned and the NBS has established itself as a national service. The article includes excerpts from different key individuals involved in the changes. First, the development director, Craig Hewison:

Hewison feels he knows why the latest restructure has been more successful. 'The chief executive, Martin Gorham, has been instrumental. He's had a long career in the health service – and one of the first things he did was visit blood centres around the country to articulate why we should be organised again, this time around functional silos.' HR has also been on the board since Gorham joined the NBS.

Hewison concedes that people felt threatened by this recent restructuring, only three and a half years after the last one, but he believes that as the dust settles, the majority of staff and managers will see the benefits. It also helped that this reorganisation wasn't as drastic as the last and clearly wasn't done for cost savings.

'We were reorganised to be better as an organisation,' Hewison says. 'There was still personal trauma, but this time we had more support. We had a national HR team,

working to national standards and national documentation, policies and procedures.'
The approach taken by NBS has been to use the knowledge of its employees to develop
their own solutions to problems rather than have them imposed by senior managers or
external experts.

The organisation began the process in 1999 when, in line with NHS policy, it ran a
staff survey. The results were as many feared: directors were not thought to be interested in staff views or well-being; workplace stress was not dealt with effectively and
workloads were excessive. The survey also highlighted a widespread belief that terms
and conditions were not fairly and consistently applied to all staff. There was scepti-
cism about whether the NBS would do anything to address this.

(Smethurst and Allen, 2003, 42)

Consider some questions on this passage:

1 What sort of approach was adopted by NBS before embarking on change?
2 How does this approach differ from our previous example of Proctor & Gamble?
3 What were the benefits of adopting this approach to change?
4 What concerns held by staff were uncovered as a result of the survey?
5 Can the managers of change satisfy such concerns?

It would be fair to acknowledge that many companies now adopt a more open approach
to the management of change. Consultation involving surveys or questionnaires of all the
staff is more common now than in the days of the previous account, in which the driver
for change often appeared to be the CEO alone. In this case, too, the chief executive went
round to listen and explain rather than tell and sell. Perhaps his long experience in the
health service made for greater empathy and understanding than newly imposed managers
from outside the business. Significantly, the openness seems to have been genuine and was
not a cover for hidden agendas of cost-cutting so often focused on staff cuts.

This bottom-up approach to change allows both more consultation and the opportunity
to identify recurrent concerns held by individuals. We can see the emergent approach here,
which accepts the benefits of clear standards for consistency while allowing for the solution
of problems at a local level. Such openness allows issues of belief and concern about the
present situation to emerge during the survey.

The difference here lies in the active encouragement, which facilitates frankness about
suspicions, attitudes and expectancies – not all of them positive. Beliefs that directors don't
care are not exceptional in an organization. Opinions about stress and workloads having
increased and the belief that terms and conditions are applied inconsistently are the beginnings of an agenda change that managers will need to address. We may notice, in fairness,
however, that it may not be possible to address perceived inequality to the total satisfaction of the objectors. However, at least the opinions of those involved have been sought
and can now be included in subsequent encounters.

Apart from the survey, 300 hundred staff drawn from different functions throughout the organization were invited to join 18 focus groups. These groups were facilitated by an outside consultant and met on four occasions to developed a mission statement, a set of values intended to help the organization see staff as a key resource and provide a yardstick against which to work. What is interesting in the remainder of the article is the views of different participants about the exercise. Next, the views of Lindsey Batson, manager of the Bath blood collection team:

> As leader of 25 staff, aiming to meet targets, stay within budgets and motivate her team members, Batson was well placed to make suggestions to the focus groups. She says that lines of communication to the top are now improved and the organisation less top-heavy.
>
> 'The culture is slowly starting to change but by definition it's an on-going process,' she says. 'We're also getting away from the blame culture and taking best practice on from other parts of the service.'
>
> How has her team reacted to the changes? 'People want to see the promises in action,' says Batson. 'My team is very open-minded. It's not that they don't ever grumble, but with these changes it helps if they can see the rationale behind it. If they can, they're very flexible and responsive.'
>
> (Smethurst and Allen, *People Management*, 20 March 2003. Reprinted with kind permission of Personnel Publications and the respective authors)

We spoke earlier about assumptions lying behind commentators' perceptions. Here the manager uses culture in two different ways within two sentences. The culture slowly changing might be construed as the whole organization, though without specifying whether it is behaviour change or perception change. The following sentence contains the reference to a particular type of culture, in this case 'blame culture', by which she could be referring to a commonly held belief or response typical of people within the organization.

In the second paragraph her comments align themselves much more closely to traditional motivational theory, in which change in behaviour favourable to individual expectancy reinforces a view that something has changed. This is coupled with the final comment that explanations sometimes make change more palatable because it is, perhaps, more comprehensible.

The article continues:

> But not everyone thinks the picture at Bath is typical. Mike Jackson, regional officer for public sector union Unison, certainly doesn't. One issue that has dogged the new organisation is that of negotiating new terms and conditions. Jackson explains, 'We've been left with two legacies: over a dozen different sets of terms and conditions and then three zones. We've been spending a lot of time since 1998 negotiating new terms and conditions. It's a real mess and it's taking a long time to resolve.'
>
> 'It's a bad, old-fashioned industrial relations atmosphere. There's a complete detachment between the senior management and what's happening at ground level. They live in a glass bubble. What they want in terms of flexible working doesn't sit easily with the constant drive for targets and budgets. There's serious tension,' he says.
>
> (Smethurst and Allen, *People Management*, 20 March 2003. Reprinted with kind permission of Personnel Publications and the respective authors)

If culture is defined as commonly held perceptions, then the union negotiator demonstrates that perceptions are themselves dependent on the subjective viewpoint of the individual. In this case involvement in the rationalization of terms and conditions lies at the heart of this reorganization, just as the new role of brand manager at Proctor & Gamble was always going to shoulder the main burden of functional changes there. The union official may well have his own expectancies, which seem not to be satisfied, and therefore seek to attribute blame to significant others.

But just when we might think that there is a commonly held union view, the article offers a contrasting perception:

> But Amicus-MSF regional officer Owen Granfield defends the organisation. Arguing that there has been a real attempt to foster a better working relationship with the staff at NBS, he says: 'I think the Unison view is perhaps coloured by the number of individuals they've had undergoing organisational change. We probably come into contact with the forces of change more often and can be more positive about them. I would say that from our perspective the NBS management is making seriously good progress.'
>
> (Smethurst and Allen, 2003, 44)

So, perceptions even from a single constituency can be unexpectedly diverse. A particular function does not determine how experience will modify beliefs or perceptions. The individual here expresses a belief that personal experience more often modifies personal assumptions and expectancies.

Finally, the article concludes with a view from the HR department:

> Head of operations Lesley Jones stresses that the review of processes, terms and conditions at NBS has been staff-led. She says: 'If we go back to our first attitude survey, the staff wanted improvements in leadership, so all senior managers have produced personal improvement plans and are in the process of going on two three-day modules on managing themselves and others.'
>
> 'In our second attitude survey, there were marked improvements on more than 80% of the areas we had asked about. In terms of benchmarking, we're above average now for NHS employers. We're not totally there but we're on the right track.'
>
> (Smethurst and Allen, 2003, 44)

We might comment on a perception from HR that planning and training can improve leadership. Leadership may well be dependent on the perceptions of those who are led as much as it is on trained leadership behaviours. Interestingly, the results of the second survey serve to reinforce a belief in the HR manager that improvement has been achieved. However, how attitudinal surveys can be accurately benchmarked is assumed here rather than explained.

Before we leave the contributors who offer so many different definitions of culture, there is one more type of contribution which may be worth examining. Theoretical works abound based on examples and illustrations, as we have seen, many of them written by participants. However, there are other works, which offer summary and overview, attempting to offer broader conclusions about this difficult term. We offer one example for closer scrutiny:

What is corporate culture?

The culture of an organization defines appropriate behaviour, bonds and motivates individuals and asserts solutions where there is ambiguity. It governs the way a company processes information, its internal relations and its values. It functions at all levels from subconscious to visible. In the world of increasingly 'flat' companies and sophisticated 'knowledge-based' products, control and understanding of an organisation's corporate culture are a key responsibility of leaders, as well as a vital tool for management if it is to encourage high performance and maintain shareholder value.

A corporate culture can be described and mapped out using different categories and classification systems, but all cultures are in fact responses to corporate dilemmas. The role of the corporate leader is to manage conflicting needs in a synergistic way, creating an environment in which opposing forces can be reconciled to create rapid and strong growth.

Culture is used by social scientists to describe a whole way of life, ways of acting, feeling and thinking, which are learned by groups of people rather than being biologically determined. Great variations occur in the behaviour of human groups with similar genetic endowments. Sir Edward Bernard Taylor attributed these to culture, 'that complex whole which includes knowledge, belief, art, morals, law, custom and any other capabilities and habits, acquired by man as a member of society.'

Corporate culture has been likened to one of those ink blots in which we see what we want to see. In corporations, culture is used to explain why nothing seems to work, or why competitors are so much more successful. Culture is thought to bestow unique competitive advantages and/or dire limitations. Could Westerners be like the Japanese even if they wished to be? Would it mean losing for ever the distinctive aspects of Western culture? This book argues that corporate culture is describable, measurable if necessary and, within limits, alterable.

(Hampden-Turner, 1990, 11)

Examine the following questions in more detail:

1   What sort of culture is being described in the first paragraph?
2   What comments would you make about the claims made in the second paragraph?
3   What sort of culture is referred to in Sir Edward Bernard Taylor's definition?
4   Is culture a set of values or a tool to be used by managers?
5   How does national culture coincide with organizational culture?

At first sight the definition offered here might seem to relate to procedures, behaviours and performances. It is fair to say that company culture could most easily be observed, measured and validated if uniform performance is the essence of culture. And yet, even within the opening sentence, it is clearly more than that. We are told that it 'bonds and

113

motivates individuals'. This would surely be more than simply replicable performances. Army drill may well appear to be a culture based on performance, something instilled and trainable. But it is clearly more than that if it also bonds and motivates. There may be soldiers, for example, whose performance in parade ground drill is faultless, but who do not necessarily find it either bonding or motivating.

But then the description moves into personification: the company is mentioned as the actor in processing information, internal relations and values. Processing information may be a laid-down performance, which is systemic and trained into individuals. But how exactly do companies process values? If culture functions at a subconscious level, how do we know that this has taken place? Why do flat organizations and knowledge-based products require culture more than traditional ones? If cultures are procedures, then they are required for the fulfilment of any function regardless of the organization's structure. Finally, how can leaders and managers use culture as a vital tool to encourage high performance and main- tain shareholder value? Is an assumption being made here that procedures assure efficiency, which in turn assures effectiveness? If so, there may also be exceptions in which happy moti- vated and culturally well-managed staff are efficient but not necessarily effective.

We can accept perhaps that cultures may include performance and attitudes, in which case they are very varied in expression, though may be monitored in the way suggested. But what evidence is there for asserting that they are responses to corporate dilemmas? It could be argued that a dilemma requires resolution and that therefore such resolutions may historically have triggered cultural solutions – solutions that are then enshrined in proce- dure or taught informally to people joining the organization. But is this the essential prerequisite of cultural values?

The definition offered by Sir Edward Bernard Taylor seems to be a summary of a popular definition of culture pertaining to the ways a tribe or society governs itself and accepts values and norms. The literature supporting social anthropology would suggest that myths and symbols are the archetypes of such cultural constructs. They are a means of interpreting what individuals do and sometimes according meaning and value. Here we might ask how this comprehensive list can be anything other than a summation of all the artefacts of soci- etal existence. But, if this meaning exists in symbol and is taught and learned, how can it be changed? It can sound as if it is the prerequisite of a static interpretation system imposed on individuals during a socialization process.

Finally, how much overlap is there between corporate culture and national culture? The terms Westerner and Japanese can be used simply as categories to identify classes of people who come from or are born in particular parts of the world. But, on closer inspection, we would have to admit that there are many cultures lying within those broad classes. Do all Japanese share the same culture or is it just surface validity to those who do not share the same identity? Westerners can include Americans and Europeans. Evidence in recent world affairs suggests that these sub-groups do not always see world affairs in the same way. Indeed, different subcultures seem to be as apparent as one, cohesive national culture. As soon as we impute a single, unitary culture, we find that it is capable of other distinctive features, which suggest that it is not as cohesive and deterministic as can sometimes be thought.

In the following section we will examine the different traditional literatures that have supported the concept of culture. We will maintain that it is possible to see some overlap between different traditions and definitions. However, we would caution that readings about culture from any of these traditions require careful examination to ensure that they are not being used to describe culture in a different theoretical context. Similarly, claims made for culture as a tool of management, especially during change, need to be scrutinized to ascertain whether the links between performance, perception and symbol exist in the way that is alleged and, still more, that those operating at a corporate level acknowledge such links.

CULTURE AS AN OPERATIONAL CONSTRUCT

Popular use of the word 'culture' can, as we have seen, embrace a number of different meanings. It may be used to indicate societal markings or identifiers – the kind of behavioural distinguishers that are used day-to-day to place an individual so that we may thereafter categorize him or her. Often such markers themselves are taken to be the culture of a group or tribe. Another common use might be in the context of the arts. Culture here is an attribute that those appreciating certain types of art are said to possess. They are cultured people because they know about and appreciate what is considered to be culture. Here culture could be described as a set of acceptable knowledge, but equally accessible if an individual wanted to know what the content of that culture was.

One writer comments on the various definitions as follows:

> The concept of culture seems to lend itself to very different uses as collectively shared forms of for example, ideas and cognition, as symbols and meanings, as values and ideologies, as rules and norms, as emotions and expressiveness, as the collective unconscious, as behaviour patterns, structures and practices, etc. all of which may be made targets to study.
>
> (Alvesson, 2002, 3)

Now, it should be clear that, if culture can be any or all of the items in this list, then we have a problem as researchers and change managers. The list is not just diffuse; it is also comprised of identifiable, measurable, testable elements, such as behaviour patterns, structures and practices, and also more abstract elements, such as ideas and concepts. An individual could learn these things and indeed they form the content of educational and instructional courses. But, when we move into the area of symbol and meaning, we are presented with a problem: how do individuals interpret meaning? Symbols can be taught to individuals. The neophyte learns that the cross is a symbol of religious meaning. But whether the individual believes the attributed meaning and interprets the sign in this way is not readily available to others to validate. Rules and norms can indeed be taught. But emotions and expressiveness belong to the individual. And, as for the collective unconscious, who could know what that contains; who has access to it?

If we confine culture as a concept to the organization, then we have narrowed down its focus to groups of people associating with each other to achieve common objectives, perhaps. But the definition of 'culture' may be as diverse as it was in a more general context. As we will discover, definitions range from 'the way we do things round here' to deeper meanings and significance grounded in a tacit knowledge, espoused and taken for granted

115

(Pettigrew, 1979; Deal and Kennedy, 1982; Pondy *et al.*, 1983; Gregory, 1983; Smircich, 1983; Frost, 1985; Meyerson and Martin, 1987; Meek, 1988; Whipp *et al.*, 1989; Turner, 1990).

However, one distinction that has been useful for understanding the generic differences has been between culture as something an organization has, compared with culture as something an organization is (Smircich, 1983). If we accept the first definition of culture as what an organization has, then we will be focusing on attributes that members of an organization are thought to possess. The advantage of this approach will be that it allows us to examine such behaviours and performances the attributes are thought to support. As we will see, the approaches to replicating such a culture would be open to the usual methods of recruitment, assessment and identification. Once included in the group, individuals can be subjected to training intended to reinforce the required performances and they in turn can be captured in the procedures and policies written into job descriptions. Thereafter, they can be monitored, appraised and rewarded in such a way that they are internalized by the individual and reinforced by managers seeking to replicate the culture consistently (Legge, 1995, 185).

If we approach culture from the alternative perspective as something the organization is, then we are looking at a tradition that can trace its roots back to the social construction of meaning and the self. The interaction of individual with group triggers perceptions and interpretations, which will give rise to attributing meaning to behaviours and linguistic acts (Casey, 1995, 57). Writers who approach the definition of culture from this standpoint regard the individual as the basis for what is sometimes described as symbolic interaction. One early contributor to this tradition is Mead (1934), who emphasized the role of language and symbols in the devolving of meaning. As symbolic meanings evolve and are shared between individuals who interact, the sharing of significant symbols and meanings can begin to involve others in the group. For later writers in the same tradition, the construction of meaning, in which individuals present themselves to each other, is an interaction that can be compared to a drama (Goffman, 1959). The problem this presents to the researcher, however, is one of identification. How do we discover what these meanings are? And then, how can such meanings be managed, if by the management of change we mean an intervention to ensure a particular behaviour or outcome? We will need to address this issue, as we will the question of how such cultures change, for symbols are sometimes offered as if their meaning was a constant, accepted by all who inhabit the context of a culture. But, if meaning is subject to interpretation, then that interpretation may not be as static and enduring as is sometimes alleged.

CULTURE AND HUMAN RESOURCE MANAGEMENT

We have already referred to the rise of what appeared to be a cohesive philosophy of managing people to replace the disparate activities that characterized personnel management practices previously. The connection between good personnel practice and the achievement of organizational objectives can now include the involvement of individuals competent to achieve the objectives and committed to the values of the organization (Beer, 1984; Fombrun *et al.*, 1984). The links can now be put in place between the HRM policies, Human Resource outcomes and Organizational outcomes (see Table 4.1, p. 94).

In this summary we can view not only the imputed connections between the management of people and desired organizational outcomes, but the inclusion once again of the culture that such a practice is intended to generate. Indeed, the reference to strong and weak cultures becomes a given in many accounts of the management of change (Georgiades, 1990; Wickens, 1987; Pascale, 1990; Hamel and Prahaled, 1994; Champy, 1995). HRM elevates culture to a level of importance in which it is both the outcome of successful management and also the instrument whereby successful managers can manage change effectively (Legge, 1995). And here we return to the problem which using the term culture presents us with: is culture something that already exists within a group of people, a function of an interaction between them, or is it something carefully constructed through, say, training and careful selection, which can be managed and protected by judicious management interventions? We need to keep asking this question, as it is not always apparent from reading the accounts of cultural change which approach is being employed or whether they are both required to achieve this cohesion of individual affect and group achievement of objectives. One writer summarizes this dilemma clearly:

> If culture is regarded as embedded in social interaction, that is as something that is socially produced and reproduced over time, influencing people's behaviour in relation to the use of language, technology, rules and law, and knowledge and ideas (including ideas about legitimate authority and leadership) then it cannot be discovered or mechanically manipulated; it can only be described and interpreted. The researcher adopting the social emergent view of culture cannot suggest how it can be created or destroyed, the researcher can only record and examine how culture may be altered in the process of social reproduction. People do not just passively absorb meanings and symbols; they produce and reproduce culture and in the process of reproducing it, they may transform it. The social emergent approach to culture also moves the researcher away from the political and ideological interests of management, towards those of the organisational community as a whole.
>
> (Meek, 1988, 293)

THE FORMATION OF CULTURES

Discussing culture in the context of the management of change presents us with some challenges: whether cultures are formed through social interaction or are attributes inherent in individuals, what happens when change affects the group and by extension the individuals within that group? We may well adopt the simple definition which we saw before, that culture is the way we do things round here (Deal and Kennedy, 1982, 4), or go for something more affective as 'the set of habitual and traditional ways of thinking, feeling and reacting that are characteristic of the ways a particular society meets its problems at a particular point in time' (Klockhohn in Ogbonna and Wilkinson, 1990, 11). But how does this occur in the first place and how can it be positively managed during enforced or imposed change at work?

One way of attempting to link the behavioural and the attitudinal aspects of culture is offered by Schein (see Figure 5.1).

117

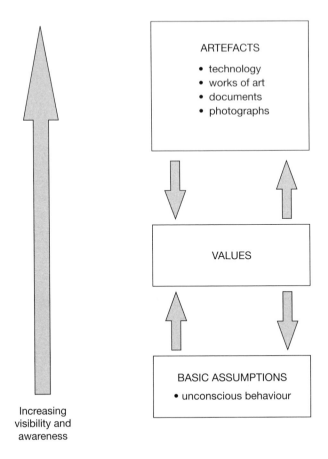

Figure 5.1 *Schein's cultural layers model*
Source: Schein (1985, 109)

At first sight the visible artefacts seem to offer a point of contact with the reality, which individuals inhabit in the organization. There may be a geographical location, a physical environment and all the support systems that enable an individual to fulfil a role and its functions such as technology, systems and procedures. All of these things have to be learned and are often taught. They will be practised and probably internalized. But they do not come value free. Apart from individual interpretation of initial experience there may also be the influence of the peer group. Values can be derived from imposed priority: out of a list of job descriptors there may be those that are regarded as important and urgent, which contrast with tasks perceived as urgent but unimportant. Casual observation of individuals at work will not always reveal which is which. Only familiarity with custom and practice is likely to reveal such prioritizing. Salespeople, for example, are usually disinterested in recording journeys made and visits completed; they prefer negotiation and closing deals. Work colleagues will probably reinforce such values. Acceptance of such a value may mean that it becomes a taken-for-granted assumption by the working group.

This brings us to the final category mentioned in Schein's schema: basic assumptions. Schein himself offers different examples of what these may be. Sometimes he lists such factors as humanity's relationship to nature; the nature of reality and truth; the nature of human nature; the nature of human activity; the nature of human relationships (1985, 86). At other times he offers specific examples of statements made in a working context more in line with Deal and Kennedy's definition above (Schein, 1990). What he does not do is identify the source of such basic assumptions. Are they inherent, or are they absorbed somehow from peer group or training? This is no mere pedagogical distinction. It may affect radically our ability to intervene successfully to change a culture. Our example taken from sales is one example. In this case most companies link payment of expenses to submission of travel details. However, such cases are not always as routine as the example there suggests. A current example may serve to illustrate the problem: there have been several references recently to 'institutional racism' in organizations, which, it is sometimes alleged, bring about a tendency to discriminate in dealings with the public. Coloured recruits joining the police force or army spring to mind here. The question is: have all police officers a basic assumption which is essentially racist? If so, is there some selection, either wittingly or unwittingly, which causes only racists to join the service, or is this a process of social-ization – sometimes referred to as canteen culture – in which the peer group communicates such a basic assumption and excludes individuals who do not accept it and behave differ-ently from the dominant group?

The concept of basic beliefs or assumptions is an enduring and compelling one. However, if it is assumed as the foundation of, say, a concept like 'corporate culture', whereabouts in an organization can it be found? Individuals have personal beliefs and constructs, which they may well bring with them to work. Indeed, there is no guarantee that personal beliefs will be jettisoned in favour of a corporate construct (Balnaves and Caputi, 1993). It is possible for individuals to survive in an environment hostile to their personal beliefs, appearing to espouse a corporate belief in order to survive or continue in membership there while retaining a personal belief at variance with the socially acceptable construct. As Legge remarks:

> Corporate culture – that shared by senior management and presented as the 'official' culture of the organization – may be only one of several subcultures within an organ-ization, and may be actively resisted by groups who do not share or empathize with its values. If the corporate culture makes no sense of the organizational realities experi-enced by the employees other than senior management, it will not become internalized outside that small group.
>
> (1995, 187)

However, we would have to admit that such conflicts between individual belief and group taken-for-granted assumptions are difficult to identify and research.

NATIONAL CULTURAL TYPING

The question of pervasive cultures inherent in groups of people is most apparent in claims made for national cultures. One such commentator is Hofstede and his work illustrates the problem presented by our concept and its role in the management of change. Most students will have come across his research, which was based on one organization, IBM, and extended through the different countries in which the company is situated. Hofstede thought that he had identified what he called five key dimensions. These he listed as follows:

- Power distance
- Individualism/collectivism
- Masculinity/femininity
- Uncertainty avoidance
- Confucian dynamism.

(Collins, 1998, 112)

Without going too deeply into each dimension in turn, we can say that each allows the researcher to adjudge along a spectrum whereabouts national groups score, similar to the way in which constructs were measured and compared in individuals (Kelly, 1955). The way in which national subjects behave may well be both identifiable and distinct, thereby allowing the observer to place subjects within such categories and then draw conclusions about national scores. However, it should be said that such behaviours can be learned. Indeed, when we go abroad to work we may be inducted into the correct procedures for meeting and greeting ethnic groups according to their expectancies of social niceties and behaviour. However, when we move to imputing values assumed to exist and underpinning such behaviours, we may find it difficult to avoid social stereotyping of the grossest kind. Gender typing alone should alert the researcher to the difficulty of identifying the basic assumptions held by men compared with women. Perceptions can change over time so that expectancies that might have applied some years ago (gentlemen always give up their seat to a lady) now no longer apply in the same way. Such subtle change makes it hard to apply the masculine/feminine dimension with any hope that it will consistently identify a national type which distinguishes between, say, Scandinavians and Asians.

Alluring though national stereotypes may be, the temptation to single out critical factors may allow only a surface validity of social behaviour, learned, perhaps, rather than inherent. But whatever the derivation of such behaviours may be, the underlying basic assumptions may not be as simple to ascribe. Collins puts the point succinctly:

> Instead of following models which attempt to explain culture as being similar to a form of unconscious mental programming, therefore, we must acknowledge that people interpret events and bend the cultural norms and mores of the cultures they inhabit, in order to address the contextual problems and events they must face. They may not discuss or think through the ramifications of their actions, but this does not mean that such actions are unconscious.

(Collins, 1998, 124)

Behaviours, however similar, may be indicative of basic assumptions, but they are not necessarily predictive either. The danger with linking action with belief and ascribing it to culture in this way makes it difficult to distinguish between what is open to management to change and what may always elude both research and manager. There have been significant attempts to highlight exactly why such research is flawed and its findings questionable. Foremost among them is McSweeney, who summarizes his article as follows:

> **The plausibility of systematically causal national cultures**
>
> The failure of Hofstede's stories — once unpacked — to show a causal link between his dimensions of a particular national culture and a specific national action is not surprising, given the earlier critique of his construction of his national cultural cameos. But, in the event, how credible is the notion of systematically causal national cultures? The critique above of Hofstede's identification methodology did not rely on a counter supposition that such causal national cultures did not exist. The analysis was agnostic on that issue. Here, however, I want to raise some doubts about the notion of national cultural social causality and so to suggest that the failure of Hofstede's model goes beyond the technical. Hence, the implication is not to devise improved identification of national cultures, but to abandon the notion of a mono-causal link between national cultures and actions within nations.
>
> (McSweeney, 2002, 109)

CULTURAL TRANSFORMATION

It is clear that, if the management of change is to include changing the culture of the organization, then we need to be clear about what it is we are attempting to change. Whatever beliefs groups hold in common lie with the individual and therefore it is with the individual that we rightly place our research endeavour. We can accept that socialization will include attempts to gain commitment to beliefs about self, work and society, often included deliberately in induction training (Van Maanen, 1978; Casey, 1995). But what happens when change occurs which lies outside the expectancy of the individual? It would be fair to say that some sort of adaptation was alluded to and researched before culture became a popular vehicle for change initiatives. Some kind of internalized adjustment is often assumed by researchers or sought by managers. It may be thought of as cognitive dissonance (Festinger, 1957) or side-bets (Becker, 1964). It may be thought to be some sort of cognitive calculus (Farrell and Rusbult, 1981; Rusbult and Farrell, 1983). But it has become more apparent during periods of threat or uncertainty at work (Greenhalgh and Rosenblatt, 1984; Lazarus and Folkman, 1984). Whatever the threat is, the individual has to make a mental calculation of how to respond to the threat and what the chances are of surviving successfully.

Some change management techniques include sessions in which individuals and groups are encouraged to share their taken-for-granted assumptions, sometimes referred to by such terms as 'unfreezing' (Lewin, 1947). The proponents of such techniques will then seek to facilitate a move away from the old way of looking at work and move towards a different set of perspectives before 'refreezing' around the newly acceptable views. Some researchers see this as a series of steps or stages, which will move, say, from preparation, to encounter, to adjustment and finally to stabilization (Nicholson and West, 1988, 9). There is an assumption here that individuals in transition are open to persuasion or training and will then simply accommodate to the required situation. We might see here an assumption that individuals will move to adapt to changes required by the organization.

121

When we examine more closely how exactly this accommodation takes place we are presented with models of evolving interpretations of change (Isabella, 1990, 31). In this example, frames of reference are suggested as the vehicle by which these changing interpretations can take place. Isabella follows the Lewin process of change and lays out four stages through which it is assumed individuals will progress: anticipation, confirmation, culmination and aftermath. She identified different stories and rumours exchanged between those subjected to change programmes at work and then examined how far there had been acceptance of the dominant interpretation or illustration of likely or expected outcomes. Once again we can see that the process described still assumes assimilation by the individual of outside sources of interpretation.

More helpful, perhaps, is the literature, which acknowledges that most change initiatives evince surprise in individuals subject to unexpected and enforced change at work. Such surprise suggests that there can be a variety of responses, some pleasant and some not so pleasant. Making sense of change means examining how change has been interpreted and discovering what exactly was thought surprising in what was done or not done (Louis, 1980a, b). At this point, basic assumptions about change can be examined – some, perhaps, confirmed and others disconfirmed. This approach has been the basis of several researchers examining the impact of enforced change and the different effects it may have on individuals or groups of individuals (Brown, 1998; Casey, 1995; Weick, 1998; McCabe, 1998). Individuals may remain convinced that their basic assumptions have been violated and that promises made by the employer have been broken (Hallier and Lyon, 1996; Rousseau, 1998). Such research may include an assumption that there is a psychological contract in which job security and career development is included.

Change, which violates these basic assumptions, may meet resistance and make acceptance of cultural change difficult to achieve. Indeed, more recent research suggests that enforced change can often scatter previously held assumptions about self, work and career. It is certain that some may resist and feel alienated. But there is emerging evidence that others may not hold such expectancies of, say, secure employment and others, even if ostensibly successful as a result of enforced change, may no longer accord trust and loyalty to the organization as they might once have done. One such successful manager explains it as follows:

> Yes, I took over 4 people and now I have staff of 21. So, I have done well for myself. At a personal level, I feel I have done very well. Yes, we went from compound-centred to billable hours. But, what's the individual getting back? Is it money, reward? Doubtful. What I feel is there has to be a feel-good factor on any project. There has to be recognition and feedback. I strive for that. But, efficiencies? There has to be a feel-good factor. You can have efficiencies, but what's in it for the individual? It hits them harder. At the lower level people feel totally stressed.
>
> (Randall, 2001, 207)

For some individuals enforced change has meant a move into a different employment contract with the same organization. One such subject moved into self-employment and continued to service the company's training needs. She summarizes how enforced change can radically affect basic beliefs about employment and find expectancies and basic assumptions about employment changed:

I think my own psychological contract has always been different from others. It reflects my own belief system. People put in long hours. But their contract is not with the organization, it is with other people in the organization. An organization is essentially inhuman. By that I mean it doesn't really exist. What we've got is senior management devising the strategy and then imposing it passing it down to other people. It's not healthy and it breeds short-termism. I always said after the take-over, 'I don't care whose name is over the door, I just work for these people.'

(Randall, 2001, 207)

Prophetic words, perhaps, which raise questions about how far the traditional psychological contract exists in the way in which its proponents suggest (Rousseau, 1998). Certainly, those who embark on imposing enforced change at work may find that the threat to basic assumptions about self, work and society triggers a diversity of responses that make the concept of a cohesive culture difficult to sustain.

CULTURE AS A METAPHOR AND METAPHORS FOR CULTURE

Before we leave the definitions of culture, it may be worthwhile offering a summary of the different ways in which writers on organizations sometimes use the word. There can be an assumption of the function of culture in the workings of organizations, which posits what it is and how it works (Alvesson, 2002, 31).

In some accounts, therefore, culture is described as 'shared social knowledge'. This is sometimes referred to as a clan culture (Wilkins and Ouchi, 1983, 469). In this account culture provides individuals with 'shared views on the utilitarian exchange relationship' and asserts that selective recruitment, socialization and ceremonial control will achieve high performance. Alvesson describes this culture as *exchange regulator*.

Another metaphor describes culture as a *compass*. Here the instrument that provides primary information about critical direction is linked to the policies and procedures required to reach the goals and the required values that underpin those performances (Weiner, 1988, 536).

Another common metaphor would be that of *social glue*. Here, the values and goals of dominant elites are assimilated by members and generate devotion, loyalty and commitment to the company (Martin and Meyerson, 1988).

Not dissimilar to the last category is culture as *sacred cow*. Often the leader is suggested as the source of such taken-for-granted values (Schein, 1985). Loyalty at a personal level requires adoption of leader values and behaviour, though whether it outlives the leader becomes a critical question.

A different approach to cultural management would be culture as *affect regulator*. Here the direct address to the emotions of employees is made by the organization. Examples offered include Disney World (Van Maanen, 1991) and Body Shop (Martin *et al.*, 1998).

More realistic to those who hold the view that corporate assumptions may be more honoured in the breach than in the observance would be culture as *disorder*. Cultural assertions by managers serve merely to emphasize the variation that individuals are already aware

123

of, but now have their attention drawn to in virtue of its evident failure to achieve cohesion (Martin, 1992; Martin and Frost, 1996).

If culture can reinforce diversity as much as enforce it, perhaps we can also view it as being like a set of blinkers, forcing vision in one direction. This is described as culture as *blinders*. Individuals are thought to be unable to envisage alternative goals, perhaps because to do so would invalidate deeply held views (Anthony, 1994, 88).

Not dissimilar to this metaphor is culture as *world closure*. Again the emphasis is on the lack of options available to members for considering any other interpretation of events than that provided by an implant of management's favourable perceptions and definitions of social reality (Knights and Willmott, 1987).

Alvesson acknowledges that there are many other ways in which culture can be viewed as different metaphors. However, we can accept that each metaphor assumes what a culture contains – procedures, performances, goals, values etc. – and what role this plays in management's attempt to control or modify these in individuals within the organization.

MANAGING CULTURAL TRANSFORMATION

In this final section it may be worthwhile to look briefly at writers who have offered schemas or models for managing cultural change. As we do so, we might be able to identify what sort of assumptions are being made about the nature and content of culture and what theoretical assumptions underlie the author's views.

Thornhill offers two such schemas side by side and entitles them 'typical frameworks for managing cultural change' (see Table 5.1).

If we were commenting on Kilmann's five steps first, we might note that surfacing norms is something that most managers of change aim to achieve. Lewin's use of sensitivity or T-groups would be an example for getting individuals and groups to be perfectly frank about their beliefs in a public forum. The move to the new state requires the identification of new

Table 5.1 *Steps for managing cultural norms*

Kilmann (1984, 1989)	Wilkins and Patterson (1985)
Five steps:	Four questions:
■ Surfacing actual norms (more or less equivalent to surfacing the culture)	■ Where are we now as a culture?
■ Articulating new directions	■ Where do we need to be going strategically as an organization?
■ Establishing new norms	■ What are the gaps between where we are as a culture and where we should be?
■ Identifying culture gaps	■ What is our plan of action to close the gaps?
■ Closing culture gaps	

Source: Thornhill (2000, 74)

norms and directions and the summary of gaps now apparent to participants. The final step would perhaps present the biggest challenge.

The Wilkins and Patterson list offers a linked set of questions, which could well be used to facilitate a work-based group discussion. Similar questions are offered by other authors intent on cultural change (Hamel and Prahaled, 1994; Champy, 1995). We might notice that the culture word is slipped into the third question, but its link to the kind of gaps which need closing is not specified.

Thornhill also offers some 'general principles for successful cultural change' (see Box 5.1).

BOX 5.1 GENERAL PRINCIPLES FOR SUCCESSFUL CULTURAL CHANGE

Accepted and appropriate patterns of behaviours are defined by values and basic underlying assumptions.

Successful organizations tend to be those where the values and basic assumptions encourage practices and behaviours which match the organization's strategies.

Where values and basic assumptions are incompatible with an organization's strategy successful cultural change may be difficult to achieve.

If an organization is contemplating change it first needs to establish whether the strategy necessitates a shift in values and basic underlying assumptions or if change can be achieved some other way.

Prior to any cultural change, senior management must understand the implications of the new culture for their own practices, artefacts and espoused values and be involved in all main change phases.

Adequate resources need to be allocated to support cultural change and maintain it once it has been achieved.

Culture change programmes must pay careful attention to the organization's power bases and opinion leaders such as trade unions and employees' associations.

Cultural change programmes must pay careful attention to the organization's existing practices or artefacts, such as recruitment, selection, retention, performance management and employee relations.

In order to create a change in culture, organizations need to decide how practices or artefacts will be amended to support the new espoused values and contradictory practices removed.

Every opportunity should be taken to reinforce the practices and artefacts and restate the espoused values of the new culture's values and basic underlying assumptions.

Source: Developed from Beckhard (1992) and
Hassard and Sharifi (1989)

We can acknowledge the debt owed to Schein's threefold levels of artefacts, values and basic underlying assumptions. However, we can also observe that the list contains summary categories, which may include behaviours and attitudes and sometimes confuse culture as an end in itself and culture as a means to an end.

Questions about opinion formers and leaders miss out the question of splits within key groups and resisters. Whose are the espoused values which all now need to follow? Are they derived and developed by some process of consensus or are they imposed by senior managers and then required of all staff members? There are no answers given here. But in the next chapter we will need to address these issues as the n-step approaches contain similar assertions, while on the whole ignoring the question of resistance.

EMERGENT APPROACHES TO CULTURAL CHANGE

We have mentioned the top-down approach, which is implied or inferred in schemas of imposed change. There is the remaining question of whether there is an alternative approach to change, which is more emergent or bottom-up. There have been several researchers who have devoted more attention to methods encouraging involvement and consultation. We have already referred to the context-related emphasis of incremental change, which requires an open view of organizations and the acknowledgement that there are no boundaries, which are not porous and constantly invaded by alternative values and influences at variance with management-espoused values.

Such writers include Pettigrew (1992) and also one of the founders of Human Resource Management as a philosophy, Beer (Beer *et al.*, 1984). In a later publication Beer *et al.* offer more of an emergent schema for facilitating change at work (see Box 5.2).

What we observe here is the more open route of involvement and consultation, which assumes the emergence of common agreement on the vision of the outcome and the means and options available to achieve that vision. It is focused on skills and actions required to achieve the vision and then refers to necessary changes in policies, procedures and structures to achieve the desired behaviours. Evaluation comes last and includes amendment, presumably to ensure that any modifications are included in the final draft. But at no time does it refer to attitudes, values or beliefs.

BOX 5.2 A SCHEMA FOR FACILITATING EMERGENT CHANGE

1. Monitor and adjust strategies in response to problems in the revitalization process.
2. Develop a shared vision of how to organize and manage for competitiveness.
3. Foster consensus for the new vision, competence to enact it and cohesion to move it along.
4. Spread revitalization to all departments without pushing it from the top.
5. Institutionalise revitalization through formal policies, systems and structures.
6. Mobilize commitment to change through joint diagnosis of business problems.

Source: Adapted from Beer *et al.* (1990)

There is an assumption that consultation itself will appeal to reason within the body of people affected. Once appealed to, that consensus should carry them forward through the subsequent steps. We will need to address the question of what happens to individuals who refuse to accept the new vision and the steps agreed by colleagues to achieve the vision.

What we can see is the focus of this change on behaviour and the omission of attitudes altogether. Authors who favour emergent change rightly emphasize the need to address objective behaviours. They play down the contradictions that individuals sometimes experience when contemplating the effect of such changes on basic assumptions about self, work and society. One writer on culture and change summarizes the problem as follows:

> The simplistic notions of strong organizational cultures and associated organizational 'excellence' have been subjected to criticism in this chapter. The intellectual and methodological bases upon which such assumptions are founded are fundamentally flawed. This means that to effect change in an organization simply by attempting to change its culture assumes an unwarranted linear connection between something called organizational culture and performance. Not only is this concept of organizational culture multifaceted, it is also not always clear precisely how culture and change are related, if at all, and, if so, in which directions.
>
> (Wilson, 1992, 91)

DISCUSSION QUESTIONS

Here are two questions to consider. They and similar variations come up regularly in examination papers:

1 'The ability to understand and manage changes in culture represents a key lever for organizational change' (Collins, 1998).

   How can culture be managed in the way suggested during periods of managed change at work?

A definition of culture will need to be addressed early on in your answer. You will probably want to look at the distinction between culture as something an organization has and something an organization is. As you do this, you may wish to include examples or illustrations of what the difference would be for day-to-day managers. In other words, what would be the most accessible elements of culture? Remember the references we saw at the beginning of the chapter to measurable, testable factors. So often, these are behaviours, performances, routine-led – the visible artefacts spoken of by Schein. You may mention that these performances can be embodied in policies, procedures and practice and are most often to be found in operations directories, staff handbooks and personnel and training handbooks.

You may then want to contrast these more accessible factors that organizations have with the perceptual elements that include attitudes, values and basic assumptions. You may want to offer an explanation of how these less accessible elements are formed in individuals and reinforced in peer groups and through interpretative experience.

The question of enforced change can then be addressed along with the fact that it may give rise to surprise and require sense-making on the part of the individual enduring contradiction in expectancies which may lie deeply in, say, a psychological contract. The question of resistance is one that needs to be addressed here. For the change agent or manager of change the question of how far to involve individuals in the change process now becomes important. Is this to be top-down, imposed change or bottom-up, emergent change? You may want to offer examples of different schemas for dealing with the steps or questions suggested as methods of proceeding in the event of adopting one or other technique.

Finally, you may want to conclude with a summary of how far culture can be managed. A definition of management may help you clarify your conclusion. The critical factor may be how far management involves willing participation of those managed and how far the performance required entails commitment to a set of values or beliefs.

2   How would you define culture in an organization? How would you attempt to access it as a manager of change?

The first part of your answer requires an exploration of the different definitions of culture as a concept. You will have seen this in the outline answer to the preceding question.

The second part of the question allows you to adopt a more pragmatic approach. But keep your focus on the word 'access'. How accessible are values, basic assumptions and attitudes in general? Are there ways of trying to identify these and what sort of techniques have been offered by practitioners to achieve this kind of revelation from individuals and groups?

The final part will be your own conclusions, perhaps based on examples and illustrations drawn from research, management accounts and, perhaps, your own experience. It may be that bottom-up change lends itself more readily to the possibility of surfacing beliefs and assumptions, just as Lewin established in his use of T-groups.

REFERENCES AND FURTHER READING

Alvesson, M. *Understanding organizational culture*. London: Sage, 2002.

Anthony, P. *Managing culture (managing work and organizations)*. Buckinghamshire: Open University Press, 1994.

Balnaves, M. and Caputi, P. Corporate constructs: to what extent are personal constructs personal? *International Journal of Personal Construct Psychology*, 1993: 119–138.

Becker, H. Personal change in adult life. *Sociometry*, 1964, *27*: 40–53.

Beer, M., Spector, B., Lawrence, P.R., Quinn Mills, D. and Walton, R.E. *Managing human assets*. New York: Free Press, 1984.

Beer, M., Einstat, R.A. and Spector, B. Why change programmes don't produce change. *Harvard Business Review*, 1990 (November/December): 158–166.

Brown, A. *Organizational culture*, 2nd edn. London: *Financial Times*/Pitman Publishing, 1998.

Casey, C. *Work, self and society, after industrialism*. London: Routledge, 1995.

Champy, J. *Reengineering management: the mandate for new leadership*. London: HarperCollins, 1995.

Collins, D. *Organizational change: sociological perspectives*. London: Routledge, 1998.

Deal, T.E. and Kennedy, A. *Corporate cultures*. Reading, MA: Addison Wesley, 1982.

Farrell, D. and Rusbult, C.E. Exchange variables as predictors of job satisfaction, job commitment and turnover. *Organisational Behaviour and Human Performance*, 1981, *27*: 78–95.

Festinger, L. *A theory of cognitive dissonance*. New York: Harper Row, 1957.

Fombrun, C.J., Tichy, N.M. and Devanna, M.A. *Strategic human resource management*. New York: Wiley, 1984.

Frost, P.J. *Organizational culture*. Beverley Hills, CA: Sage, 1983.

Georgiades, N. A strategic future for personnel. *Personnel Management*, 1990 (February): 43–45.

Goffman, E. *The presentation of self in everyday life*. New York: Doubleday, 1959.

Greenhalgh, L. and Rosenblatt, Z. Job insecurity: towards conceptual clarity. *Academy of Management Review*, 1984, *9*: 439–447.

Gregory, K. Native view paradigms: multiple cultures and culture conflicts in organizations. *Administrative Science Quarterly*, 1983, *28* (3): 359–376.

Guest, D.E. Personnel and HRM: can you tell the difference? *Personnel Management*, 1989 (January): 48–51.

Hallier, J. and Lyon, P. Middle managers and the employee psychological contract: agency, protection and advancement. *British Journal of Management*, 1996, *7*: 107–123.

Hamel, G. and Prahaled, C.K. *Competing for the future*. Boston, MA: Harvard Business School Press, 1994.

Hampden-Turner, C. *Corporate culture for competitive edge*. London: Hutchinson, 1990.

Harvey, D.F. and Brown, D.R. *An experiential approach to organizational development*. Englewood Cliffs, NJ: Prentice Hall, 1992.

Hassard, J. and Sharifi, S. Corporate culture and strategic change. *Journal of General Management*, 1989, *15* (2): 4–19.

Hofstede, G. *Culture's consequences*. Beverley Hills, CA: Sage, 1980.

Hofstede, G. *Cultures and organization*. Maidenhead: McGraw Hill, 1991.

Isabella, L.A. Evolving interpretations as a change unfolds: how managers construe organizational events. *Academy of Management Journal*, 1990, *33* (1): 7–41.

Kelly, G.A. *The psychology of personal constructs*. New York: W.W. Norton, 1955.

Kilmann, R.H. *Beyond the quick fix: managing five tracks to organizational success*. San Francisco, CA: Jossey Bass, 1984.

Kilmann, R.H. *Escaping the quick-fix trap: how to make organizational improvements that really last*, San Francisco: Jossey Bass, 1989.

Knights, D. and Willmott, H.C. Organizational culture as management strategy: a critique and illustration from the financial service industries. *International Studies of Management and Organization*, 1987, *17* (3): 40–63.

129

Lazarus, R.S. and Folkman, S. *Stress, appraisal and coping.* New York: Springer, 1984.

Legge, K. *Human resource management: rhetoric and realities.* Basingstoke: Macmillan Business, 1995.

Lewin, K. Frontiers in group dynamics. *Human Relations,* 1947, *1*: 5–41.

Louis, M.R. Surprise and sense making: what newcomers experience in entering unfamiliar organizational settings. *Administrative Science Quarterly,* 1980a, *25*: 226–251.

Louis, M.R. Career transitions: varieties and commonalities. *Academy of Management Review,* 1980b, *5*: 329–340.

McCabe, D. Making sense of quality: towards a review and critique of quality initiatives in financial services. *Human Relations,* 1998, *51* (3): 53–73.

McSweeney, B. Hofstede's model of national cultural differences and their consequences: a triumph of faith – a failure of analysis. *Human Relations,* 2002, *55* (1): 89–118.

Martin, J. *The culture of organizations: three perspectives.* New York: Oxford University Press, 1992.

Martin, J. and Frost, P. The organizational culture wars: a struggle for intellectual dominance, in S. Clegg, C. Hardy and W. Nord (eds) *Handbook of organizational studies.* London: Sage, 1996.

Martin, J. and Meyerson, D. Organisational cultures and the denial, channelling and acknowledgement of ambiguity, in L.R. Pondy, R.J. Boland and H. Thomas (eds) *Managing ambiguity and change.* New York: Wiley, 1988.

Martin, J., Knopoff, K. and Beckman, C. An alternative to bureaucratic impersonality and emotional labor: bounded emotionally at The Body Shop. *Administrative Science Quarterly,* 1998 (June), (special issue: Critical Perspectives on Organizational Control).

Mead, G.H. *Mind, self and society,* ed. Charles Morris. Chicago: University of Chicago Press, 1934.

Meek, V.L. Organizational culture: origins and weaknesses. *Organizational Studies,* 1988, *9* (4): 453–473.

Meyerson, D. and Martin, J. Cultural change: an integration of three different views. *Journal of Management Studies,* 1987, *24*: 623–648.

Nicholson, N. and West, M. *Managerial job change: men and women in transition.* Cambridge: Cambridge University Press, 1988.

Ogbonna, E. and Wilkinson, B. Corporate strategy and corporate culture: the view from the checkout. *Personnel Review,* 1990, *19* (4): 9–15.

Pascale, R. *Managing on the edge.* London: Viking, 1990.

Pettigrew, A.M. On studying organizational cultures. *Administrative Science Quarterly,* 1979, *24* (4): 570–581.

Pettigrew, A.M. *Shaping strategic change.* London: Sage, 1992.

Pondy, L., Frost, P.J., Morgan, G. and Dandridge, T.C. *Monographs in organizational behaviour and industrial relations: organizational symbolism.* Greenwich, CT: JAI Press, 1983.

Randall, J.A. *Enforced change at work: the reconstruction of basic assumptions and its influence on attribution, self-sufficiency and the psychological contract.* Unpublished Ph.D. thesis, University of St Andrews, 2001.

Rousseau, D.M. The problem of psychological contract. *Journal of Organizational Behaviour,* 1998, *19*: 665–671.

Rusbult, C.E. and Farrell, D. A longitudinal test of the investment model: the impact of job satisfaction, job commitment and turnover on variations in rewards, costs, alternatives and investment. *Journal of Applied Psychology*, 1983, *68*: 429–438.

Schein, E.H. *Organizational culture and leadership*. San Francisco, CA: Jossey Bass, 1985.

Schein, E.H. Organizational culture. *American Psychologist*, 1990, *45* (2): 109–119.

Schein, E.H. in D. Collins, *Organizational change: sociological perspectives*. London: Routledge.

Smethurst, S. and Allen, R. Blood simple. *People Management*, 2003, *9* (6) (March): 42–44.

Smircich, L. Concepts of culture and organizational analysis. *Administrative Science Quarterly*, 1983, 28 (3): 339–358.

Thornhill, A., Lewis, P., Saunders, M. and Millmere, M. *Managing change: a human resource strategy approach*. Harlow, FT: Prentice Hall, 1999.

Turner, B.A. *Organizational symbolism*. Berlin and New York: de Gruyter, 1990.

Van Maanen, J. People processing: strategies of organizational socialization. *Organizational Dynamics*, 1978, *7* (1): 18–36.

Van Maanen, J. The smile factory: work at Disneyland, in P.J. Frost, L.F. Moore, M.R. Louis, C.C. Lundberg and J. Martin (eds) *Reframing organizations*, Newbury Park: Sage, 1991, pp. 58–76.

Van Maanen, J. Displacing Disney: Some notes on the flow of culture. *Qualitative Sociology*, 1992, *15* (1): 5–35.

Weick, K.E. (1998) Improvization as a mindset for organizational analysis. *Organization Science*, 1998, *9* (5): 543–555.

Weiner, Y. Forms of value systems: a focus on organisational effectiveness and cultural change and maintenance. *Academy of Management Review*, 1988, *13*: 534–545.

Wickens, P. *The road to Nissan*, London: Macmillan, 1987.

Whipp, R., Rosenfeld, R. and Pettigrew, A. Culture and competitiveness: evidence from two mature UK industries. *Journal of Management Studies*, 1989, *26* (6): 561–585.

Wilkins, A.L. and Ouchi, W.G. Efficient cultures: exploring the relationship between culture and organizational performance. *Administrative Science Quarterly*, 1983, *28*: 468–481.

Wilkins, A.L. and Patterson, K.J. You can't get there from here: what will make culture change projects fail, in R.H. Kilmann, M.J. Saxton and R. Sepa (eds) *Gaining control of corporate culture*. San Francisco, CA: Jossey Bass, 1985.

Wilson, D.C. *A strategy of change*. London: Routledge, 1992.

Chapter 6

N-step models

Practice, performance
or preference?

TOPIC HEADINGS

- Stepped change approach
- Theoretical underpinnings of n-step approach
- Phase analysis and Organizational Development
- Benefits of the phase model
- Examples of implementation

INTRODUCTION

The way in which change in organizations is handled will obviously affect the outcome in both the long and short term. Once the theoretical background to change has been assessed, most managers of change will be looking for a plan which can be simply and easily implemented. Accounts of change by those involved in it are not difficult to find. Those who have survived and done well or those who instituted the change often write about their experiences. We may suspect that they have a vested interest in portraying the experience in a positive light. What we are looking for is the underlying rationale that the manager of change used in implementing the change process.

Fortunately, there are several examples now emerging from the public sector. In the last 10 years, politicians have been interested in implementing change in the Civil Service and the public sector more generally to ensure that greater efficiency is achieved in all that they do. Governments are attracted by the promises that such savings can be made by adopting the new formulas of private sector change and breaking out of what was seen as an inflexible way of managing public services (Harrison, 1992; Hood, 1991; Huxham and Vangen, 1996). To give a flavour of what the literature contains we will look at one account in full and then address the question of claims made by different n-step approaches to change.

It would be no surprise to discover that positive accounts on the management of change come from literature extolling success and drawing conclusions about how change should

133

be implemented on the basis of their experience. One such account features the Tactical Air Command in the United States. The manager of change in this case was a General Bill Creech:

> The results speak for themselves:
> When Creech left TAC, 85% of its planes were rated mission capable, up from 58% when he arrived; he had taken TAC from the worst to the best of all air force commands.
>
> Fighter jets were averaging 29 hours a month of flying time, up from 17.
>
> TAC was capable of launching double the number of sorties it could when Creech arrived.
>
> The elapsed time between the order of a part and its delivery had dropped from 90 to 11 minutes.
>
> The crash rate had dropped from one every 13,000 flying hours to one every 50,000. And the reenlistment rate for first-time mechanics had nearly doubled.
>
> TAC accomplished all of this with no new money, no more people and a workforce with less experience than the workforce in place through the years of decline.
>
> (Osborne and Gaebler, 1992, 257ff.)

Consider the following questions about the background of the change example we are offered here:

1   What sort of change is featured here?
2   What sort of factors might effect an increase in the supply of parts?
3   Why would the crash rate be significant?
4   What does the enlistment rate suggest about previous problems?
5   How can a less experienced workforce become more efficient?

The background of this change suggests that the structures of the organization needed to be addressed. The supply of parts seems to be holding up the serviceability of jets and perhaps affecting their availability to fly sorties. If this surmise is correct, then we can see a link between the ready supply of parts and their release to crews for fitment, thereby, perhaps, enabling crews to turn round fighters more quickly and expeditiously.

More interesting is the possible link between this problem and the incidence of crashes. Perhaps the link is something to do with faulty parts on aircraft, though this point could be accounted for by aircraft being grounded rather than flown with mechanical faults. In 1987, the number of fatalities for General Aviation pilots in the UK amounted to 27. Twenty of these were pilot error – the majority (17) running out of fuel. Very few, in other words, were caused by faulty parts. Indeed the system used in aviation is predictive maintenance, which means that parts are replaced at due date, whether the aircraft has been in action or not. So, replacement of worn parts would reinforce the low flying rate but not entirely account for the fall in accidents.

Finally, the release of experienced workers – presumably mechanics, though the account does not say who they were – and their replacement with less experienced people again leaves questions unanswered. It could be argued that older workers were less efficient and newer ones more enthusiastic. It could say that more experience is not necessary to achieve efficient results. The question of levels of competence therefore remains unanswered here.

Of his own success Creech states:

When I left TAC, I had more control over it than my predecessors. I created leaders and helpers at all those various levels. Without that kind of network below you, you're a leader in name only.

It's not really that hard to run a large organization. You just have to think small about how to achieve your goals. There's a very fine limit to how much leadership you can exercise at the very top. You cannot micromanage – people resent that. Things are achieved by individuals, by collections of twos and fives and twenties, not collections of 115,000.

In his six years at TAC, Creech doubled its productivity. He did so simply by recognising human nature: people work harder and invest more of their creativity when they control their own work. Manufacturing businesses that embrace participatory management say it typically increases their productivity by 30 to 40 percent. Sometimes the increase is far higher. 'The extra commitment of the self-motivated doesn't make just a 10 to 20 per cent productivity difference. Someone who is fully engaged in his or her chosen work can do in months what routine attendance to a task might not accomplish in years.'

(Osborne and Gaebler, 1992, 258ff)

Consider the following questions:

1 What points are being made here about the connection between people and productivity?
2 What constraints are there on leadership?
3 What similarity is there between the armed services and manufacturing?
4 What problem might there be in continuing to achieve the productivity increases mentioned in the article?

The writer and the General both refer to the link between self-motivated people and the increase in productivity. From the original story we might conclude, therefore, that the older workers were unmotivated and unlikely to yield the required results because of lethargy and lack of commitment. In contrast, new workers adopt and adapt without question and their enthusiasm makes up for their lack of experience.

The General accepts that such motivation is necessary in all the 115,000 workers, as 'you can't micromanage'. His task was to create a network of leaders and helpers. He does not explain what exactly thinking small means with regard to the work that these people do for him. Perhaps it means redrawing job descriptions or giving autonomy to individuals to make decisions, which they were precluded from making in the past.

However, the account goes further and draws conclusions about results achieved in the manufacturing sector. In the first place we might question how far the armed service can be compared with manufacturing industry. The background of the services would be command and control, whereas we might expect more discretion available to workers outside the military. Perhaps the author is claiming that, for all workers, there has to be an autonomy to make decisions to achieve greater productivity, whether they are in industry or the services. Alternatively, it could be saying that all individuals need to demonstrate initiative so that they make the important decisions and achieve greater productivity. Leaders need to choose these people and then encourage them to get on with it.

One point that we will find comes up consistently in these discussions about increased productivity is that it is easy to see how they may come about initially. But can this level of increase be sustained over the long term? If we go back to the original example: the old, tired and lethargic work force have got used to doing things in an inflexible and defensive way. This may well be the problem which, over the years, has brought about low productivity. The leader steps in to renew the supply of new, motivated labour and makes sure that the decision-making chain does not obstruct this new entrepreneurialism in any way. Initially, if the plan works, a newly emergent organization will suddenly yield impressive results of the kind described in the article. However, once the gap between old practice and new practice has been closed, where will the source of new productivity gains come from? This question is rarely addressed by those who offer this as an outcome of imposed change. However, it seems unlikely that such results will be found year on year indefinitely.

THE STEPPED CHANGE APPROACH

It is appropriate at this point to examine a typical set of prescriptions sometimes suggested as suitable for implementing a change programme at work. In this case they are entitled the Ten Commandments of implementing change. We will look at them as a list first and then examine each step in turn:

1. Analyse the organization and its need for change
2. Create a shared vision and common direction
3. Separate from the past
4. Create a sense of urgency
5. Support a strong leader role
6. Line up political sponsorship
7. Craft an implementation plan
8. Develop enabling structures
9. Communicate, involve people and be honest
10. Reinforce and institutionalize change.

(Kanter, 1991, 382)

Whenever we are confronted with a prescriptive or normative list, we are entitled to ask what it contains and why it is drawn up in the sequence presented. Are these steps to be undertaken in the order suggested by the writer? Is there a sequence, which means that one step should be concluded before the next is embarked upon? Could one of the steps be omitted without any difference being made to the final outcome? The author gives no direct answer to these questions.

Certainly there is a mix of action points here, some of which are general statements of good practice, e.g. Communicate, involve people and be honest. We might expect this to apply to all that we do, yet in the list it comes in the penultimate position.

In contrast we find specific tasks, which need to be achieved early on, perhaps, but which are general in their content: Create a shared vision and common direction. Is this something that should involve all participants or just the managers of change themselves? We might expect that this vision would inform the implementation plan. However, the implementation plan comes in seventh position in the list. There are a number of anomalies occurring within the list of steps. We will examine each step in turn and attempt to develop an understanding of what might be involved.

1 Analyse the organization and its need for change

Stating the obvious should make the meaning of this step self-evident. No manager of change would seek to embark on change without first asking this question, surely? And yet on closer inspection the words do not of themselves denote exactly what is involved here. We could be being asked to conduct any one of the following:

■ A full financial audit of the organization
■ A structural survey in which different departments and their staff are identified
■ A skills audit of the organization's personnel
■ A marketing analysis of the business within the industry.

Then, again, where has the need arisen for change? It is rare for the demand for change to be aspirational and unconnected with a demand from within or outside the organization. So, whose perception has triggered this demand for change? One book that expands the steps for us offers some advice in implementing the Ten Commandments. Their explanation is as follows:

> Change strategists and implementers should understand an organization's operations, how it functions in its environment, what its strengths and weaknesses are and how it will be affected by proposed changes to craft an effective implementation plan. If this initial analysis is not sound, no amount of implementation know-how will help the organization achieve its goals.
>
> At this early stage of the change process, implementers may also want to systematically examine the forces for and against change. Change will not occur unless the forces for it are stronger than those resisting it.
>
> (Jick and Peiperl, 2003, 177ff)

Apart from leaving us with no idea how the need for change can be manifested by gaining results from surveys or other data, the authors move seamlessly into the implementation plan. They omit the one option that might apply: nothing can be done. It seems that change management can overcome obsolescence by astute assessment of strategic potential.

Finally, they offer uncritically an explanation of change couched in mechanistic terms: we are here using the metaphor for change derived from the discipline of science – the forces for change. As with the example we have used earlier of the forces affecting flight: if thrust outweighs the counteracting force of drag, then the aircraft will increase in speed. If drag increases and the force of thrust does not increase, then the aircraft will slow. As we have commented earlier, we have not been shown how the organization can be compared with such an example – and if it is, what these forces are exactly. We might identify any of the major pieces of data as indicative of force-like characteristics, but still not have demonstrated that we have control of or access to any force that can counterbalance what we perceive as a detriment to the organization.

The need for change is most often presented as being reasonable and demonstrable. The implication of this approach will always leave opponents of change seeming to be unreasonable and intractable. Perhaps this may account for the rare mention of resistance from those involved in the content of predictive change. Once they have seen the evidence, which the change strategists and implementers offer, for the need for change, then they, too, will be convinced that a programme of change is inevitable and embark on it more willingly.

2 Create a shared vision and common direction

Those who come from a promotional or marketing background may immediately relate this statement to the idea of image – something that evinces a response in the viewer, perhaps a required or planned response. Advertising offers many examples in which the creator of the image has made assumptions about what will attract or repel the viewer. Those who wish to sell holidays, or any other commodity, will examine the motivators of those they want to entice or gain commitment from. They will examine the benefits that those individuals expect to have satisfied and then seek to embody these in an illustratively striking way. As we shall see in the chapter on TQM and BPR, the trend to embody common endeavours in a simple and direct statement is frequently commended in popular literature (Hamel and Prahaled, 1994; Champy, 1995).

The proponents of this approach sometimes explain it as follows:

> One of the first steps in engineering change is to unite an organization behind a central vision. This vision should reflect the philosophy and values of the organization and should help it to articulate what it hopes to become. A successful vision serves to guide behaviour and to aid an organization to achieve its goals.
>
> (Jick and Peiperl, 2003, 178)

It would be easy to be sceptical about the idea of vision. Great endeavours require a sense of what is intended in the achievement of a goal, large or small. However, the second part of the statement moves from the overall strategy into the tactical application of the vision: create a common direction. The authors acknowledge this point:

> While crafting the vision is a classic strategist's task, the way that this vision is presented to an organization can also have a strong impact on its implementation. Employees at all levels of the organization will want to know the business rationale behind the vision, the expected organizational benefits and the personal ramifications – whether positive or negative. In particular, implementers should 'translate' the vision so that all employees will understand its implications for their own jobs.
>
> (Jick and Peiperl, 2003, 178)

Perhaps we can detect a move into number seven in the list: Craft an implementation plan. It could be that the implementers have already made decisions about the implication for individual jobs, which will be communicated with the general vision. While such implications may be obvious to the outside observer, they may just strike individuals affected as a conclusion rather than a recommendation or, better still, an invitation to engage in open discussion. The discussion that we have had about open organizations and the crucial importance of engaging involvement of those affected so that change is seen as emergent rather than imposed now comes into play. The danger here is that those who devise the vision come to assume that its implications will be obvious and accepted by those involved. We might ask, therefore, how realistic it would be to involve those affected in the development of the vision itself. Evidence of this occurring is slight.

3 Separate from the past

The discussion that we had on the nature of culture now returns to the agenda. Is culture something that we have or something that we are? If it is the former, then we have accepted that it may be vested in attributes that we have and the way in which we do things at work. If it is inherent in learned behaviours, then it might be thought that the question now is only how do we retrain the individuals to accomplish the new behaviours? Before we leave this apparently easy option, we might ask whether or not the new behaviours required by the new vision are attainable or not. We make this point not just because some of these new behaviours may be unrealistic – this is always a danger in any change programme. There is also another question: can individuals be expected to undertake prescribed behaviours at all? The literature surrounding learning organizations might suggest that it is possible (Senge, 1990). However, perhaps we ought to look at the question of aptitude. How fair is it to expect individuals who have spent all their working life in one mode of operation to adapt with a short training course to something that they may find radically different from their past experience?

If we accept that culture is something we are, then it becomes a question of perception. How do individuals perceive the value of what they do? Could it just be that the mechanics of Tactical Air Command, whose story we heard at the beginning of the chapter, perceived that they were doing a good job. Obviously General Creech did not believe this himself and went about implementing a plan to improve performances significantly. Interestingly, this included recruiting many new operators who, perhaps, were unaffected by the perceptions of long-term workers on 'what works round here' (Deal and Kennedy, 1982). However, it demonstrates how difficult it may be to gain the commitment of older more experienced workers to change. The literature surrounding n-steps is often very positive about the response of workers to change. It may just be that this attempt to separate from the past is exactly the concern that workers have. Interestingly, the proponents of change accept this in their summary:

> However, while it is unquestionably important to make a break from the past in order to change, it is also important to hang on to and reinforce those aspects of the organization that bring value to the new vision. That is, some sort of stability – heritage, tradition or anchor – is needed to provide continuity amid change. As the changes at many companies multiply, arguably this past-within-the-future becomes even more essential.
>
> (Jick and Peiperl, 2003, 178)

4 Create a sense of urgency

How much notice do most individuals need that change is essential? Should the pilot put the plane into a nose-dive to convince passengers that the safety demonstration is for real? What sorts of passengers are impervious to the appeals of a pilot to pay attention? And the answer is from simple observation, frequent fliers. Now such lack of concern suggests that they have seen it before. Perhaps it is true that those who have experienced many changes are less impressed by change implementers who come in claiming great prospects for changes ahead. Experience can blunt expectancy and leave individuals feeling loath to get involved again in something that they had no say in last time and will have no say in again, perhaps.

Few changes happen without the threat to job security and some changes begin with that immediate decision to get rid of a certain number of staff. Emotions may be mixed about the putative benefits of change. Frankly, most of the benefits noised abroad by the implementers may not have been realized and, by the time they are, the implementers have moved on. Not surprisingly, this experience can only breed cynicism in those who have seen such management of change in the past.

Perhaps it would be fair to say that even a hint of change will create its own urgency and that urgency itself will generate both problems and opportunities for implementers, both internal and external alike.

5 Support a strong leader role

We have already discussed the idea of strong cultures and questioned what exactly such a phrase might mean. It is right that we should ask similar questions about the concept of a strong leader. One writer who has made it a focus of her work has been Karen Legge. She summarizes her thoughts as follows:

> The role of transformational leader is often presented as centred in changing compliance into commitment. The transformational leader (invariably a man) is the hero of the hour, fending off Japanese attack and rallying the troops to achieve success against the odds (read Jaguar, BA, etc.). He may be presented almost as an icon of critical

modernity, as questioning the old order of inefficient non-participative bureaucracies, dinosaurs of state industry, distinctly non-dancing giants, to use Kanter's phrase (e.g. Richard Branson, Bill Gates). Such 'critical' anti-heroes in fact have more in common with 19th century entrepreneurs and are fully in tune with the meta-narrative of capitalism and all that that entails in terms of performativity.

(Legge, 1995, 311)

If we accept that a strong leader is a decisive leader, making decisions which are necessary and sometimes uncongenial, then we might question the contention that such a role needs to be supported at all. The role models offered would seem to be quite capable of discharging these roles for themselves. So, what can the commandment be referring to? Perhaps there is a feeling here that the individual currently in a leadership role does not have the necessary decisiveness and therefore needs someone more decisive to take over during the period of change. Perhaps it means that the individual currently in post will need to be supported by the board as he or she undertakes the difficult decisions that will bring controversy and discontent from those who reject or obstruct it. Then, pulling together will be critical to make change stick. Alternatively it may mean that the change needs a leader, perhaps from outside, who will require support in order to survive the rejection that his or her ideas and plans may meet from inside.

The significance of a clear leadership role could scarcely be underestimated. However, who should exercise the role remains to be clarified. As we shall see in the chapter on change agents, the role itself may require a separation of functions between different people, both insiders and external specialists.

6 Line up political sponsorship

Political sponsorship may conjure up visions of money and commitment road-shows in the minds of some readers. The idea of running for public office without a manager to plan and line up opportunities for the candidate to meet and influence key voters or opinion formers will be important in any successful campaign for political office. But perhaps the Commandments do not see their aphorism quite in these terms.

For some writers the secret lies in identifying who these key players are and then approaching them with a view to finding out whereabouts they are in terms of the proposed changes. The view is that those seeking to gain commitment should have a plan of their own, which they can share with their targeted contacts. It may include such elements as:

- Identify target individuals or groups whose commitment is needed
- Define the critical mass needed to ensure the effectiveness of the change
- Develop a plan for getting the commitment of the critical mass
- Create a monitoring system to assess the progress.

(Beckhard and Harris, 1987)

With it the authors offer a sample Commitment Chart, which enables the progress to be indicated (see Figure 6.1).

141

Key players	No commitment	Neutral	Accommodate	Facilitate
1		X —————————	—————————	→ O
2		X —————	→ O	
3		X —————————	—————————	→ O
4		O ◄—————	X	
5			XO	
6	X —————	→ O		
7		X —————————	—————————	→ O
8		XO		
9	X —————————	—————————	→ O	
10			O ◄—————	X

Figure 6.1 *Commitment mapping*
Source: Beckhard and Harris (1987, 94–95)

The idea of a concerted campaign charted in this way will appeal to those who see the management of change as a systems approach campaign 'to win minds and hearts'. The drawback will be that rumour and counter-rumour may attend a proactive programme of intervention such as is suggested here.

Perhaps a less contentious style might include leaders of official or unofficial groups within the organization. Certainly, the results of the Commitment Chart, if accurate, might also alert the change team to individuals who might be willing to facilitate group work or play some other positive role within the programme.

7 Craft an implementation plan

The challenge here lies in identifying what is the content of this stage. What exactly is the involvement of those affected? If the tactical implications of the strategic plan have already been fixed, then the implementation plan may be little more than deciding what should now happen, when and how. In this case nothing much more than a gant or pert chart may be needed to identify key events and allot their sequence.

But, if the stage of deciding what the tactical plan should include has not been attempted, then this stage becomes very significant. All those who want to attempt emergent change need to embark on a programme of involvement precisely at the point where decisions are to be made about what is to happen and how it is to take place. Indeed, it is precisely accounts of how this can take place successfully that is most lacking in the literature of evidence supporting this endeavour. Two researchers whose work summarizes much that is best in the emergent tradition of change management puts it as follows:

> [Moreover], this study calls into question any easy unitary notion of managing change and competition. Quite the reverse, the research reveals the operation of a range of highly interconnected, sub-processes, which are commonly overlooked or assumed. The implication for management is that it has to master not just the readily apparent need to manage the demands of business analysis but also its siblings of politics and educa- tion. This calls into question therefore the ability of those responsible not only to

problem-sense but also to: raise the energy for change; justify the need for change and legitimize chosen courses of action; negotiate the pathways of change for organizations; stabilize successful programmes; set in motion processes which will lead to the generation of relevant knowledge; and resolve the many contradictions which arise between these sub-processes.

(Pettigrew and Whipp, 1991, 292)

The involvement is essential, but its achievement is complex and time-consuming. The question of who has ownership of the plan becomes pivotal to the perception of top-down or bottom-up among those on whom change is visited.

8 Develop enabling structures

The question of reinforcement in the context of both individual learning and organizational change has been mentioned in previous chapters of this book. Indeed it is hard not to conclude that the theory of individual change has been extrapolated to include change in groups and teams.

We might also include here our previous discussion on the structure–actor debate. As we can see, the structures mentioned could be enabling in the sense of structural changes to the way in which different factors are arranged in the organization. Perhaps a new department is to be set up to handle queries or manage parts of the change.

But we could also be looking at the need that individuals have to manage change – and that could be change of knowledge, changes in skill, changes in the way we approach problem-solving or client-handling issues. One example of this might be training and development programmes, which might themselves be described as enabling structures.

Again, we can say that the literature is light on evidence offering example and illustration of such enabling structures. Their presence is often assumed and taken for granted. But the actual way they are set up and managed is not always clearly apparent to those who are interested in what has been successful and what has not worked so well with those undergoing programmes of change.

9 Communicate, involve people and be honest

We have already commented on the underlying need for patency during a change process. Proponents sometimes offer a checklist for the agents of change. Here is one such list:

In general, a constructive change announcement:
Is brief and concise.
Describes where the organization is now, where it needs to go and how it will get to the desired state.
Identifies who will implement and who will be affected by the change.
Addresses timing and pacing issues regarding implementation.
Explains the change's success criteria, the intended evaluation procedures and the related rewards.

Identifies key things that will not be changing.

Predicts some of the negative aspects that targets should anticipate.

Conveys the sponsor's commitment to change.

Explains how people will be kept informed throughout the change process.

Is presented in such a manner that it capitalizes on the diversity of the communication styles of the audience.

(Jick and Peiperl, 2003, 182)

The reader might be forgiven for feeling that the sponsors have initiated this list and that those who receive it may therefore feel like 'targets'. We might also consider how far it is feasible to be totally honest when it is possible that some individuals may be about to lose their jobs. These events may be impossible to reveal openly when they concern individuals and their families.

Second, in emergent change processes the outcome depends on the involvement of the participants. Now certain latitude in terms of time and cost implications will need to be negotiated if such a scheme is to have any significance with those who undergo change. The conclusion of this quotation acknowledges the difficulty of achieving this:

Too often, 'communication' translates into a unilateral directive. But real communication requires a dialogue among the different change roles. By listening and responding to concerns, resistance and feedback from all levels, implementers gain a broader understanding of what the change means to different parts of the organization and how it will affect them.

(Jick and Peiperl, 2003, 183)

10 Reinforce and institutionalize change

Reinforcement as a concept reaches into the theory surrounding learning for children (Piaget, 1932) and its application in the motivation theory that finds its place in management studies. The proponents are clear how this should take place in the organization:

Throughout the pursuit of change, managers and leaders should make it a top priority to prove their commitment to the transformation process, to reward risk taking and to incorporate new behaviours into the day-to-day operations of the organization. By reinforcing the new culture, they affirm its importance and hasten its acceptance.

(Jick and Peiperl, 2003, 183)

The subjects of the action in this excerpt remain managers and leaders. Their intervention now is one of reward for new behaviours, always assuming that they can identify these easily. The question of what happens to those who fail to exhibit these new behaviours is not divulged. We notice, however, in the final sentence, that the concept of culture re-emerges and we can only assume here that the term is used in its sense of behaviours, rather than beliefs.

As we have seen in the chapter on culture, many writers who address transition or transformation or reframing at work assume that the process of assimilation by workers will take place (Nicholson and West, 1988; Isabella, 1990). The question of resistance receives minimal attention in much of the literature devoted to n-step approaches to change at work. This causes some writers to describe them as 'undersocialized' models of change (Collins, 1998, 84).

Our final point here would be the lack of detail in the prescription to institutionalize change. Reward systems are themselves the result of complex connections between systems and people and the evidence suggests that individual perceptions of reward change over time and therefore cannot be depended on to operate in any predictive way (Fletcher, 1993).

THEORETICAL UNDERPINNINGS OF N-STEP APPROACHES

In this section we want to examine the assumptions that underlie prescriptive, stepped approaches to change. In their simple format, stepped approaches can be simple, functional steps involved in a programmed or systemic format – one which has perhaps been designed to operate in a predictive way. Alternatively, there could be a generic approach to problem-solving in a more complex operating environment. Collins offers what he calls 'a typical example of schematic change models':

> Develop strategy
> Confirm top level support
> Use project management approach:
>> Identify tasks
>> Assign responsibilities
>> Agree deadlines
>> Initiate action
>> Monitor
>> Act on problems
>> Close down
> Communicate results.
>
> (Collins, 1998, 83)

Collins sees three common features of n-step guides as being:

- A 'rational' analysis of organizational change
- A sequential approach to the planning and management of change
- A generally upbeat and prescriptive tone.

We have already noted that the assumptions made in the Ten Commandments we have reviewed exhibited all three features. In summary, we have discussed the difficulties of achieving the outcomes suggested exactly in the way described. We may detect a heavy dependence on the structural elements of change. Tasks have an internal validity in that their sequence has a logic. However, in terms of gaining top-level or any other support, we might suspect that achieving such a consensus might be more difficult. In reality, the question of resistance again remains unanswered. What happens when significant members

145

of the top team have reservations and fail to give the support required? The prescriptive process does not explore this eventuality at all.

But, before we leave the stepped approaches to change, we may look at an article which has offered a different way of looking at and describing the change process and the way in which it unfolds.

PHASE ANALYSIS AND ORGANIZATIONAL DEVELOPMENT

Stepped approaches to change should not be thought of as solely a phenomenon triggered by the excellence literature of strategic human resources management. The earlier example of Kurt Lewin could be considered a well-known example of stepped change. And yet, as we say this, the steps themselves contain a world of emergence which is not often remarked upon. Unfreezing alone suggests that the T-groups or sensitivity groups encompassed a discursive process in which facilitators required time to allow discussion, accept dissent and seek to consolidate consensus. That exercise of openness offers every opportunity to participants to express basic beliefs, concerns and objections before embarking on the task of moving to change and their response to its prospects.

Two writers who have summarized this more open approach to change contrast what they see as the more expansive descriptor of the stages of change as phases, rather than steps (Bullock and Batten, 1985). In terms of the distinction, they suggest that a phase differs from a step in that the latter suggests a discrete element which requires completion before the next stage can commence and that steps suggest a rigid sequence which cannot be varied, rather like the functional models we looked at earlier in the book. Phases may be used more loosely and run concurrently. We can use a phase to encompass a range of activities, say, and therefore see phases as more organic and flexible. In their own words they describe it as follows:

> Phases is a more appropriate term than steps for describing the flow of events in OD work. Steps implies discrete actions, while phases better connotes the reality of OD practice – a cycle of changes. Although it is useful for our understanding of OD practice to conceive of distinct phases, in actual fact they blend and overlap.
>
> (Bullock and Batten, 1985, 387)

The authors propose seven criteria for identifying and evaluating phase models in OD:

1 The phase description must view change longitudinally

The change referred to here includes cultural change to include shifts in understanding and perception. Only when that has been achieved has the change been completed, in the authors' opinion.

2 The phase conception must be continuous

Similar to their first point, change processes are 'dynamic and perpetual', therefore they underlie random events and provide continuity in gradual and continuous process.

3 There must be some fluidity in the phase definition

It is rarely possible to define discrete start and finish point and elements within each phase will be variant and variable.

4 Phases must be linear

Phases should not be reversed. The sequence will be logical even though elements within the phases may overlap and extend in time.

5 The OD phase must be activity based

In the mind of the authors, OD is not a passive science but is punctuated by proactive interventions by change agents.

6 The phase description must have generality across many situations

Phase descriptions that are bounded by specific application become difficult to transfer into other applications successfully, so descriptors should be general rather than specific.

7 The phase model must be relevant and useful for understanding any given change effort

Comparability is the final factor the authors identify as important to the phase descriptor.

We could say that these criteria are indicative rather than predictive. They arise from practitioners reviewing and evaluating their experience of attempting to manage change. They attempt to avoid the constricting elements, which characterize the more simplistic claims of n-step approaches and alert practitioners to the need of seeking transferability, if others are to benefit from their experience.

The authors identify seven theoretical approaches among the different examples offered of change management models. We offer them here in summary format:

1 Planning model

The example we examined earlier in Collins is listed here and such models often include: develop the need for change; establish a relationship; clarify the problem; examine goals and alternatives; implement the change effort; stabilize the change; and terminate the relationship. We might expect a similar approach to govern the steps undertaken by an external consultancy.

2 Problem-solving model

The focus here is somewhat more specific, perhaps to a process or distinct element. It often includes: problem awareness; problem identification; information gathering; solution generation; decision; implementation; and review. The authors acknowledge that this model is often to be found within the context of a larger model of change.

3 Need-satisfaction model

Need satisfaction suggests an older literature, which finds its context in the debate on motivation (McClelland, 1975). It includes: need identification; initial diagnosis and strategy; and actions. It suggests that the organizational model is organic rather than mechanical.

4 Growth model

Again the metaphor here is organic and in some cases the idea of plant growth and its stages are delineated: seeds; nutrients; first fruits; and preserving the grass roots (Brugliera, 1976). Structuralists might struggle to make sense of this imagery.

5 Ice model

Perhaps the most famous example of change models is offered here: unfreezing; moving; and refreezing (Lewin, 1947). As we have noted above, the process was rather more complex to implement than the simple terms describing it initially suggest.

6 Transition model

Here a six-phase model is offered: diagnosis; defining the end state; defining the transition state; change strategies; evaluation; and stabilization (Beckhard and Harris, 1977). Put more simply, that might be rendered as: where are we; where do we want to be; and how are we going to get there? It is not dissimilar to the incremental approach to change that we saw in early chapters.

7 Primary activity model

Here an intervention strategy is offered. Argyris is suggested as a proponent of this model. The stages undertaken in the intervention are described as: generating valid information; allowing free, informed choice; and fostering internal commitment. These activities he envisaged as unfolding in a primary intervention cycle: diagnostic phase; choice phase; and internal commitment phase.

Bullock and Batten summarize the coincidence of each model against the seven criteria and this table can be found in the original article (1985, 396). What is more interesting, however, is the summary and overview in which they seek to identify key phases and elements within each phase which encompass the many models they have identified (see Table 6.1).

The authors then conflate all the models and demonstrate where they fit and how far they are commensurate with the phases and elements included in their outline model. This can be found in full in the original article (1985, 402–405).

Table 6.1 *Outline of the four-phase model*

Change phases	Change processes
1 Exploration	a Need awareness b Search c Contracting
2 Planning	a Diagnosis b Design c Decision
3 Action	a Implementation b Evaluation
4 Integration	a Stabilization b Diffusion c Renewal

Source: Bullock and Batten, (1985, 400)

BENEFITS OF THE PHASE MODEL

It could be said that the phases themselves are unexceptional and are merely summary categories for the beginning, middle and end of a logical sequence in any intervention intended to achieve the management of change. And yet the descriptors are comprehensive enough to embrace an emergent style that is often applauded but less often adhered to. Bottom-up change, if it is intended to bring out consensus and commitment from all involved in change, requires that at least the attempt be made to include this openness.

If we examine the elements listed in the Change processes column, then we can appreciate the difference that such an open approach could make to the acceptance of change. Under Exploration, need awareness and search can be the prescriptive preserve of management alone. Alternatively, the prospect of calling on a wider resource born of experience among the constituents of change would suggest a broader and perhaps more politically acceptable outcome. Similarly, under Planning, do diagnosis, design and decision have to be the preserve of senior managers or outside consultants? Most people have experienced change in their working lives. Perhaps the lessons learned should not have to be relearned but be the basis of a shared consolidation of experience, expertise and knowledge. In the third section of Action, so often the temptation to adopt the top-down approach emerges. Plans are drawn up and budgets allocated. What need of further consultation can there be? Then the final stage of evaluation can follow using the same criteria as was used to implement the plan.

However, what is distinctive in this account of change is the possibility of overlapping phases in place of distinct and separate steps. As the programme unfolds its lessons can be learned and acted on before the end of the action phase. Initial cohorts who have completed the implementation can be evaluated and lessons learned can be implemented for subsequent groups going through the change programme. In this way Integration can include not just the shakedown of the programme, but also its further extension, triggering more effective renewal elsewhere. In fairness to the proponents of the learning organization, this has

149

to be the closest example of a cycle of learning generated within an organizational programme of change feeding subsequent lessons drawn into subsequent subjects of change.

The idea of phases overlapping means that the initial cohort can itself become a vanguard of learning in which, once the completed cycle of phases is concluded and conclusions drawn, other cohorts embark on what can be a continuing reflective process. However, examples of such management of change strategies remain the exception rather than the rule.

Our central finding in relation to managing change is that there are no simple universal rules which arise. In fact the reverse is true. Leadership is acutely context sensitive. This is manifested in a number of ways. The very choice of leader clearly relates to who makes the choice and the circumstances in which they do so. The democratic process sits uneasily with the idea of management as decisiveness exercised by the few. However, it must be said that a change programme that takes account of evaluation and applies its early findings directly to subsequent phases must have a better chance of acceptance if not ultimate success. Even those experienced in emergent change strategies admit that it is difficult to achieve:

> The critical leadership tasks in managing change appear to be much more fragmentary and incremental than the popular preoccupation with business wizardry in the 1980s allow. Leading change requires a flow of actions, which are appropriate to their context. Put simply, different eras produce the need for different types of leadership. Such requirements do not necessarily imply a single leader. The need may be for more than one leader over time if performance is to be maintained. Equally important may be the creation of a collective leadership at a senior level, which may then be supported by the development of a sense of complementary leadership at lower levels. Leading change involves action by people at every level of the business.
>
> (Pettigrew and Whipp, 1991, 280ff.)

Nobody said that this process was easy. However, a programme that allows for subjects to modify it from their own experience may have distinct advantages over predictive and imposed schemas of change.

UPBEAT OR DOWNBEAT?

We opened this chapter with an example of the upbeat assertions which characterize many contributions to the change literature. Less obvious is evidence, which is more realistically conducted in organizations struggling to achieve change. One researcher whose name exemplifies this tradition is John Storey and I include here a brief excerpt from an account of change at Jaguar under the leadership of Sir John Egan. The results of the turnaround achieved are often rightly acknowledged for Jaguar's success in bringing quality circles to a brownfield manufacturing site. The actual detail of its success is less often quoted.

Jaguar certainly had devised an interconnected programme of measures. A human resource management post was created in 1985 and a campaign was launched to win 'minds and hearts' (as it was unabashedly called). This comprised all the main elements we discussed in the previous chapter: an emphasis on direct communications; more careful selection; task level participation; and investment in training and development. To promote identification with the company, 'family days' were introduced. The new selection initiatives included psychometric testing for hourly paid recruits. The trust in HR by most top managers as the way to proceed was very much in evidence:

'We see HR as the front arm, the leading arm of personnel. To get the best out of people you have to get them wanting to come to work and wanting to win. Industrial Relations to us is a supporting activity only. That's the difference between us and, say, Ford or Austin Rover. They would like to move from Industrial Relations but don't know how. We are the other way round, we are an HR company with an Industrial Relations function acting in support of that. We may not yet be Nissan but we are nevertheless distinctive in the way we approach HR.' (Director, Jaguar)

Yet even this special case revealed problems for HRM. Communication and participation were sought through team briefings, attitude surveys and a quality circle (QC) programme. But these have not been installed unproblematically, even at Jaguar. There was considerable resistance to both the survey and the circles. For example, 56 circles were introduced between 1982–6 and the figure plateaued at this level. A major push from management increased the total number to 82 by 1987. But despite this at Brown's Lane, the main site, no hourly paid involvement in quality circles had been achieved. All 35 circles at this location were on the staff side. This reflects the resistance by senior stewards. The 82 circles across the company meet once a month for an hour but there is some pressure to have this increased to once a fortnight. Noteworthy also is top management's persistence. Despite nearly a decade of experience with QCs and the attendant resistance, there was in 1987, a renewed target of 200 circles across three sites.

(Storey, 1992, 59ff.)

Such honesty should alert us to the difficulty of penetrating the complexities of practice and perception among an established work force. It may also alert us to the fact that upbeat accounts of new working practices often emanate from greenfield sites (Wickens, 1987). Pettigrew acknowledges the reality which managers have to deal with day to day. He describes it as 'embeddedness'. Culture is a context in which individuals adjudge what is significant and what is to be resisted:

An understanding of embeddedness – the location of behaviour and institutions with the social settings which condition and constrain them – can boost our understanding of the range of influences which affect organizations and should have a critical impact on the analysis of organizations.

(Martinez-Lucio and Weston, 1992, 216)

For some authors this definition of cultural embeddedness gives rise to what others see as oversocialized change. If symbols, myths and meaning are so deeply embedded in custom and practice, then it is not surprising if even the most spirited of efforts to induce change meet with at best partial success and at worst total impasse.

We return to a definition of culture which cannot be deconstructed simply by management messages and may even elude the emergent practices that seek to engage individuals and groups in radical reappraisal of beliefs and assumptions about self work and society (Casey, 1995). In the words of other contributors to the debate:

> Meanings are themselves embedded in quite distinctive class, regional and national cultures. Each occupation [has a] quite distinctive pattern that is connected in unique ways to external meaning systems. These patterns may render cultures beyond managerial capacity to influence let alone control.
>
> (Ackroyd and Crowdy, 1990, 3)

The final word on Jaguar belongs to the man who initiated change at the car company:

> Most change is longitudinal. Managers cannot recreate the world anew to suit new ideas or fashions. Previous decisions may leave management little scope for new strategic approaches. Greenfield sites can suddenly appear as the most attractive option.
>
> (Storey, 1992, 59ff.)

Our conclusions, therefore, are that the complexities surrounding change remain within the original debate on the definition of culture: what is it, can it be changed, and if so can that change be managed in any directive way? The simple stages offered by stepped change approaches may suggest that such managed change is both logical and feasible. However, we should expect to encounter resistance, which may not yield to rational argument or reward inducements or even the openness that characterizes the best practices of emergent change strategies. Some sobering findings of a survey in 93 medium- and large-size firms can be summarized as follows:

> Implementation took more time than originally allocated (76 percent).
> Major problems surfaced during implementation that had not been identified beforehand (74 percent).
> Coordination of implementation activities (e.g. by task forces, committees, superiors) was not effective enough (66 percent).
> Competing activities and crises distracted attention from implementing this strategic decision (64 percent).
> Capabilities (skills and abilities) of employees involved with the implementation were not sufficient (63 percent).
> Training and instruction given to lower level employees were not adequate (62 percent).
> Uncontrollable factors in the external environment (e.g. competitive, economic, governmental) had an adverse impact on implementation (60 percent).
>
> (Alexander, 1985)

Perhaps the implementation of change programmes may not be as easy as some prescriptive and normative methods suggest. Change agents may need a programme that offers the best opportunity of involvement and ownership for all those affected by the change programme.

DISCUSSION QUESTIONS

There are two questions which may occur with some regularity and they frequently feature one or more of the n-step approaches. It is as well to be familiar with the three stages offered by Lewin in terms of their contribution to both later practice and OD practitioners, many of whom learned their skills facilitating Kurt Lewin's T-groups. It may also be an advantage to learn the Ten Commandments, which we have gone through in the present chapter.

In general, questions vary from straight comparison between n-step approaches and the discussions surrounding their internal and external validity. You will therefore find it useful to rehearse the arguments of how far the steps are logically sequenced and how far they are transferable between the different types of change, which he discussed in earlier chapters.

To give you slightly different questions I offer the following:

1   The steps in some problem-solving models of change frequently contain some variation of:
   ■ Problem awareness
   ■ Problem identification
   ■ Information gathering
   ■ Solution generation
   ■ Solution evaluation
   ■ Decision
   ■ Implementation
   ■ Review.

   How helpful are these steps in providing a guide for the management of change? Cite examples and evidence to support your argument.

You may note that the list comes from the book by Collins (1998, 83). The key words lie in the first two bullet points: problem awareness/identification. Problem-solving in this sense lies at the heart of functional or systemic change. The reason for this is that functions and systems have been designed with an internal rationale and solving the problem will be dependent on diagnostics – finding out what has gone wrong and putting it right. A simple example would be the breakdown of an engine or machine. Tracking the source of the fault will be a systematic perusal of the constituent parts of the mechanism. Sometimes a simple flow chart or fault-checker is sufficient for the problem solver to undertake this task success-fully. In this case the repair can be affected and then a test run conducted to see whether it has been achieved successfully.

The situation is different in the case of non-systemic situations. If we move away from structural change to the actor side of the organization debate then this becomes easy to demonstrate: human beings do not respond as simply to change as mechanistic systems do. Here, the techniques, which change agents may have found worked successfully in one group, may not be as successful in another context. We can refer here to the debate on embeddedness and cultures as perception rather than behaviours.

If we combine structure and actor elements in change then the management of change becomes altogether more complex. Apart from a multiplicity of departments and groups, each of which may have their own perceptions of what is occurring, there is also the question of complexity, which may defy the simple problem-solving schema offered here.

We may note a similar direction and occasional coincidence of terminology between the simple schema and, say, the Ten Commandments. Indeed, the same need for analysis opens the list. But the focus here is the organization. What follows then addresses the political aspects of managing change rather than the more simple aspects or information, solution and decision, which follow in the problem-solving list. Similarly, we can see a similarity between the implementation plan and implementation. However, the review stage is certainly more complex in Kanter's Commandments and necessarily addresses enabling structures and reinforcement factors.

At best, then, we might say that there could be some change programmes that are structural and therefore may lend themselves to the more simple model. However, anything more complex, involving different departments and staff, will not yield results as simply as the model suggests. We may discuss whether even the Ten Commandments provide for the variance of human response that may accompany change, particularly the all-too-often neglected subject of resistance. But, overall, the simple model would not serve in the context of continuous change and does not directly address the needs of emergent or bottom-up change strategies at all.

2   Exploration, Planning, Action and Integration are the four phases of Bullock and Batten's model, which 'allows the semi-standard reporting of virtually all OD case studies'. How far do you agree with this assertion? Choose one example of an n-step approach and assess how closely it coincides with the four-phase model.

The question gives you the four phases and you may want to examine what the authors mean by each word. The process described has about it a comprehensiveness, which even allows the simple problem-solving schema to be fitted into the four phases. Bullock and Batten then look at the seven main models of change, which they outline, and again the models fit into the phases, though in some cases not all phases are fully addressed. Stated as briefly as it often is, for example, the Lewin three-step approach has a similar flow of exploration in the unfreezing stage and we could assert that the final, refreezing stage could be conceived of as the integration phase. However, the central stage of Lewin's may include both action and planning, though this planning could have occurred during the exploration stage, also.

More insightful are the change processes offered by Bullock and Batten, in which the emergent strategies are much more clearly apparent: the need awareness, search, decision and diffusion elements all allow of an openness which is not so readily apparent in n-step approaches. So, if we can see similarities between OD case studies and the four phases, they are very general and facilitated by the general categories offered by Bullock and Batten.

You may want to use the Ten Commandments to answer the second part of the question. We could note that the imperative characterizes the list here. It is a set of directions, something prepared by a change manager for other change managers. The subjects of change usually have these elements imposed on them. 'Analyse' could be construed as the initial work undertaken, say, by an outside consultant with very little of the emergent and exploratory about it. We might argue that planning and action phases could include much of the central elements of the Commandments, though it could be said that these are themselves a mixture of moral counsels, political techniques and management tasks presented in no apparent logical order.

In summary we might suggest that the Commandments are a series of management dicta in which a certain sequence can be seen, but which are not as carefully thought through as the four phases are. Indeed, the phases have about them an internal logical sequence which allows them to overlap with each other, but does not allow for replacement or omission of any of the steps in the sequence. We could not say the same of the Ten Commandments, which quite clearly contain elements that need to be sustained throughout the change rather than being a distinct step in themselves (e.g. Communicate, involve people and be honest). Any similarity between the Commandments and the four phases would therefore be based on surface validity.

This question has not asked about the difference between step and phase. A distinction is often asked for in examination questions. You will want to note that the question of steps often suggests a sequence of unitary actions, which are often dependent on each other in the sequence presented by the writer. Phases contain further elements explaining what each contains. They can be run to overlap one another and different groups can proceed through in stages, allowing the organizers to accept learning from earlier groups, which can be used to benefit successive participants in the change programme.

REFERENCES AND FURTHER READING

Ackroyd, S. and Crowdy, P.A. Can culture be managed? Working with raw material: the case of English slaughtermen. *Personnel Review*, 1990, *19* (5): 3–13.

Alexander, L. Successfully implementing strategic decisions. *Long Range Planning*, 1985, *18* (3): 91–97.

Argyris, C. *Intervention theory and method: a behavioural science view*. Reading, MA: Addison-Wesley, 1970.

Beckhard, R. and Harris, R.T. *Organization transitions: managing complex change*. Reading, MA: Addison-Wesley, 1977.

Beckhard, R. and Harris, R.T. *Organization transitions*. Reading, MA: Addison-Wesley, 1987.

Brugliera, M. The self-help roots of Northcare. *Journal of Applied Behavioural Science*, 1976, *12*: 397–403.

Bullock, R.J. and Batten, D. It's just a phase we're going through: a review and synthesis of OD phase analysis. *Group & Organization Studies*, 1985, *10* (4) (December): 383–412.

Casey, C. *Work, self and society*. London: Routledge, 1995.

Champy, J. *Reengineering management: the mandate for new leadership*. London: HarperCollins, 1995.

Collins, D. *Organizational change: sociological perspectives*. London: Routledge, 1998.

Deal, T.E. and Kennedy, A. *Corporate cultures*. Reading, MA: Addison-Wesley, 1982.

Fletcher, C. *Appraisal*. London: IPM, 1993.

Hamel, G. and Prahaled, C.K. *Competing for the future*. Boston, MA: Harvard Business School Press, 1994.

Harrison, S., Hunter, D., Marnock, G. and Pollitt, C. *Just managing power and culture in the NHS*. London: Palgrave, 1992.

Hood, C. A public management for all seasons? *Public Administration*, 1991, *69* (1): 3–19.

Huxham, C. and Vangen, S. Working together: key themes in the management of relationships between public and non-profit organizations. *International Journal of Public Sector Management*, 1996, *9* (7): 5–17.

Isabella, L.A. Evolving interpretations as a change unfolds: how managers construe key organizational events. *Academy of Management Journal*, 1990, *33* (1): 7–41.

Jick, T.D. and Peiperl, M.A. *Managing change: cases and concepts*. New York: McGraw-Hill, 2003.

Kanter, R.M. Transcending business boundaries. *Harvard Business Review*, 1991, (May–June) *69* (3): 151.

Legge, K. *Human resource management: rhetoric and realities*. Basingstoke: Palgrave, 1995.

Lewin, K. Frontiers in group dynamics. *Human Relations*, 1947, *1*: 5–41.

Martinez-Lucio, M. and Weston, S. Human resource management and trade union responses: bringing the politics of the workplace back into the debate, in P. Blyton and P. Turnbull (eds) *Reassessing Human Resource Management*. London: Sage, 1992.

McClelland, D. *Power, the inner experience*. New York: Irvington, 1975.

Nicholson, N. and West, M. *Managerial job change: men and women in transition*. Cambridge: Cambridge University Press, 1988.

Osborne, D. and Gaebler, T. *Reinventing government: how the entrepreneurial spirit is transforming the public sector*. Reading: Addison-Wesley, 1992.

Pettigrew, A. and Whipp, R. *Managing change for competitive success*. Oxford: Blackwell, 1991.

Piaget, J. The origins of intelligence and children. New York: International University Press, 1932.

Senge, P.M. *The fifth discipline: the art and practice of the learning organization*. London: Century Business Publishers, 1990.

Storey, J. *Developments in the management of human resources: an analytical review*. Oxford: Blackwell Business, 1992.

Wickens, P. *The road to Nissan*. London: Macmillan, 1987.

Chapter 7

Programmed approaches to organizational change

Rhetoric and reality

TOPIC HEADINGS

- The rhetoric of radical programmed change
- The rhetoric of quality programmed change
- Total Quality Management and underpinning theory
- Business Process re-engineering revisited
- Postscript on New Public Management

INTRODUCTION

We have already begun to piece together the various elements that may underlie change at work. We have identified the different ways of looking at the organization. The traditional approach of Organizational Development traditionally led from a structured approach: organizations are considered to be constructed almost in an assembled model of pieces, which fit together and cooperate with one another. The basis of this model may well be span of control: how many people are needed to fulfil a particular function, be it marketing, production, service or finance, and how many supervisors and managers are required to monitor and evaluate their work effectively?

We have noted the contrasting view of those who take a view of organizations being comprised of actors: individuals each of whom have their own aspirations, skills, knowledge and experience, who coalesce during working time to achieve particular goals. This brings us into the world of the individual: motivation, competence, commitment, attitudes and taken-for-granted assumptions.

We can accept that there is a link between the individual and the larger functional body. It is the smaller working group. Here, group dynamics and team working become the focus for our scrutiny. The issues for practising managers and trainers become the ability of the individuals in a working team to grapple with the daily demands, which are at once routine and functional but also responsive to the reactive and unexpected. The profusion of problem-solving, leading and facilitating team courses is a testament to the urgency with which the managers look for the means of optimizing the efficiency and effectiveness of people. There is no let-up in the search for the ideal dynamic which will yield optimum business results through people.

The context within which these internal endeavours take place remain the essentially less manageable element of the equation. We have already noted that the proponents of emergent change are more consistent in their emphasis on embeddedness (Pettigrew, 1990). These can be the external demands, which govern success in any market requiring managers to assess likely customer demand and possible competitor response.

In this chapter we have chosen to group commentators who have offered programmed approaches to the management of change. Their philosophies are not just stepped or phased approaches in which the right formula of, say, training and interventionist management is alleged to achieve success. Here, the driver is often external and its impact on the organization may require a specific, programmed approach to ensure successful survival of external threat.

We will consider Total Quality Management (TQM), Business Process Re-engineering (BPR) and also the movements in the public sector sometimes described as New Public Management (NPM). It would be fair to say that they have captured the public imagination beyond the constituency of users who have been subjected to their methodologies, for their proponents have been successful in capturing the attention of managers and practitioners alike.

We will begin this section of the chapter by offering a number of quotations from proponents of each movement and consider the questions that could be asked about some of the assertions being made.

THE RHETORIC OF RADICAL PROGRAMMED CHANGE

Explanations of the drivers of change vary in the assumptions they make about its causes. They often share a similar move from a general assessment made about the dynamics of the market or need of an industry towards a particular solution, which the author's work then addresses. We will start with a general example of this technique:

> Moreover, the pace of change has accelerated. With globalization of the economy, companies face a greater number of competitors, each of which may introduce product and service innovations to the market. The rapidity of technological change also promotes innovation. Product life cycles have gone from years to months. Ford produced the Model T for an entire human generation. The life cycle of a computer product introduced today might stretch to two years but probably won't. A company in the pensions business recently developed a service to take advantage of a quirk in the tax laws and interest rates. Its anticipated market life was exactly three months. Coming to this market late by just thirty days would have cut the company's selling time for the service by a third.
>
> The point is that not only have product and service life cycles diminished, but so has the time available to develop new products and introduce them. Today, companies must move fast, or they won't be moving at all.
>
> (Hammer and Champy, 1995, 23)

Consider the following questions:

1   How do the authors define globalization?
2   How would you define it?
3   What evidence is given for the reducing life cycles of products and services?
4   How is a market life of three months calculated?
5   What opportunity does the threat of computer-aided design offer managers?

The term 'globalization' is freely used by gurus, hero managers and journalists alike. It is rarely defined in any way that would allow us to compare the claims made about it between and even within author's claims for it as a predictive phenomenon. We may believe that it means a growing market awareness among consumers, or we may assume that it means that similar IT technologies are available to all worldwide sectors of businesses alike. But even here there is a distinction between markets and industry/businesses, which suggests care in extrapolating claims in one sector that are assumed to apply in others.

At best we might accept that global trends suggest that people and money pass more freely across geographical and physical boarders than was possible in the past. We might accept that technologies like the personal computer and the internet make it unlikely that such ease of communication will abate or be successfully countered in any way that we can see now. However, how that impacts on particular markets may depend on different factors sometimes less obvious to observers, even those apparently close to a business or a local market.

The claim for reducing life cycles in both products and services would seem to be a well-substantiated claim and the examples offers by the authors would seem self-evident. However, a car designed for a generation? Did Ford really lay claim to that as an aim, or not? Some products have extended their life cycle in spite of better technical specification being available elsewhere. Brand-naming and status usage may offer protection from sudden erosion of market share. However, whether local markets can be defended from erosion over an extended period has yet to be substantiated.

In fact, market life is extremely difficult for anyone to calculate. Estimates of how many end-users there are in a locality may suggest what the likely demand will be. However, the designers of products and services can be surprised by the difference between the expected respondents initially targeted and the actual user profiles that respond in the market take-up.

We have already commented on the impact of technology on design, engineering and manufacture. Each of these business functions has found itself linked to the computer world. The time taken to produce from Research and Development to packaging and promotion has been greatly reduced by computerized processes. However, it should be pointed out that the same technology is available to all and a case could be made that barriers to entry in any market could have been unwittingly or wittingly reduced by the implementation of facilitative software applications. In other words, as we will see later in this chapter, the benefits offered in early implementation of technological advantage may be easily replicable by imitators, too.

We mentioned earlier in this chapter the need to examine the learning points offered by authors as they lay out their general claims of irresistible change elements in business. Our authors conclude their claims as follows:

> Executives think their companies are equipped with effective change-sensing radars, but most of them aren't. Mostly what they detect are the changes they expect. The brand managers at a consumer goods manufacturer we know assiduously tracked consumer attitudes in order to detect shifts that might affect their products. Their surveys kept giving them good news, but market share took a sudden drop. They did more surveys. Customers loved the products, but market share kept tumbling. It turned out the problem was that the company's sloppy order fulfilment process was infuriating its retailers, who responded by cutting its shelf space, but neither the brand managers nor anyone else at the company had a broad enough perspective to detect and deal with this problem.
>
> The changes that will put a company out of business are those that happen outside the light of its current expectations and that is the source of most change in today's business environment.
>
> (Hammer and Champy, 1995, 23–24)

Consider the following questions:

1 What comment would you make about customer surveys?
2 Who else might the company have been speaking to in order to discover the nature of the problem they were experiencing?
3 How should the problem of order fulfilment have been dealt with?
4 What leap of logic lies in the assertions of the final paragraph?

It certainly seems strange that no customers stated that the products were good, but hard to get hold of, and that the supplier always seemed to be out of stock. Asking the wrong question or the wrong people may have constrained the company's ability to respond to more extensive sources of knowledge about its customers.

It does seem strange that no one else in the company received any messages that retailers were experiencing frustration in acquiring the product. Whoever takes the orders might normally have expected to hear complaints from this source. Sales forces would tend to hear a barrage of complaint of which each would be aware. Would none of them have raised it with senior management? It would seem unlikely. The account begs more questions than it answers.

However, we can begin to see the conclusions that a writer might now draw: the communication question will now receive an airing – people should communicate better and training in communication might now be recommended. Alternatively, we might be looking at the restructuring of the ordering system and its ability to pick up on complaints. Perhaps another field on the computer program would enable the order processor to make a note of supply problems and a responsible manager could capture these in a file for review each day. Here, we might be offered a system and people problem needing to be solved.

Finally, we might accept the claim that unexpected threats are those that cause people most concern and discomfort. We can accept that reactive change can absorb much time and effort, perhaps because there are no systems designed to take care of such exceptions. However, that most companies go out of business due to such unexpected change would seem difficult to assert from the evidence offered in the author's account.

For the authors the lessons are simple and straightforward:

> Our diagnosis of America's business problems is simple, but corrective action that it demands is not as easy to implement as the solutions that have already been tried. Our diagnosis goes to the heart of what a company does. It rests on the premise that a company that is better than others at the meat and potatoes of its business – inventing products and services, manufacturing or providing them, selling them, filling orders, and serving customers – will beat the competition in the market place. We believe that in general, the difference between winning companies and losers is that winning companies know how to do their work better. If American companies want to become winners again, they will have to look at how they get their work done. It is as simple and as formidable as that.
>
> (Hammer and Champy, 1995, 26)

In this example the authors emphasize the efficiency factors of productivity and the advantage that greater efficiency must bring to the business outcomes of pricing and profitability. It is all about processes, procedures and plans being tightly managed and being better than the competition at managing this. Much that will be offered us in terms of effective ways of improving company performance may be attributed to such external drivers as globalization but then often alight on a particular element of efficiency management which, it is alleged, lies at the heart of restoring world-class performance and effectiveness.

So far, then, we have been presented with the traditional mix of people and systems, which have to be managed proactively to close the gap between efficiency and effectiveness factors. We will be asked to address the problems that occur when our own conviction that custom and practice is good enough cause us to fail to see that world demands and customer demands are moving on and leaving us behind the competition. The answer offered will often be twofold: be aware of technological and other improvements that you need to implement, and be aware that customers and markets may be asking for something else altogether.

For some writers, however, there is a deeper cause of failure to respond to market demands with appropriate change strategies. Here is an example of this type of analysis of the problem underlying obsolescence:

> Every manager must face a cold hard fact: Intellectual capital steadily depreciates. What you, dear reader, know about your industry is worth less right now than it was when you began reading this book. Customer needs have changed, technological progress has been made, and competitors have advanced their plans while you have been pursuing these pages. (No, don't stop reading! Just make sure you spend even more time thinking

161

about how your industry is changing.) Here's our definition of a laggard: A laggard is a company where senior management has failed to write off its depreciating intellectual capital fast enough and has underinvested in creating new intellectual capital. A laggard is a company where senior managers believe they know more about how an industry works than they actually do and where what they know is out of date.

Success reduces genetic variety. To the extent that success confirms the firm's strategy ('if we're rich, we must be doing the right thing'), managers may come to believe that doing more of the same is the surest way to prolong success and that any competitor that is not doing it 'our way' can't be very smart. And if the competitor is relatively resource poor, well, that's even more reason to dismiss the up-and-comer.

(Hamel and Prahaled, 1994, 55)

Consider the following questions:

1 What do the authors mean by 'intellectual capital'?
2 What are the implications of the word 'laggard'?
3 What are the implications of 'writing off' depreciating capital?
4 What are the dangers of using the term 'genetic' in the context of change management?
5 What would the last paragraph be a sign of in the opinion of the writers?

I imagine that most readers might assume that the word 'intellectual' applies to human beings. It is used here in coordination with the word 'capital'. We can understand that capital is derived from the financial sector and refers, say, to an investment required in a successful business. So, if we are right, then the conclusion drawn here is that having the right ideas will enable human beings to be successful. The authors go on to assert that intellectual capital depreciates. The statement is general and closed. It does not admit of alternative assertion that some human capital does not depreciate, for example. That rather makes it look as though, using the analogy of a car, depreciation cannot be remedied. The best thing to do with such a vehicle is write it off.

The impression evoked by the writers may be reinforced by the reference to the word 'laggard'. Again, to most readers that may suggest a laziness and moral ineptitude which have put the company in its current parlous position in the first place. Are these senior managers alluded to perhaps as an example of this depreciated intellectual capital? If, so how can the capital be improved?

And so, in the final paragraph we have the reference to 'genetic variety'. This again is not closely defined by the authors and could perhaps apply to variety of personality type or modes of thought or potential/aptitude. Whatever it is, the prospects for reform would not be promising as the genetic message from which the metaphor is derived is in its original context the message that dictates the physical make-up of each individual. Genetic, as in the composition of the genes, is not within the power even of the owner of the genes to change. It begins to sound, then, as though the owner of the genes, if found unsuitable for the changing environment, does not have too many options for change, indeed may have none at all. Extinction is not an option that can be managed using this metaphor.

If we accept the example offered of managers' beliefs and assumptions as to what governs success, then we might allow that reframing is possible. However, as we have discussed, the evidence for reframing is not as compelling as is sometimes suggested. It could also take a long time to achieve.

For some authors there are suggestions of dos and don'ts for those managers who wish to be successful in managing radical change in their organization. It might be as well to examine an example of each of these before moving on to consider less radical proposals of programmed change at work. Here are the values required for success in the opinion of one writer:

> To perform up to the highest measure of competence, always.
>
> To take initiatives and risks.
>
> To adapt to change.
>
> To make decisions.
>
> To work co-operatively as a team.
>
> To be open, especially with information, knowledge and news of forthcoming or actual problems.
>
> To trust and be trustworthy.
>
> To respect others (customers, suppliers and colleagues) and oneself.
>
> To answer for our actions, to accept responsibility.
>
> To judge and be judged, reward and be rewarded, on the basis of our performance.
>
> (Champy, 1995, 79)

Consider the following questions:

1   How would you describe the ten statements in the list?
2   What sort of performances are being asked for here?
3   What sort of relationship is this between employer and employee?
4   How would you test for these in a recruitment or selection situation?
5   What might be the implications of the final statement?

We might note here that most of the statements are aspirational. They could be seen as targets, but it would be difficult to envisage how they could be used as standards of performance. We will discuss the distinctions underlying this discussion later in this chapter. However, this means that most of the targets laid out here would be subject to the judgement of another person, probably a manager.

An example here might be 'to work co-operatively as a team'. It is clear that teams themselves will not always agree among themselves about what is a good course of action or the solution of a problem. So, the judgement on what makes a good team member could be affected by negative interventions, even if these are justified by results. Different leaders value different roles in teams, while evidence suggests that team roles may be fairly static (Belbin, 1981). This means that the role admired by one leader may be downplayed by another.

The same problem of objectivity arises in the case of trust and trustworthiness: since trust is a personal response to a leader based on individual considerations, it is hard to see how a general demand can be made on individuals in this way. Indeed, the tenor of many of these aphorisms makes them a set of moral aspirations rather than a clear guideline to objective performance.

Certainly, the relationship would appear to depend much more on the perceptions of the employer as to the employee's worthiness. In this respect it would be difficult to set up reliable criteria to support these requirements. They are not testable, measurable or validatable in any objective performance, but must depend on the judgement of another over time. In new employees they are therefore almost impossible to test for. That might make us wonder how they could be used to make valid choices at critical moments in the employment contract, such as appraisal and review.

Finally, worded as it is in the list, the final statement could be construed as a flexible contract in which reward will be made according to the satisfaction of the user. Such statements are paralleled in advice to buyers of shares and securities: this investment can go down as well as up. If the servant pleases his or her Master, the reward could be generous. If not, expect to get rather less than you had hoped for.

For those who do not come up to expectations, then the same fate as the depreciated car might be the outcome. The don'ts list is equally definite in its prescriptions:

> Don't live too long with people who refuse to change their behaviour, especially if their work is important to achieving your reengineering goals. Your tolerance of old behaviours signals that you are not serious about the change.
>
> The above applies to all people, managers as well as workers. This is a new democracy.
>
> Don't expect people to change how they behave unless you change what they do; that is, their work must be designed to allow them to act differently.
>
> Don't expect cultural change to happen immediately. Although you may achieve some early results, a complete cultural change is measured in years (hopefully just a few) rather than in months.
>
> Don't articulate a new or updated set of values and then delay reengineering your management processes to support them.
>
> (Champy, 1995, 109)

Consider the following questions:

1   What are the implications for a worker with reservations about change?
2   How far would democracy be an accurate word to describe this process?
3   Who will be making the changes in work procedures?
4   What sort of cultural change does the writer assume?
5   How could a new set of values be 'articulated'?

It becomes clear in this final list that the cost of failing to change appropriately would be serious indeed. Resistance would be futile as the change is to happen and it is not just a question of acquiescence but full compliance and commitment from all those affected. Indeed, delay in dispensing with the services of the unwilling could be interpreted as a signal that resistance will be tolerated. This sacking is intended *pour encourager les autres*.

It would be fair to say that democracy has been used to suggest a system of voting based upon a majority vote in favour or against, before matters of state are implemented. Here, the decision lies with the reader or putative implementer of the change programme. It is interesting perhaps that the majority may suggest that the writer assumes that all reasonable workers have already agreed with the change and that therefore only the unreasonable objector is acting outside the democratic consensus.

The manager of change is suggested as the agent of job redefinition in this scenario. The references to empowerment and autonomy of workers to decide how they arrange their work to achieve the objectives does seem to apply here. Perhaps the new behaviours are so significant that the new culture requires that they be implemented uniformly and without variance.

We might note that the wording here seems to suggest that the new set of values is imposed, perhaps having been formulated by the implementers of change. Again, this would be a different view from that held by those who believe that culture emerges from basic assumptions held about work (Schein, 1985, 1990). Here, the values themselves are laid down by the owners of change and expected from the actors involved in carrying out the change in different, defined behaviours.

Cultural change in this account would suggest an imposed change programme of required behaviours, which will be accompanied by believing and espousing the right underlying assumptions about the new terms and conditions at work. Here, culture is not an emergent set of values, which comes about through modified, if managed behaviours. It is a required mindset of beliefs, which will be held like a credal formula by all who want to continue to work in the organization. This is more like a religious foundation than the democratic model of organization.

THE RHETORIC OF QUALITY PROGRAMMED CHANGE

We have spent some time offering examples of radical change programmes with examples of the rhetoric that sometimes supports them. We should allow that not all programmed changes are as extreme as those we have examined and indeed, historically, there were more reasoned and reasonable attempts to intervene to achieve greater efficiency and effectiveness at work.

We will now look briefly at this tradition of programmed change, which arguably outlasted Business Process Engineering – though, at the time, BPR succeeded TQM as a programme for change. One writer attempted to present the main contributors to this movement for Total Quality and he summarizes the contributions of the four main contributors whose names are frequently associated with TQM. Here is one of his early explanations of the movement:

> Everyone experiences – almost accepts – problems in working life. This causes people
> to spend a large part of their time on useless activities, correcting errors, looking for

things, finding out why things are late, checking suspect information, rectifying and reworking, apologising to customers for mistakes, poor quality and lateness. This list is endless and it is estimated that one third of our efforts are wasted in this way.

Quality, the way we have defined it as meeting the customer requirements, gives people in different functions of an organisation a common language for improvement. It enables all people, with different abilities and priorities, to communicate readily with one another, in pursuit of a common goal. When business and industry were local, the craftsman could manage more or less on his own. Business is now so complex and employs so many different specialist skills that everyone has to rely on the activities of others in doing their jobs.

(Oakland, 1989, 13)

Consider the following questions:

1   What is the focus of this approach?
2   Why is it necessary?
3   How has the estimated waste been calculated?
4   What is the benefit of the approach?
5   What sort of business now requires this approach?

The starting point of the writer is clearly everyday problems experienced by people at work. The advantage of the TQM approach will be to examine the kind of problems being experienced and try to define learning outcomes, which can be applied to avoid or alleviate the problems being experienced.

Waste and error account for much that would come under the heading of interference costs in all businesses. They can be substantial and can depend on how far individuals are aware of their implications and also how far it is within their power to do anything about them. It is clearly an effort worth making, as on their own they rarely appear in company accounts. They are that missing element which is hidden from view, but which could be giving rise to substantial costs. An example would be staff turnover costs – the amount paid for every member of staff who needs to be replaced. There is recruitment, selection, induction training, perhaps uniform and equipment, all of which must be paid each time another member of staff has to be replaced.

Interestingly, some companies and industries have attempted to calculate the costs involved in such interference. However, it is difficult to be exact and here the writer does not say how the average offered has been calculated.

The idea of a common endeavour for reducing such losses evidently appeals to the proponents of this programme for quality assurance. They are insistent that all individuals need to be involved in it, not just those who have been engaged in manufacturing or producing the products or services themselves. This is a corporate endeavour and senior managers are, if anything, more responsible for the success of such initiatives rather than less. Indeed,

Deming calculates that 94 per cent of quality problems lie at the door of senior management, though he does not divulge exactly how he came to this figure.

Interestingly, the writer seems to be suggesting that bureaucratic and hierarchical organization itself requires such attention to securing the objectives of consistent quality. We may accept that it is easier for the single craftsman to achieve monitoring and evaluation of his or her own efforts. However, it seems that the point being made here is that the division of labour in its increasing complexity makes the quest for quality even more critical.

We will be looking in more detail at the suggested implementation and techniques that underwrite the practice of TQM in the next section. However, before we leave this section it might be worthwhile to compare the claims made by the writer for the way in which TQM should be approached and contrast it with the claims we have seen made for the implementation of Business Process Re-engineering. The author and his colleagues, who have been involved in the implementation programmes, comment on situations which can often occur and what successful implementation will require:

> Goals are imposed which are seen or known to be unrealistic. If the goals perceived by the subordinate are in fact accomplished then the subordinate has proved himself wrong!
>
> Where individuals are stimulated to commit themselves to a goal and where their personal pride and self-esteem are at stake, then the level of motivation is at a peak. For most people the toughest critic and the hardest taskmaster they confront is not their immediate boss, but themselves.
>
> Directors and managers are often afraid of allowing subordinates to set the goals for fear of them being set too low, or loss of control over subordinate behaviour. It is also true that many do not wish to set their own targets but prefer to be told what is to be accomplished.
>
> TQM is concerned with moving the focus of control from outside the individual to within; the objective being to make everyone accountable for their own performance and to get them committed to attaining quality in a highly motivated fashion. The assumptions that a director or senior manager must make in order to move in this direction are simply that people do not need to be coerced to perform well, that work is natural, and that people want to achieve, accomplish, influence activity and challenge their abilities. If there is belief in this, then only the technique remains to be discussed.
>
> (Oakland, 1989, 25ff.)

We may compare these beliefs and assumptions with the assertions of the proponents of BPR, which we saw earlier. The underlying principle seems to be one of assimilation: the worker will set his or her own targets and then internalize them. Managers do not need to fear the slackening of effort here. There is a feel of the Y manager whose beliefs are benevolent about worker involvement and therefore the style of management required is not directive but rather delegational (McGregor, 1960). Resistance is not addressed, not because it will not occur, but because involvement will overcome resistance. Individuals will see the good sense of gaining their own control over their own work. Coercion is not an issue in a world of work in which individual acceptance is the key.

At the heart of both claims for programmed change at work lie the claims and counterclaims of competence and commitment. The motivational assumptions may be that

167

competent workers do not need to be coerced. And, if they are not competent, then training should be offered.

The alternative account starts with the assumption that committed workers will fulfil the expectations of the organization and its management. If individuals are not committed, then they can have no part in this new world of totally committed workers who will bear any burden and pay any price in achieving excellence, to the delight of the customers and the optimum benefit of the shareholders.

In the following section we will examine the theoretical underpinnings for the claims made by proponents of programmatic change and the evidence offered so far of its successful achievement.

TQM AND UNDERPINNING THEORY

Before embarking on a search for the detail that the different approaches to TQM have in common, it is worthwhile examining the context in which it was born. One of its best-known proponents is W. Edwards Deming, who summarized this in a Foreword he wrote to a book describing how his techniques were presented in America in the 1980s (Walton, 1989). Here Deming sees a decline in Western industry expressed in a shrinking trading balance between the United States and the rest of the world, which he sees as a trend stretching over the previous 20 years. He is quite clear in the basic cause of this occurrence:

> The cause of the decline is that management has walked off the job of management, striving instead for dividends and good performance of the price of the company's stock. A better way to serve stockholders would be to stay in business with constant improvement of quality of product and of service, thus to decrease costs, capture markets, provide jobs and increase dividends.
>
> Management in America (not all) has moved into what I call retro-active management: focus on the end product – look at reports on sales, inventory, quality in and quality out, the annual appraisal of people; start the statistical control of quality and QC-Circles for operations, unfortunately detached from management's responsibility; apply management by numbers, MBO (management by objective), work standards.
>
> (Oakland, 1989, ix)

If we were to see this analysis in its context, then we might say that the output measurements and review systems were then the predominant focus of managers' attention and that they had taken for granted the process of manufacture in its internal workings.

To illustrate this in his seminars, Deming involved managers in a simple activity, which allowed participants to randomly select from a box of white and red beads. The red beads were designated as unwanted by the customers who had paid for white beads. Each scoop made was analysed and the results posted under the names of the participants with the number of red beads selected. Three participants were designated inspectors and the results tabulated and compared (see Table 7.1).

The purpose of the exercise was to demonstrate to participants that the scores became the focus of comment. How had one participant fared compared with another? Why was

Table 7.1 *Results of participants' selections*

Name	Day 1	Day 2	Day 3	Day 4	Totals
Tom	21	28	19	27	95
Mary	19	14	25	30	88
Harry	9	15	24	22	70
Jane	17	10	15	25	67
Sheila	23	24	23	26	96
George	14	17	22	22	75
Total output	*103*	*108*	*128*	*152*	*491*
Average output	17.2	18.0	21.3	25.3	81.8

one further behind than the rest? This reinforced to his audience Deming's point that focusing on results in a statistical way deflects managers away from asking why there was such variance in the first place.

For Deming, then, TQM is a philosophy and it can be summarized as 'a concept applicable to the whole organization':

> It is a philosophy and a set of techniques aimed at creating and maintaining a constancy of purpose towards the improvement of products and services. The basis of TQM is cross-functional co-operation, largely through sales and marketing interacting with production, coupled with an obsession about quality service for the customer.
>
> (Wilson, 1992, 93)

Before we examine the techniques involved in more detail, we would do well to examine the hypotheses on which it is based. Wilson provides a useful diagram derived from Deming, which illustrates this well (see Figure 7.1).

Define customer needs

We might remark that this element of Deming's model places the context of TQM away from the statistical into the source of products and services: customer needs. Today such a simplistic step might be taken for granted. For its time, Deming and his colleagues felt the need to place it centrally in their argument for implementing the process of TQM.

Improve organizational quality towards meeting those needs

The obviousness of the second step might also be taken for granted in manufacturing and service industries today. Indeed, the whole focus of TQM was not just to reassemble manufacturing processes to achieve this objective, but also to ensure that all supporting disciplines within the company should reinforce that objective, too. So, service, support in the field,

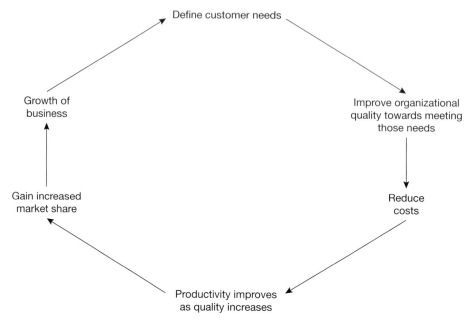

Figure 7.1 *Steps in the TQM process*
Source: Wilson (1992, 94)

training and customer care should all be seeking to adjust their contribution to ensure a seamless product and service to the customer. No part of the process should be beyond the demands of quality assessment.

Reduce costs

This is the interesting step, which should give rise to careful consideration. It begs the question: where will that cost saving be found? If we accept Deming's analysis on the state of industry throughout the West or in the United States as having lost sight of its purpose, then it may well be that unnecessary costs have been incurred in focusing on monitoring the process and comparing the performance figures, rather than identifying where the detail of the process might be improved. Tightening up on the procedures to ensure they coalesce may indeed yield a cost saving.

We may agree that poorly coordinated production and service provision can have given rise to error and wastage in the past or to reworking required by customers who were inadvertently in receipt of the red beads instead of the white, which they had paid for. Such interference costs should indeed be alleviated by the implementation of a programme to iron out such problems.

But, having reached a level of performance, which is now consistent, how much more improvement could be achieved? Once the level is reached, then in theory there are no errors and waste of the kind we previously experienced and the costs squeezed out of the system will now be more difficult to find.

Productivity improves as quality increases

We can follow on with the logic of this assertion with the points we have made earlier: the improvement here will achieve a level to the point where the quality is achieved. If, say, we have now achieved ISO 9000 in both output and process, then that is where our cost base now consolidates. The initial take-up of the process of improvement may indeed offer improved savings while it is still in process of being implemented. At the point of achievement, however, unless something else is improved over and above the standard aimed for, the saving can reasonably be expected to cease.

Gain increased market share

At this point the assumption made should be correct provided that the improvements made to product and service now coincide with what the customer wanted. The assumption takes no account of the fact that, while the improvement process was being put in place, the customer's requirements could have changed. Alternatively, another supplier could have achieved the standards before us. In either case the expected yields in terms of sales may be less than expected.

Growth of the business

How business grows may be a function of internal factors such as extra capacity, or external factors such as increased market demand. Both could indeed be the outcome for a successful supplier of product or service. However, neither of those outcomes is guaranteed. A market may become saturated – in which case there is no more growth, however good the product may now be. On the other hand, there may be demand but the capacity is not within the company's power to develop – perhaps for reasons of lack of resources or opportunity.

Define customer needs

This brings us back to our first point. But it again begs the question: how exactly is this need reassessed? It could be argued that, once reached, the new standard becomes an accepted outcome and is indeed quite difficult to get moved on. Achievement of a standard can become an end in itself and the effort to rethink and start the cycle all over again may be more than the change agents want to embark on.

The customer as the driver of change in this model of the TQM process is clear and the logic has a surface validity about it. However, the objections lie inherently in a series of causal connections that may not be realized in quite the way the model suggests.

THE CONTENT OF TQM

The concept of identifying the critical factors inherent in any production function is not new to the management of work. We could argue that the scientific managerialism laid out by Taylor (1913) was equally focused on identifying the best practice for any particular function and then gauging reward around its achievement by individual workers. However,

171

the key to TQM as a programmed approach to change relies on defining the key functions and standardizing their implementation by those who undertake them:

> Quality and productivity improvement through standardisation and statistical process control is a modern success story. Economically feasible methods for controlling the uniformity of output enabled the use of interchangeable parts, which, in turn, made possible industrial mass production, economies of scale and improvements in wealth and welfare (Womack *et al.*, 1990).
>
> (Lillrank, 2003, 215)

What we observe here is a focus on the analysis of tasks and job elements in such a way that their description can be drawn up precisely into standards of behaviour which under-write patterns of performance and ensure that they are conducted uniformly by all individuals who have to discharge them. These designed and designated performances can then be codified or drawn up into policy and procedures and enshrined in Staff Handbooks, Personnel and Training Policies and Operations Manuals throughout the organization.

A simple example will illustrate this point. If you travel by air you will be impressed by the smooth approach and touchdown achieved in the majority of landings. The landing configuration is defined closely for those wishing to train as a pilot. These are: a 3-degree glide path; straight down the centre line of the runway (veering no more that 2.5 degrees either side); with a horizontal variance of no more than 50 feet plus or minus from the descent path. Once you know this standard, you will train to it, be tested on it and adhere to it in every landing you complete as a pilot. And so, in many sectors, particularly where safety is a critical factor, defining key behaviours and reinforcing them is vital to securing a required quality of outcome.

Of course, not all behaviours are as predictable as this example suggests. Most routine, functional tasks may well lend themselves to such normative approaches. However, there will be areas of human endeavour which require the exercise of discretion by the actor. Negotiation, sales and many other social interactions between human beings does not always lend itself to predictive behaviours. Here, more discretion is required from the individuals concerned and, indeed, practised techniques can be defeated by unexpected responses. The management of routine behaviours is therefore more feasible because performance can be measured and therefore compared (Burns and Stalker, 1961). Standard operating proce-dures will enable the validation of performances to be rationalized (Cyert and Marsh, 1993). Some exceptions can be envisaged and therefore practised to prepare for landing, say, with a different power setting (March and Simon, 1958). But once the area of discretion becomes great or the external conditions become unstable, then the procedures need to be drawn up with more discretion given to the individual operator (Eisenhardt and Martin, 2000, 1106).

In such examples routines evolve and change because they are not mindless but emer-gent accomplishments (Lillrank, 2003, 218). At this point we move from standards, towards target, tolerances and ranges of behaviour. The distinction is made between variation and variety (2003, 221). The former refers to the idea of a range of behaviours on the same standard routine. The latter refers to a variety of different routines called on as occasion demands. Much more discretion is required to be exercised by the individual actor and the acceptability of the performance becomes the evaluation by the end-user rather than validation by those monitoring the performance according to written procedures. Lillrank offers a threefold distinction, which moves from the very rigid predicted performance, through the more discretionary routines and finally to what he calls non-routine situations. The fact that there are fewer validatable behaviours in this latter category does not mean that it will lack methods of evaluation by end-users or providers (see Table 7.2).

STEPS IN THE TQM PROCESS

We have already examined stepped approaches to change in the previous chapter. The proponents of TQM offer their own lists for achieving successful implementation. Like most lists, they include a mixture of the practical and the aspirational. Deming's Fourteen Points are as follows:

1. Create constancy of purpose for improvement of product and service
2. Adopt the new philosophy
3. Cease dependence on mass inspection
4. End the practice of awarding business on price tag alone
5. Improve constantly and forever the system of production and service
6. Institute training and retraining
7. Institute leadership
8. Drive out fear
9. Break down barriers between staff areas
10. Eliminate slogans, exhortations and targets for the workforce
11. Eliminate numerical quotas
12. Remove barriers to pride in workmanship
13. Institute a vigorous programme of education and retraining
14. Create a structure in top management that will push every day on the above 13 points.

(Oakland, 1989, 287)

Table 7.2 *Standard, routine and non-routine processes*

	Standard	Routine	Non-routine
Acceptance criteria	Single variety	Bounded variety set	Open input set
Assessment	Acceptance test	Classification	Interpretation
Conversion rules	Switch, algorithm	Algorithm, grammar, habit	Heuristics
Repetition	Identical	Similar but not identical	Non-repetitive
Logic	Binary	Fuzzy	Interpretive

Source: Lillrank (2003, 222)

As we can see, there are some items in the list that are themselves hortatory and which can only be described as aspirational. Such aims can only be a target which the organization and its managers aim for but may not reach. Deming himself inveighed against what he saw as the prevailing management mindset of quotas and Management by Objectives. These he found predictive and inflexible and he believed that managers and workers needed to look anew at what they were trying to achieve and be open-minded about how to achieve it consistently, reassessing its quality and fitness for purpose.

We can also see that he perceived the removal of obstacles to that quality as a twofold endeavour, which included the need for consistency both in competencies and in commitment. His inclusion of management in this revitalization programme was at the time a different message of involvement and leadership in which managers were intended to become standard-bearers themselves.

QUESTIONS ARISING FOR TQM PRACTITIONERS

It would be fair to say that the initiative that Deming and his colleagues put in place commanded considerable attention during the 1980s both in the United States and throughout the industrialized world. As such, the ability to test the practicality and the underpinning theory of TQM allows writers to summarize concerns and objections to this programmed approach to change under the following headings offered by Wilson (1992, 101ff.):

Intangible benefits

The focus of some efforts to achieve a stated standard such as BS 5750 or ISO 9000 can become an end in itself rather than a means to the end of quality achievement. The focus of steps and stages of inspection and outside intervention can subvert from the transformational process, which the proponents suggest is the main benefit of undertaking TQM.

Sectional interests

TQM can find a disparity between managers who are very committed and those who are not. Some writers suggest that this increases the chance of fragmentation and localized commitment to the overall strategy (Cyert and Marsh, 1993).

The customer comes first and is also judge

Sometimes the effort to achieve internal standards can be a source of tension, with the ultimate need to satisfy TQM requirements perceived as a distraction from satisfying current customers. Indeed, managers may well be heard to say, 'I thought we were here to satisfy customers now, not be deflected by getting another plaque on the wall.'

The sponge phenomenon

Managers may find that resources and time are required to effect the required changes. The training needed longer to bed down; courses needed to be extended; extra tuition was needed in an area that had not been foreseen and so on. The programme is a consumer of financial and other provision that detracts from current need in the business, and can be seen as a solution to all internal organizational problems.

Recreating the rigid organization

Achieving the standard becomes an end in itself and, once achieved, leaves individuals feeling that nothing more need be done. Customer care now becomes a routine, refer-to-the-handbook operation, as policy and procedures are cast in stone and deferred to as the sole arbiters of day-to-day decisions.

The distinction between means and ends becomes blurred

During the programme the end result can be lost sight of by participants, as the elements needed to achieve the end are focused on as an end in themselves. Facilitative leadership is needed here and may not be available at the time.

TQM can make things worse

Diverting attention from an inherent problem not necessarily directly connected to the quest for TQM could be just enough to topple the company into demise. Research into organizations attempting the change suggests that this is a very possible scenario (McKiernan, 1992).

Lack of evidence

It is always difficult to support causal connections between validation and evaluation. The fact that training has been conducted does not ensure that success in satisfying the customer is guaranteed. It might have been achieved without the training. Assured techniques of successful implementation do not always transfer readily from one company or sector to another.

MANAGEMENT COMPETENCIES AND TQM

Before moving on from the specifics underlying production and consistency, we ought perhaps to mention the UK's Management Charter Initiative. In the early 1990s there was a movement to define the different elements of competencies that managers might exercise in their jobs so that training could be more carefully crafted to support those designated tasks.

Different units of competence were delineated to include handling information, handling people, planning and structuring work, and each of these units was broken down into its constituent elements and in turn each element was broken down into its individual competencies. A simple example might be that of communication, often identified as a competence that managers need. The specific communication might be with groups compared with individuals. If we took the latter, then we might focus on particular types of individual interviews: selection; disciplinary; grievance; and appraisal. Now, for each interview we

175

could delineate the structure of that interview, which the manager would be expected to have experience in or be prepared to undertake.

The system was designed to coincide with the traditional levels of management and was designed to fit into the NVQ levels appropriate to first-line manager, middle manager and senior manager requirements. Initially, it was supported by internal and external validators and could be used to gain accreditation through providing evidence of achievement at work or even prior experience, if evidence of expertise could be provided to the assessors. At the time it seemed to offer a management standard that could validate standards across business sectors and so offer evidence of transferable skills for managers moving on in their careers.

It would be fair to say that the initiative lost its way amid the different perceptions that managers had about the context of the work they were being asked to undertake in different sectors. Wilson summarizes this succinctly:

> The notion of a universal list of competences appeared alien to a number of managers and their companies. Many companies which supported the charter initially began to press for the competences to be 'tailored' to suit the demands of their particular business. The tendency to assume that every business is unique and to exert pressure for course syllabuses to be tailored will be no surprise to any reader who runs an educational programme (e.g. MBAs) supported by one or more organizations. Understandably each organization wants its specific problems addressed in the syllabus.
>
> (1992, 109ff)

Consistency of performance is a means to an end. As an end in itself it can become self-defeating. TQM can provide a means for reassessing internal procedures. But the link with increased effectiveness can never be taken for granted.

BUSINESS PROCESS RE-ENGINEERING REVISITED

It seems that the transformation offered by the internal efforts to achieve consistent quality was not enough for the proponents of BPR (Champy, 1995; Hamel and Prahaled, 1994; Hammer and Champy, 1993). For them re-engineering is the fundamental rethinking and redesign of business processes to achieve dramatic improvements in critical, contemporary measures of performance, such as cost, quality, service and speed. So far, then, we appear to have a focus on the traditional productivity factors, which would be the concern of any traditional manager who wanted to improve performance.

But, as we have seen, the proponents of BPR do not wish to wait too long to find radical achievements yielded in the improvement of performativity. If possible, we do not want to live with people who do not demonstrate the changes required and the thought and commitment behind them. It is time to be radical with the way we organize the new organization.

We have already seen that the rhetoric of this change management programme had moved on from the incremental change envisaged by TQM. Traditional hierarchies as defined in, say, the Management Charter Initiative are renamed to identify more closely with the new roles they will play in the business:

Self managers – people who may not think of themselves as managers but, in the last analysis, they answer only for the quality of their own work.

Process and people managers – those who answer for the work of others.

Expertise managers – people whose responsibility is the care and development of the company's intelligence.

Enterprise managers – all those with profit and loss responsibility.

(Champy, 1994, 4)

We can see the innovation of definition of management based not on hierarchical position but on a more dynamic role including the empowered nature of their jobs. More difficult to interpret are some of the diagrams that accompany the texts (see Figure 7.2).

As students of HRM will know from the popular discussion at the time, such diagrams offer no clear indication of whether they are illustrating a theory, a model or a map (Noon, 1992). And, indeed, the double-headed arrows suggest that the map can offer illustration but not direction for management strategists.

So, too, we might find it difficult to derive much more than a general interaction of important elements from the diagram in Figure 7.3.

We may detect some elements of TQM. But included here are market and strategic alliances that are hinted at but not adumbrated clearly.

What seems to predominate is the demand for competition in linking technology, skills and product share. Again, how that logic can be achieved in detail is not divulged (see Figure 7.4).

EMERGING EVIDENCE OF UNEASE

There is some evidence emerging that all is not well with those on whom such change is visited. Radical change to working lives can often mean very different demands made on

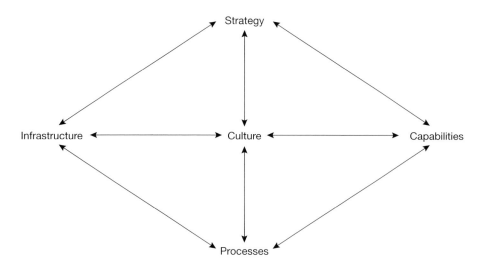

Figure 7.2 *Diagram of interrelated factors affecting change*

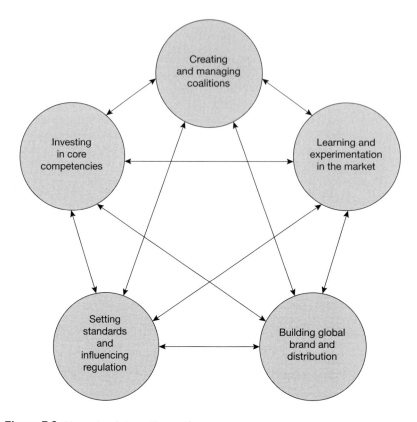

Figure 7.3 *Managing integration paths*
Source: Hamel and Prahaled, Managing migration paths in Competing for the Future,
Boston, MA, 1994, p. 186. Reprinted by permission of Harvard Business School Press.
© 1994 Gary Hamel and C.K. Prahaled; all rights reserved

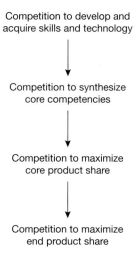

Figure 7.4 *Links between competitive drivers*
Source: Harvey and Brown (1992, 212)

people who have served faithfully in such organizations as banks and building societies, for example, finding themselves transferred to call centres. The attendant impact and its effects on stress and staff turnover emphasize how difficult it is to implement radical change without engendering discomfort or worse to the individuals involved (Knights and McCabe, 1998).

More general reviews of research drawn from many contributors have found similar responses from subjects (Willcocks and Grint, 1997). In their own words:

> Business process re-engineering is revealed as essentially political in rhetorical and practical manifestations. Its claims for newness are exaggerated and its application generally less startling in its outcomes than its promotional literature predicts.
>
> (1997, 105)

More recent researchers find that, while senior managers are likely to be much more bullish in their assessments of the impact of change and its success in the business, those lower down the hierarchy are likely to take a much more sober view (Doyle *et al.*, 2000). Their article is entitled 'Mixed results, lousy process: the management experience of organizational change'. Among their conclusions they state:

> The argument advanced here suggests that an adequate theory of organizational change should take into account not only organizational process and context, but also the lived experience of those involved in processing change initiatives and the pressures, tensions, contradictions and constraints under which they function.
>
> (2000, S72)

If there is unease and stress occasioned by radical change at work, there are some writers who would see this as a likely outcome from a movement whose very language is couched in violent formulas and metaphors redolent of warfare and offensive strategies (Grint and Case, 1998). In summary, one overview puts it succinctly as follows:

> In their haste to jump on the BPR bandwagon, executives abandoned a tried and trusted approach to organizational redesign, the socio-technical school, in favour of a new fad which ignored 'soft' issues such as the quality of working life and prevailing values and relations. It could be said that a rather different part of the story is that the successes of the re-engineering are counted in how better integrated tasks become and the greater empowerment of employees. However, these should not be confused. This improvement of integration and coordination of work may be desirable but it is not the same as broadening the scope of autonomy or the variety of work that employees enjoy (Willmott, 1995).
>
> (Genus, 1995, 79)

POSTSCRIPT ON NEW PUBLIC MANAGEMENT

We have already referred to the movement referred to as New Public Management (NPM). The rhetoric surrounding programmed approaches to change found appeal among politicians and public sector managers who thought that gain could be derived from efficiency savings and the 'cutting of waste'. It is important to note that the same assumptions lie at the heart of NPM as were described by proponents of Business Process Re-engineering. However, there was sometimes a confusion between the processes themselves, which were thought to be capable of being improved in order to yield financial savings and the belief that public servants could find a new entrepreneurial spirit.

We have seen in the previous chapter that the two factors are sometimes assumed to go hand in hand and that, once released from the dead hand of bureaucratic restraint, natural entrepreneurialism will emerge in day-to-day decision-making. Such accounts offer a triumphalistic version of events which prove that such will be the case (Osborne and Gaebler, 1992). Deconstructing what might be regarded as the constraining role of rules and regulation might have seemed quite feasible at first and usually addressed the definition of clear standards and the introduction of competition into the public sector (Hood, 1991; Pollitt, 1995).

Other voices suggested that the changes could not be successful without embracing the deeper cultures that underlay public practices at work (Peters and Savoie, 1994; Bate, 2000). However, even early attempts to achieve this desired goal brought with it a surface resistance (Harrison et al., 1992). The basic assumptions that are held by public servants make it difficult, if not impossible, for an easy transition to take place (Randall, 2001). Indeed, some would suggest that such a transformation is unlikely to take place given the requirement that individuals not only change the way they work but the way they think about and evaluate their work as well:

> Neo-managerialism fosters the idea that public managers are (and should be) self-interested, opportunistic innovators and risk-takers who exploit information and situations to produce radical change. In other words, the neo-managerialism underpinning liberation and market-driven management cultivates the notion that public managers should assume an entrepreneurial leadership role.
> Guy Peters and Osborne & Gaebler are among a cacophony of voices linking entrepreneurialism to improved government performance.
>
> (Terry, 1998, 197)

SUMMARY

We suggest that the fault-line that runs through the discussion of managing change at work is to be seen here as we consider programmed approaches to change. When we looked at culture we saw it defined sometimes as what an organization had – attributes on which behaviours are constructed – and what an organization is – the perceptions that govern the way in which events are interpreted.

The same fault-line runs through the programmed approaches themselves. The lists of change factors often include both elements of behavioural change and belief change side-by-side. Sometimes it is assumed that if one changes then the other will change with it. As we saw with stepped approaches to change, the question of resistance is lightly touched on, if at all. And, in the case of some of the more radical approaches to change, resisters would not be allowed to survive very long.

Each programmed approach to change has about it a freshness and innovation that commends it to those who want to manage radical change at work. However, the same constraints remain to be overcome and they lie at the heart of why individuals work and how they evaluate what they are trying to achieve for themselves and others.

DISCUSSION QUESTIONS

1   Total Quality Management (TQM) is dependent on improving quality to meet customer need while reducing cost. What are the potential flaws in the theoretical assumptions underlying this management philosophy?

You may want to begin your answer by placing TQM in its context of management by objectives and quotas, which Deming, for example, inveighed against. The focus of managers was analytical, according to him, and they had lost sight of the need to examine closely the processes of production in detail.

You may then introduce Wilson's diagram (see Figure 7.1) showing the steps in the logic which underwrites the programmed approach that TQM embodies. This will give you the opportunity of examining the links between those steps and the assumptions being made by the proponents of TQM. You will want to show how these steps may not be as self-evident as the diagram suggests.

Second, you may want to look at the eight-point list from Wilson (see pp. 101–102), in which he examines the evidence for the programme's effectiveness. You may want to comment on how the standards themselves can become an end in themselves and indeed a level of performance, which itself may become as rigid as the previous practice it was intended to replace. You may also want to comment on the cost of achieving these standards and the expending of time and resources that their achievement may require.

Finally, you may want to look at the assumptions about individual and group motivation to change in general and the factor of different responses from different managers and groups to the prospect of this or any other change. This raises the enduring question of how feasible it is to speak of 'management' in the same breath as we speak of 'change'.

2   Total Quality Management (TQM) is a technique for managing efficiency improvement whilst Business Process Re-engineering (BPR) is the same technique applied to effectiveness in the organization.

    How far would you agree with this statement?

You may want to start your answer with a description of TQM and BPR and the diagrams and list of steps involved in implanting these programmed approaches to change at work. It will be important to be clear about the differences you perceive between the two approaches.

As always with questions containing a statement, you are well advised to examine the assumptions being made in the statement and the assumptions that underlie it. If, for example, your definition of efficiency is the attention to the improvement of the productivity factors of time, quality, quantity and cost, then it is clear that there is some coincidence between that and what TQM proposes. Although, having said that, you may want to point out that the trigger for these changes is clearly customer demand and its objective is to satisfy that demand and thereby expand the business. So, it would not be fair to say that TQM is some sort of internally focused approach to change at work.

We then come to the question of BPR. Is this radical change different in essence from TQM? Could it not be similar in that it seeks to satisfy customer demands and so find an immediate advantage among the customer base with distinguishing value-added benefits transforming the business? What would the proponents of BPR do differently from the proponents of TQM? We may conclude here that the differences are based around the ability or willingness of radical change managers to live over-long with the resisters to change. Indeed, perhaps the best answer would be for them to replace older workers with those who will adopt and adapt to new ways more willingly and more quickly. Certainly there is evidence that greenfield sites, which by definition can make such a fresh start, offer more evidence of such a change being more successful than sites in the same sector seeking to implement programmed approaches to change (Storey, 1989, 1995).

The statement makes a false distinction, which confines efficiency to one programme and effectiveness to the other. It would be fair to say that both programmes attempt to address both. However, the methods they might adopt would find a different approach to how people are expected to change and what measures managers might take to achieve compliance.

REFERENCES AND FURTHER READING

Bate, P. Changing the culture of a hospital from hierarchy to networked community. *Public Administration*, 2000, *78* (3): 485–512.

Belbin, R.M. *Management teams: why they succeed or fail*. Oxford: Butterworth Heinemann, 1981.

Burns, T. and Stalker, G.M. *The management of innovation*. London: Tavistock, 1961.

Champy, J. *Reengineering management*. New York: HarperBusiness, 1995.

Cyert, R.M. and Marsh, J.G. *A behavioural theory of the firm*. Englewood Cliffs, NJ: Prentice Hall, 1993.

Doyle, M., Claydon, T. and Buchanan, D. Mixed results, lousy process: the management experience of organizational change. *British Journal of Management*, 2000, *11* (Special Issue): S59–S80.

Eisenhardt, K.M. and Martin, J.A. Dynamic capabilities: what are they? *Strategic Management Journal*, 2000, *21*: 1105–1121.

Genus, A. Re-engineering business processes in practice, in I. McLoughlin and M. Harris (eds) *Innovation, organizational change and technology*. London: International Thomson Business, 1995.

Grint, K. and Case, P. The violent rhetoric of re-engineering: management consultancy on the offensive. *Journal of Management Studies*, 1998, *35* (5): 557–577.

Hamel, G. and Prahaled, C.K. *Competing for the future.* Boston, MA: Harvard Business School Press, 1994.

Hammer, M. and Champy, J. *Re-engineering the corporation.* London: Nicholas Brealey Publishing, 1995.

Harrison, S., Hunter, D., Marnock, G. and Pollitt, C. *Just managing power and culture in the NHS.* London: Macmillan, 1992.

Hood, C. A public management for all seasons? *Public Administration*, 1991, *69* (1): 3–19.

Knights, D. and McCabe, D. Dreams and designs on strategy: a critical analysis of TQM and management control. *Work, Employment & Society*, 1998, *12* (3): 433–456.

Lillrank, P. The quality of standard, routine and non-routine processes. *Organization Studies*, 2003, *24* (2): 215–233.

McGregor, D. *The human side of enterprise.* New York: McGraw Hill, 1960.

McKiernan, P. *Strategies of growth: maturity, recovery and internationalization.* London: Routledge, 1992.

March, J.G. and Simon, H. *Organizations.* New York: Wiley, 1958.

Noon, M. HRM: a map, model or theory, in P. Blyton and P. Turnbull (eds) *Reassessing HRM.* London: Sage, 1992.

Oakland, J. *Total quality management.* Oxford: Butterworth Heinemann, 1989.

Osborne, D. and Gaebler, T. *Reinventing government: how the entrepreneurial spirit is transforming the public sector.* Reading, MA: Addison Wesley, 1992.

Peters, G. and Savoie, D.J. Civil service reform: misdiagnosing the patient. *Public Administration Review*, 1994, *54* (5) (September–October): 418–425.

Pettigrew, A.M. Is corporate culture manageable?, in D.C. Wilson and R.H. Rosenfeld (eds) *Managing organizations: text, readings and cases.* London: McGraw Hill, 1990.

Pollitt, C. (1995) Justification by works or by faith: evaluating the new public management. *Evaluation*, 1995, *1* (2): 133–154.

Randall, J.A. *Enforced change at work: the reconstruction of basic assumptions and its influence on attribution, self-sufficiency and the psychological contract.* Unpublished Ph.D. thesis, University of St Andrews, 2001.

Schein, E.H. *Organizational culture and leadership.* San Francisco, CA: Jossey Bass, 1985.

Schein, E.H. Organizational culture. *American Psychologist*, 1990, *45* (2): 109–119.

Storey, J. *New perspectives in HRM.* London: Routledge, 1989.

Storey, J. *Human resource management: a critical text.* London: Routledge, 1995.

Taylor, F.W. *The principles of scientific management.* New York: Harper, 1913.

Terry, L.D. Administrative leadership, neo-managerialism and the public management movement. *Public Administration Review*, 1998, *58* (3): 194–200.

Walton, M. *The Deming management method.* London: Mercury Books, 1989.

183

Willcocks, L. and Grint, K. Re-inventing the organization? Towards a critique of business process engineering, in I. McLaughlin and M. Harris (eds) *Innovation, organizational change and technology*. London: International Thomson Press, 1997.

Willmott, H.C. The odd couple? Reengineering business processes and managing human relations. *New Technology, Work and Employment*, 1995, *10* (2): 89–98.

Wilson, D.C. *A strategy of change*. London: Routledge, 1992.

Womack, J.P., Jones, D.T. and Roos, D. *The machine that changed the world*. New York: Rawson, 1990.

Chapter 8

Project management
Facilitation or constraint?

TOPIC HEADINGS

- The project and its management
- Management by Objectives
- Ways in for the change agent
- Implementing change programmes
- Evaluating change

INTRODUCTION

It would be fair to point out that project management is often regarded as being central to the success of change management. However, much of the academic literature refers to it as a counsel of perfection, but rarely offers much direct advice on how it should interface with change programmes at work. As an introduction to academic reading, therefore, we might be excused for not offering a how-to chapter for people embarking on a career as a management consultant or change agent. It would also be true to say that accounts of change by those who have conducted it or written about it rarely contain much detail on the instruments used to manage different types of change.

This leaves the author with a difficult path to tread. Our treatment thus far has been to examine the accounts born of experience and subject them to questions in order to uncover unsupported claims made by the writers or probe theoretical assumptions not revealed in the selected narrative. There is, for example, a profusion of work offering good practice in general terms, sometimes using illustrations that may or may not be applicable to diverse situations. There are also detailed books offering technique and example but little empirical evidence for application and utility. We will attempt to build a bridge between both types of writing.

It could be said that project management requires a skills set outside the work of the change manager. All we need do, then, is engage the services of a project manager with a suitable software package. And yet actual control of the change programme requires not just planning, promotion and communication, which are central to the work of traditional management, but also coordination and control (Fayol, 1949). Experience would suggest that any change programme would involve costs and require outcomes. The more individuals, both external and internal, become involved in such programmes, the more such costs will spiral. Change agents and managers will therefore need to think carefully about the kind of instruments needed both to coordinate and control and also to inform all those taking part in the programme of their part in it and where it fits into the larger aim and objective of the change programme.

So, we will keep to the format that we have established in previous chapters and attempt to offer the reader both examples and an opportunity to consider how and when different instruments might be appropriate to use. In the words of one practical guide:

> Those who are experienced in managing large-scale organisational change tend to have a wide range of myths and cautionary tales about the challenges of making things happen. One project manager, working in a large organisation, had a series of old sepia photographs on the wall behind his desk. The first, taken for an old newspaper, showed two halves of a nearly completed bridge missing one another by nearly a metre. The project manager had added the caption 'Poor Co-ordination.' Another showed a train that had crashed through its buffers. This one was captioned 'Running over Target.'
>
> The message was clear. The principles of effective project management may seem, to the uninitiated, a rather abstruse and perhaps pedantic set of disciplines. And yet, if we fail to apply these principles to managing change, the effect may be catastrophic.
>
> (Leigh and Walters, 1998, 123)

WHAT IS A PROJECT AND HOW IS IT MANAGED?

The first challenge to the manager of change is to clarify what exactly a project is. After all, we could be simply planning a software implementation or an update programme for a small in-house team; alternatively, we could be looking at major structural change throughout a large and complex organization. In this sense, we might suggest that a series of related events required to achieve the overall objective could be considered as a project. One of the to-do volumes that offers practical examples of different instruments defines it more fully thus:

> A project can be looked upon as an undertaking that has a set of activities that are linked together over a period of time to achieve an established goal or goals. Project management is concerned with the management of these activities to ensure that the goals are attained to the right quality, on time and within budget. A project has three chief attributes:
>
> a clearly defined objective
> infrequent, unique or unfamiliar to the enterprise undertaking its execution
> complex, often having an intricate physical performance and time structure.
>
> (Pearson and Thomas, 1991, 103)

All of this sounds easy to understand and indeed obvious. However, the evidence for achieving such an aim might seem to suggest that it is not as easy as it at first sounds. Indeed, one author suggested that the following results would not be untypical of IT projects:

Well over 25% of UK IT projects are well over budget and running late.

30% of large IT projects are over time and over budget (KPMG report).

46% of IT applications are delivered late.

48% over budget.

Too much emphasis on planning and control, not enough on management skills:

Team building

Communication

Negotiation

Training.

(Morley, 1991)

Some authors go so far as to emphasize that the barriers to success are not technical, but are people problems (Kearney, 1990). And most writers now acknowledge that the wider implications of change have not always been considered fully enough when projects were embarked on. The conceptualization and planning stages are reinforced in most schemas on change (Buchanan and Boddy, 1992; Paton and McCalman, 2000). We need to put projects into the organizational context in order to assess their full impact on all concerned. Such change processes are sometimes expressed diagrammatically (Leigh and Walters, 1998, 166; Paton and McCalman, 2000, 83).

We will not include these here, however, as such illustrations can become both intricate and difficult to interpret by those who were not directly involved in drawing up the information on which they are based. Examples of such techniques as stream analysis can be found in several volumes (Leigh and Walters, 1998, 170; Hayes, 2002, 98). Suffice it to say that a project is not just the diagrammatic arrangement of productivity or efficiency factors, but also the combination of people, systems and techniques required to coordinate the resources needed to complete progress within the established goals. As such, the areas of expertise required are more extensive than mere draughtsmanship. In the opinion of one commentator they include:

Managing scope (defining boundaries)

Managing time

Managing money

Managing quality

Managing communications

Managing human resources

Managing contracts/supply

Managing risk.

(Dinsmore, 1990)

We have already referred to the element of scope and the need to delineate this aspect clearly at the outset. The next three elements in the list are standard management control indicators that we would expect to find at the heart of project management. The final four in the list summarize the need to involve participants and find ways in which the information governing the project can be put across to those involved. We can include, if we wish, the costs involved to alert participants to the effect on budgets or other critical resources. These in themselves may well also serve to indicate risk of overruns on time, quality, quantity or cost.

SOME EXAMPLES TO WORK ON

Diagrams can be simple descriptions of a process or a before–after sequence of events. Sometimes, as we have seen, they are simply illustrative of general links described by their author and show connection between elements but uncertainty about the direction or interaction that takes place (examples of diagrams containing double-headed arrows have been commented on in previous chapters).

Variations on this type of diagram include different steps containing directions and enclosed in different shapes to indicate the function intended to be taken by the reader (see Figure 8.1).

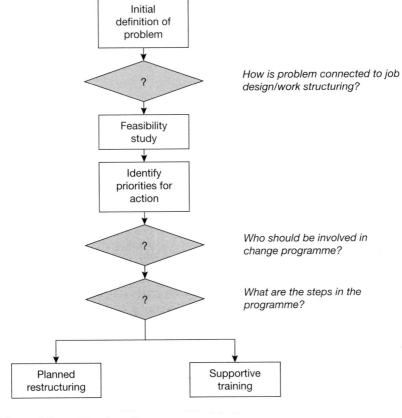

Figure 8.1 Decision flow diagram
Source: Adapted from Birchall (1975, 98) in Buchanan and Boddy (1992, 13)

What we see here offers process steps in the rectangular boxes and decision steps enclosed in diamond shapes. We could describe such causal connections as illustrating stages in a process, say, of decision-making or production. A similar flow or sequence can be seen in relationship maps (see Figures 8.2 and 8.3).

Projects that are a series of dependent events, required to be conducted in a specific sequence, obviously lend themselves to a charted approach. One such chart is sometimes referred to as PERT (programme evaluation review techniques). For example, see Figure 8.4.

Discrete and dependent events are here laid out in a sequence, which enables the reader to identify a series of different events perhaps conducted by different individuals or departments. Our earlier concern about the crucial nature of communication might be partially answered by such a diagram.

However, there is still information missing which might be useful for those involved to know. How long, for example, should each of these events take? When exactly should they start and finish? We can see a sequence, of course. But, if we were responsible for the sales training, it would be as well to know when exactly the recruitment stage would be completed so that we can plan the start of the training. But, perhaps more crucially, they

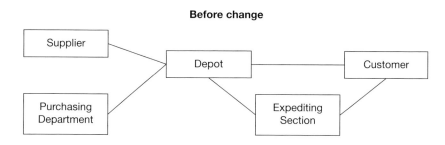

Figure 8.2 *Structure diagram before change*

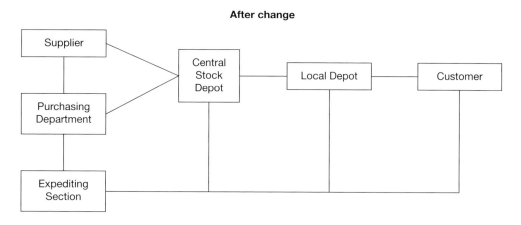

Figure 8.3 *Structure diagram after change*

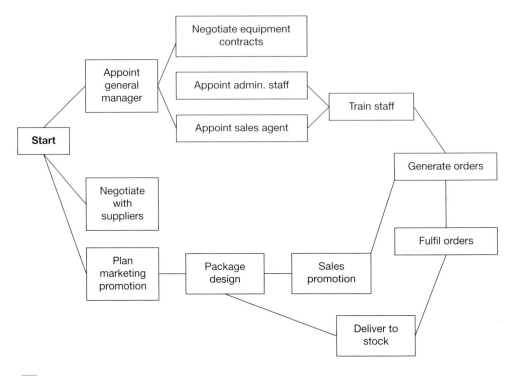

Figure 8.4 *Precedence network*

are expected to bring in orders – we might want to know how long we have to prepare them before the results are expected by the company (in some cases it could be as long as nine months before sales might come through).

TRYING IT OUT

Here is a case study designed by a group of postgraduate students, previously employed in the NHS. They assure me that the details are close to the kinds of choices available to those managing projects in the Health Service today.

Introduction

Back injuries sustained at work are one of the major causes of nursing staff sickness in the NHS. In addition to the personal costs for individuals, there are substantial costs to individual hospitals in providing staff to cover sick absence or in recruiting replacement staff for those who leave nursing through injury. Increasingly NHS hospitals are having to pay compensation to employees who have suffered work-related injuries: these payouts can be substantial, the largest to date being £680,000 to one individual.

It will become a statutory requirement for all staff involved in direct patient care to be given training in 'Moving and Handling'. You are required to organize the implementation of the training programme to nursing staff at St Ebbe's Hospital as a pilot exercise. If successful, the training will be extended to other staff groups. There are 300 nurses at St Ebbe's.

On completion of the training, staff will have learned new techniques requiring the use of lifting equipment such as mechanical hoists. This equipment has already been supplied to the hospital but is currently in storage awaiting the training programme. As part of the implementation programme, evaluation is required to ensure that staff who have received the training are implementing the new techniques correctly.

Timescale

Five months from September to January.

Budget

The budget of £12,500 is to cover only the hiring of external trainers and any locum staff required to cover the wards.

Training

Basic training (which all staff must have) takes 2 days.

Advanced training (needed to become an internal trainer – i.e. a member of St Ebbe's staff who will be able to train their colleagues) takes 5 days in total (such staff do not have to go through the basic training as well).

External trainers can provide basic training for 12 trainees at a time or advanced training for 6 trainees at a time.

Internal trainers can only provide basic training and can only teach 6 trainees at a time.

Facilities

The hospital has two suitable equipped rooms for training. These are available at no cost Monday–Friday and can hold a maximum of 1 trainer and 12 trainees.

Clinical services

Clinical services have to continue as normal while the training programme is in progress. This means that you may have no more than 6 staff away from the wards on any one day. For every nurse over and above 6 attending training you must allow for the cost of locum cover.

Costs

External trainers cost £200/day each, whether they are training or evaluating. The cost of internal trainers is part of the establishment cost of the hospital.
Locum staff for the wards cost £100/day each.

Evaluation

Evaluation can only be carried out by an external trainer on the wards.

Organizational objectives

1 All 300 nursing staff to be trained and the training programme evaluated by the end of the 5-month period and within the budgetary allocation.
2 On completion of training all staff to have been evaluated.

Please calculate how to achieve this objective and then draw up a schedule to demonstrate to staff when and where training will take place.

Initial options

You may like to look at the first option of using external trainers to train all 300 nurses at £200/day:

Number of training events would come to 25 as the external trainers can take 12 trainees at a time.

Each course will cost £400.00 in external trainers' fees.

This would give a total cost of: .... £10,000.00.

However, on every course 6 locums would have to be paid for at £100.00/day.

So that would be 6 × £100 × 2 (days) = £1200.00 × 25 = £30,000.

Total cost: .... £40,000.00.

Start again:

The alternative might be to train 6 internal trainers.

Cost for this: .... £1,000.00.

If we use 1 room for 2 day courses, say 2 per week then we incur no establishment costs for the trainer and 6 nurses incur no locum costs.

At the end of 20 weeks we will have trained the original six + 12 per week × 20 weeks.

This comes to 246 nurses trained for the original training cost.

This means that we need to train the remaining 54 nurses so we need 9 additional courses to do this. We have a second room available but this time we will need to pick up the interference cost of locums.

9 courses is 18 days on each of which £600.00 locum costs will be incurred.

Total: .... £10,800.00 + £1000.00 = £11,800.00.

We are actually £700.00 under budget here which is the amount we have left for evaluation. This would allow 3½ days of an external consultant's time.

We have chosen to express it in a straightforward two-axis diagram, which includes a cumulative total along the bottom row to allow the manager to alert finance to the likely take-up of costs [see Figures 8.5 and 8.6].

MANAGEMENT BY OBJECTIVES

Managing change could be said to be little different from any other form of management: we have a joint objective, in which all participants have some part to play or contribution to make. It would help all involved if we could define that objective clearly so that everyone understands what the group is committed to.

The next step might be to break down the overall part into the elements which apply to different parts of the organization. So, in a traditional manufacturing company production will derive their targets from the organizational objectives; marketing and sales will start to assess what the implications are for them if the production targets are to be placed in the market; finance will need to assess how far current processes can cope with the increase in invoices etc. Each of these parts of the organization can draw up a suitable instrument expressing what the productivity factors will look like for the coming trading period.

All we now need to do is apportion the group objective among the team members comprising the group. Sales people will have different targets according to their territories, and secretaries will have their own need to identify new priorities and work schedules with appropriate procedures to support their workflows.

Once the planning process is complete, individuals can have their own targets expressed weekly, monthly and cumulatively in the trading year ahead. Budget and actual columns will then alert all participants to any variance between what was planned and what is actually unfolding and then take appropriate executive decisions to make good the shortfall. Managers can pass information up the chain so that the Board are in possession of the vital information that indicates the organization's current state of health financially and in business terms.

Authors who subscribe to the traditional Organizational Development philosophy sometimes define it as:

A process whereby the superior and subordinate managers of an organization jointly identify its common goals, define each individual's major areas of responsibility in terms of results expected and use these measures as guides for operating the unit and assessing the contribution of each of its members.

(Harvey and Brown, 1992, 417 from *An experiential approach to organizational development*, 4th edn. Reprinted with kind permission of Pearson Education)

Weeks 1–7

Figure 8.5 *Hospital training budget spreadsheet*

The figure reproduces a rotated spreadsheet (columns A–AA). Column A holds the row labels (Week, Course, Room 1, Room 2, Total, Cumulative). Each week provides two courses (A and B), each with a **Cost** and a **Nos** column. The legible contents are:

Week	Course	Room 1 Cost	Room 1 Nos	Room 2 Cost	Room 2 Nos	Total Cost	Total Nos	Cumulative Cost	Cumulative Nos
1	A	£1,000.00	6			£1,000.00	6	£1,000.00	6
1	B	£1,200.00	6	£1,200.00	6	£1,200.00	12	£2,200.00	18
2	A	£1,200.00	6	£1,200.00	6	£1,200.00	12	£3,400.00	30
2	B	£1,200.00	6	£1,200.00	6	£1,200.00	12	£4,600.00	42
3	A	£1,200.00	6	£1,200.00	6	£1,200.00	12	£5,800.00	54
3	B	£1,200.00	6	£1,200.00	6	£1,200.00	12	£7,000.00	66
4	A	£1,200.00	6	£1,200.00	6	£1,200.00	12	£8,200.00	78
4	B	£1,200.00	6	£1,200.00	6	£1,200.00	12	£9,400.00	90
5	A	£1,200.00	6	£1,200.00	6	£1,200.00	12	£10,600.00	102
5	B	£1,200.00	6	£1,200.00	6	£1,200.00	12	£11,800.00	114
6	A	£ -	6			£ -	6	£11,800.00	120
6	B	£ -	6			£ -	6	£11,800.00	126
7	A							£11,…	(cut off)

Weeks 15–21

Figure 8.6 *Hospital training budget spreadsheet*

The figure reproduces the continuation of the rotated spreadsheet (columns BG–CH). Each week again provides two courses (here labelled B and A), each with a **Nos** and a **Cost** column.

Week	Course	Room 1 Nos	Room 1 Cost	Room 2 Nos	Room 2 Cost	Total Nos	Total Cost	Cumulative Nos	Cumulative Cost
15	B	6	£ -	6	£ -	6	£ -	222	£11,800.00
15	A	6	£ -	6	£ -	6	£ -	228	£11,800.00
16	B	6	£ -	6	£ -	6	£ -	234	£11,800.00
16	A	6	£ -	6	£ -	6	£ -	240	£11,800.00
17	B	6	£ -	6	£ -	6	£ -	246	£11,800.00
17	A	6	£ -	6	£ -	6	£ -	252	£11,800.00
18	B	6	£ -	6	£ -	6	£ -	258	£11,800.00
18	A	6	£ -	6	£ -	6	£ -	264	£11,800.00
19	B	6	£ -	6	£ -	6	£ -	270	£11,800.00
19	A	6	£ -	6	£ -	6	£ -	276	£11,800.00
20	B	6	£ -	6	£ -	6	£ -	282	£11,800.00
20	A	6	£ -	6	£ -	6	£ -	288	£11,800.00
21	B	6	£ -	6	£ -	6	£ -	294	£11,800.00
21	A	6	£ -	6	£ -	6	£ -	300	£11,800.00

When we read the accounts and examples given we can acknowledge that the systems put in place will be open to monitoring using instruments in the way we have discussed in this chapter. However, there may be aspects of change missing from the accounts. An example may illustrate this:

> BM Corporation phased in a programme over two years. MBO began with a two-day training session conducted by an external consultant and attended by every member of management including the CEO. The training programme continues for future and new managers. To emphasise that MBO is not a one-shot programme, the CEO still stresses MBO in employee publications and annual state of the company presentations
>
> Employees formulate objectives for each year's budget and the direct supervisor reviews performance at quarterly intervals. A new feature of BM's programme is to calculate the dollar value of written objectives. BM also introduced 'stretch' objectives. These are objectives identified by an employee's manager that are most critical to the organisation's goals. A cash bonus system is tied to attaining stretch objectives.
>
> (Harvey and Brown, 1992, 421 from *An experiential approach to organizational development*, 4th edn. Reprinted with kind permission of Pearson Education)

Consider the following questions:

1   What sort of learning can be supported in a two-day training course?
2   Why were all members of management at the training?
3   What does training for all newcomers indicate?
4   Why do employees formulate their own objectives?
5   What are stretch objectives?
6   Why is a cash bonus introduced with this scheme?

Two-day courses are fairly short in terms of management development courses. It is likely, therefore, that they are instructional training courses. Individuals attending would be expected to learn new processes and become familiar with new procedures and how to use them at work. In the context of MBO, therefore, there would not be much more time available to the trainer that would permit detailed instruction and then exercises to validate that the new knowledge was in place. There would not be time to discuss at length the impact of the new procedures for working conditions and the implications this may have for the conditions under which work is both done and monitored by managers.

We have already seen that many of the n-step approaches include a reference to the importance of senior managers attending courses to reinforce that the content is important and serious as far as the company and its senior managers are concerned. It has another advantage, too: senior managers can monitor how accessible the training is and how well it is received.

The rolling programme suggests that merely including new procedures in the company will not be sufficient. New members of staff will need to be initiated into the programme specifically for this important monitoring process.

A new approach to targets requires individuals to say specifically what each believes he or she will achieve in a trading year. The advantage of this to managers might be that they gain commitment from individuals as they may be in the best position to know what they will be able to achieve. Second, individuals will be more likely to feel committed to objectives that they have defined themselves. Third, should those targets not be achieved, then the individual must give account of their failure to achieve them.

'Stretch' objectives or targets, as their title suggests, are intended to give individuals 'something to go for'. Some individuals may be disinclined to offer such demanding objectives for themselves, so the manager may define them instead. Needless to say, certainly in a sales environment, such extra targets would be reinforced by offering commission, possibly at a higher rate than for standard achievement of quotas. How relevant the context of the job might be to accepting such incentives could be questioned and is certainly important to discuss with those directly affected. This final point coincides with the reinforcement referred to in many change schemas we have seen thus far.

The authors accept that there have been mixed results for the practical and functionalist approach to Management by Objectives. It should lend itself to the management and monitoring tools that we have discussed. However, it may not address other important issues that can affect the successful completion of a project for managing change. In their own words the authors acknowledge this lack:

> Some MBO programmes also may have problems because management fails to recognise that proper implementation of MBO requires new improved managerial skills and competence. Steven Kerr has criticised MBO and has pointed out several limitations. He questions whether joint goal setting among equals is possible, whether subordinates at lower levels are free to select their objectives, whether MBO aids in evaluating and rewarding performance, whether setting objectives as explicitly as possible is always functional and finally whether MBO is really applicable in a dynamic and changing environment.
>
> (Harvey and Brown, 1992, 421 from *An experiential approach to organizational development*, 4th edn. Reprinted with kind permission of Pearson Education)

There are two references to aspects of project management hinted at in this passage, which should now be addressed: first, new, improved managerial skills and competence and, second, the dynamic changing environment. These bring us back to issues referred to previously and which are now apposite in the context of implementing change. It can be viewed as a functional task, or as something requiring developmental skill of a very high order.

A BROADER VIEW OF PROJECT

Thus far we could say that our review of some of the instruments used to monitor the implementation of a change programme can be seen in the narrow perspective of the to-do list, which is expressed in a diagrammatic way and then measured according to the chosen criteria of performativity. There are several examples we could offer that demonstrate the very closely focused to-do list (Collins, 1998, 83; Buchanan and Boddy, 1992, 9). One of the larger consulting firms specifies the implementation cycle for change projects thus:

Develop a strategy
Confirm top level support
Use a project management approach
Identify tasks
Assign responsibilities
Agree deadlines
Initiate actions
Monitor
Act on problems
Close down
Communicate results.

(Buchanan and Boddy, 1992, 9)

The focus here could apply to changing a computer software program, or restructuring the organization or changing job descriptions in a company. And it is here that we can consider the distinction between the functional changes, mechanical redesign and the more complex and possibly contested changes involving people. The sequence of logic in the list here is compelling. As a checklist for the on-site operator it is impeccable as a guide for sequencing actions. However, we might be forgiven for thinking that it falls into the 'under-socialized' category of management checklists.

We may compare this hands-on approach with the consultant's overview, which gives a map of the important elements that are to be addressed during change (see Figure 8.7).

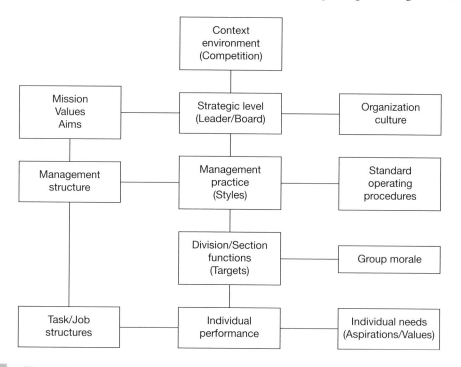

Figure 8.7 *Linked issues in a change programme*

For an even more involved and comprehensive model see Figure 8.8.

In all such examples we might be inclined to observe that an overview containing so many aspects of change and possible interrelations between them may be useful for a consultancy team but perhaps a little confusing for those involved in the change at the functional level of the organization.

If we return to a simpler model perhaps the steps of the process may be expressed more openly. Some large corporations have had to adopt more of a consultancy style among their managers, many of whom are considered as internal agents of change as part of their day-to-day duties. One example is BT and they offer the following list:

> Identify problem
> Gather data
> Analyse data
> Generate solutions
> Select the solution
> Plan for implementation
> Implement and test
> Continue to improve.

> (Buchanan and Boddy, 1992, 10)

Here the sequence is similar to other problem-solving schemas popular with writers on the management of change (Collins, 1998, 83). However, the early items in the list allow of

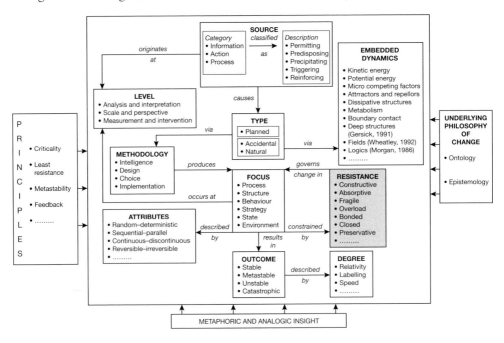

Figure 8.8 *Building blocks for change*
Source: Stickland, F. (1998) The dynamics of change, *p. 137. Reprinted with kind permission of Routledge*

an approach more open to the inductive approach of jointly examining the basis of the problem. A similar list can be found in most taxonomies of change seen through the problem-solving lens (Ahituv and Neumann, 1986). Most writers allow that the systemic processes work well with such iterative procedures as stock control or financial accounting. But, for the soft social skill areas, something a little more exploratory might offer a better opportunity for identifying human concerns and objections to surface (Gunton, 1990, 222).

For those writers who place their emphasis on the context of change, meaning the situation in which the change takes place, words like truth, trust, love and collaboration are often used (Buchanan and Boddy, 1992, 14). But how can prescriptive routes governed by lists for action engender this? Some authors point out that some of the terms that have gained currency in recent years, such as 'participation' and 'empowerment', are not essentially new in consultancy and management practice (Pettigrew, 1985). The example is sometimes given of Coch and French (1948) who were able to demonstrate that different groups within a company undergoing change responded differently according to whether they were allowed no participation, some participation or what they called total participation. The authors continue:

> A significant proportion of management commentary since Coch & French can be seen as attempts to offer further detailed advice on how to involve employees more effectively in the running of their organizations and in the effective implementation of change. This applies to the 'quality of working life' movement of the 1960s and 1970s (Buchanan, 1979), to the 'quality circle' movement of the 1970s and 1980s and to 'high involvement management' practices in general (Lawler, 1986). The more recent writings of Tom Peters (1989) reflect the same advice in his advocacy of self-managing teams as the basic organizational unit and the redefined role of participative or 'facilitative' first-line supervision.
>
> (Buchanan and Boddy, 1992)

We could add here that the date 1948 is contemporaneous with Lewin and his use of sensitivity groups and the attempt to unfreeze assumptions held by groups of workers about their jobs and the move to other ways of seeing employment in the organization. Such an open approach requires a different set of skills in the agent or manager of change. Kotter and Schlesinger summarize them as follows:

> Education and counselling
> Participation and involvement
> Facilitation and support
> Negotiation and agreement
> Manipulation and co-operation
> Explicit and implicit coercion.
>
> (1979)

The concepts here at least suggest a more proactive role for those who are subjected to change. The challenge then becomes how to stimulate or facilitate such change. Are there

199

equally helpful guidelines to assist the manager of change to derive the knowledge of deeper meanings and associations held by members of staff?

WAYS IN FOR THE CHANGE AGENT

One of the most useful recent books to appear comes from a writer whose textbooks are well known in the subject of the management of change, Colin Carnall. His book *The change management toolkit* is a valuable compendium of techniques and offers instruments that may be useful either in survey format or in more open sessions with groups. He addresses the depiction of organizations, the approaches available and the strategic review that many authors refer to but few illustrate as clearly as this book does.

Knowing what is current practice and adjudging what is currently being achieved in an organization is one area that he covers comprehensively. Perceptions of current HR or marketing practice are alike the gauge of individual and group surprise or lack of it in the face of change (Louis, 1980; Brown, 1995; Weick, 1979). What is about to be visited on those subjected to change may or may not come as a surprise. It all depends on what they expected and how they evaluate what they currently have in their working lives and experience (Carnall, 2003a, 32ff.).

Individual responses can be canvassed more directly and the questions drawn up by Carnall are again contained in useful lists, which may be valuable to change agents who would like to discover what individuals expect before they intervene rather than wait for the response afterwards. If administered to individuals for written answers then they will be constrained by the usual caveats about confidentiality and anonymity of questionnaires that are administered at work (Belson, 1981; Oppenheim, 1992). Questions about personal preferences in job, work and career have been popular subjects for surveys and the type of questions they contain can exhibit cultural factors that do not transfer easily from one work group to another (Porter and Steers, 1974). A selection of statements may demonstrate this point:

> I understand the objectives of this organization
> Performance is regularly reviewed by my boss
> This organization sets realistic plans
> All individual work performance is reviewed against agreed standards
> People are always concerned to do a good job
> This organization has a capacity to change
> The salary I receive is commensurate with the job that I perform.
>
> (Carnall, 2003b, 40–43)

Consider which of these statements is likely to yield specific information and which might be more difficult to support with specific evidence.

If we were looking to gather specific information, then probably the second and fourth statements offer the best opportunity to examine what respondents experience at work. Presumably it would be possible to check how often appraisals are conducted in an organization. Similarly, agreed standards are more often written down in operations manuals and personnel and training manuals, though how specific they are may depend on whether they apply to functional tasks, which may be more measurable than more conceptual and theoretical underpinning knowledge of, say, management functions.

The first statement contains the non-testable word 'understand' and would require an interview to establish what exactly a respondent understood were objectives of the organization. Whether plans are realistic or not might then be evidenced by the difference between achieved targets or budget and actual outcomes, though overall responses might still be a matter of individual opinion.

The fifth and sixth statements call on opinion again, which may be useful as a gauge of perception shared with others or held alone. However, of the two, the second could be said to be totally unknown. It may be an inspired guess based on intuition and it may be significant, especially if shared by others in a group or team.

The final statement should raise a smile with any researcher who has asked such questions of people at work. One researcher cited a group of subjects in which 75 per cent of respondents believed that they were in the top 10 per cent of performers (Fletcher, 1993). The research did not divulge whether the respective managers concurred with such self-recommendation or not.

The responses to the questionnaires are graded by respondents according to a standard Likert scale. Although such results may be challenged as to reliability, the author makes the point that the responses may still be a useful guide to current perceptions within an organization and its working groups and demonstrate how they may be assessed more fully to indicate strengths and weaknesses in the context of change (Carnall, 2003b, 57ff.).

FACILITATING DISCUSSION

The process of managing projects has become more open to the involvement of participants, perhaps through the influence of those researchers who have been convinced that this is the only way to engage minds and hearts of those involved (Pettigrew, 1985; Schein, 1988) and through the long experience of continuous change that has assailed workers in many sectors.

We have already referred in previous chapters to researchers who have challenged the belief – which continues to inspire those who would want to impose change on organizations for political reasons – that change is easily effected (Pollitt, 1995; Hood, 1998; Robinson and LeGrand, 1994). There appears to be a more considered approach to direct interventions in favour of a more reflective approach for those involved. A recent selection of writing by Attwood *et al.* contains several accounts of such change, involving a frankness that informs change agents who otherwise might not understand the basic assumptions of those they seek to change:

Putting the elephant on the table
A difficult discussion is going on between a number of organizations concerned with the care of people with learning disabilities about organizational arrangements that will support better daily living for service users. The conversation is somewhat desultory and there is a clear sense that important things are not being said. Suddenly the person in charge of

the provision of social services says: 'There is an elephant in the corner of this room! I think I had better put it on the table!' He then explains that the elected members of his local authority will not countenance any new organizational solution to the problems under discussion that result in social services staff being employed by any other than the local authority. There is an uncomfortable silence, followed by a general acknowledgement that, though this is difficult, knowing that this is the case releases everyone to think about what is practically possible given the power realities of the situation.

(Attwood *et al.*, 2003, 93)

Before you read on, consider what are the implications of this intervention for the change agent who is required to implement it?

We have already referred to basic assumptions and the role that they can play in enforced change at work (Randall, 2001). Surfacing such taken-for-granted beliefs may be difficult if addressed directly by researchers or change agents. Indirect means offer a better chance of hearing what needs to be said to explain, say, a disinclination to refer to or discuss topics openly. In the above example we could say that such a revelation has been made very openly. Perhaps the politicians referred to do not harbour this objection. However, at least the change agent can probe further to discover whether the third parties referred to do hold such a belief or whether it is only the perception of the speaker.

The purpose of such discursive involvement of those involved in change, both subjects and agents, is to allow a consensus to develop or emerge that will allow a clearer under-standing of what is acceptable, what is feasible and what is not. Gaining participation in change is the desired goal, which any project manager will find facilitates any kind of change at work. There are many OD practitioners who have affirmed consistently that dealing with resistance to change requires such a long-term investment in listening to and learning from those involved in change at work (Nadler, 1993; Watson, 1966). One author lists the features and benefits of such strategy as follows:

Resistance will be less if:
- Participants feel the project is their own (not imposed by outsiders)
- Project has whole-hearted support from top officials
- Participants see change as reducing their present burdens
- Project accords with values/ideas of participants
- Project offers new experience, which interests participants
- Participants feel their autonomy and security is not threatened
- Participants have joined in the diagnostic efforts
- Project is adopted by consensual group direction
- Proponents are able to empathise with opponents
- Provision is made for feedback during the project
- Participants experience acceptance, support, trust and confidence between each other
- Project remains open to revision and accommodation to desired amendments.

(Watson, 1966)

We have examined several ways in which such involvement might be achieved before a project for change is undertaken. It remains for us to examine how change can best be implemented by retaining such involvement and how the effects of change can be evaluated.

IMPLEMENTING CHANGE PROGRAMMES

It would be fair to say that examples of change in detail are hard to find in the sense that many case studies available are mostly written by practitioners themselves or managers and consultants after the event. Such case studies can be found in writers on strategic management (Harrison, 2003), in standard textbooks on the management of change (Carnall, 2003a; Burnes, 2000) and from change management readers, whether from an OD background (Harvey and Brown, 1992) or an HR perspective (Jick and Peiperl, 2003). Current HR and personnel journals are replete with accounts of successfully managed change, again usually written by the agents and managers of change. They are no doubt accurate accounts of the perceptions of those who write them, but they tend to focus on the wider perspective of the financial context of the change, the strategic considerations that arose for senior management and the planning that took place with the change agents.

Lacking from many accounts of change is the voice of the participants and those who have run the events at the front line. Such accounts as there are tend to have been written by researchers and participants after the events themselves (Casey, 1995; Randall, 2001). As such we are often left with a summary account which gives the impression of unalloyed success. The following is not untypical:

> If Marshall was the most important player in emphasising customer service, then the Putting People First (PPF) programme was the most important event. Approximately 40,000 BA employees went through the PPF programmes. The programme urged participants to examine their interactions with other people, including family, friends and, by association, customers. Its acceptance and impact was extraordinary, due primarily to the honesty of its message, the excellence of its delivery and the strong support of management.
>
> Employees expressed their pleasure at being treated with respect and relief that change was on the horizon. As one front line ticket veteran said, 'I found it fascinating, very, very enjoyable. I thought it was very good for British Airways. It made people aware. I don't think people give enough thought to people's reaction to each other. . . . It was hard hitting. It was made something very special. When you were there, you were treated extremely well. You were treated as a VIP, and people really enjoyed that. It was reverse role, really to the job we do.'
>
> (Jick and Peiperl, 2003, 33)

The programme was followed by other events for managers, such as a five-day residential programme for 25 managers at a time called Managing People First:

> MPF stressed the importance of, among other topics, trust, leadership, vision and feedback. On a smaller scale, MPF stirred up issues long neglected at BA. One senior

manager of engineering said, 'It was almost as if I was touched on the head . . . I don't think I ever considered culture before MPF. Afterwards I began to think about what makes people tick. Why do people do what they do? Why do people come to work? Why do people do things for some people they won't do for others?' Some participants claimed that the course led them to put more emphasis on feedback. One reported initiating regular meetings with staff every two weeks, in contrast to before the programme when he met with staff members only as problems arose.

(Jick and Peiperl, 2003, 33)

While such accounts are touching in their optimistic review of some personal impressions, the overall evaluation of the training inputs remains unaddressed in the accounts themselves. One senior manager from personnel gave a similar positive overview of the enthusiasm engendered on the two-day events held for all staff members and many articles were published in practitioners' journals applauding significant change achieved in the management of the project (Georgiades, 1990).

Management consultants have a slightly different narrative style that combines the parameters of successful implementation with a hortatory style, encouraging the reader to embark on the necessary shock tactics to wake up participants:

Managers need to make people experience harsh reality first-hand. That's the kingpin to knocking over the cognitive hurdle. People remember and respond most effectively to what they see and experience – 'seeing is believing'. In the realm of experience, positive stimuli reinforce behaviour while negative stimuli change behaviour. Simply put, if a child puts their finger in a pudding and it tastes good, they will put their finger back in it again and again. No parental advice is needed to encourage that behaviour. Conversely, if a child puts their finger on a burning stove, they will never do it again – no parental pestering is required.

Tipping point leadership builds on this insight in two ways to inspire fast change that is internally driven of people's own self accord.

To break the status quo, employees must be put face to face with the problem. When New York senior police officers were told to stop commuting to work by car and take the 'electric sewer' (the subway) instead, they immediately saw the horror citizens were up against – aggressive beggars, gangs of youths jumping turnstiles, jostling people and drunks sprawled on the benches. With that ugly reality, the officers could no longer deny the urgent need for change in policing methods.

(Kim and Mauborgne, 2003, 29)

The content of the article here relies on traditional behavioural approaches of individual response to pleasure/pain stimuli and then moves seamlessly into the realm of group perceptions based on enforced change at work and will then draw conclusions about the need for change agents to manifest similar rude awakening to harsh reality.

Academic writers more often attempt to ground their proposals in the theoretic assumptions underpinning the discipline they contribute to. One such example is the writing on psychological contract, referred to earlier in this book. The idea of transactional and relational elements of a imputed or implied internal contract held by workers has been a subject of contestation between those who support the idea of internalized cognitive calculus (Rousseau, 1998; Lazarus and Folkman, 1984; Rusbult and Farrell, 1983) and those who believe that a contract between individuals and a diffused organization is impossible to support (Guest, 1998). However, the attempt to see this contract as a context for thinking about changing individual behaviour is offered by some writers as a way of thinking about and managing change (see Table 8.1).

What is striking here is the similarity in essence to some of the more directly illustrated points in the previous excerpt. The writer here expands the steps and inserts stages and suggestions for achieving the 'new contract'. However, the new contract itself seems to rely heavily on the managers with their staff being inducted and trained in its content. HR procedures and managers then combine to reinforce required behaviours. In short, much

Table 8.1 *Transforming the psychological contract*

Stage	Intervention
Challenging the old contract	
Stress	Provide new discrepant information (educate people). Why do we need change?
Disruption	
Preparing for change	
Ending old contract	Involve employees in information gathering (send them out to talk with customers and benchmark successful firms).
Reducing losses	Interpret new information (show videos of customers describing service and let employees react to it).
Bridging to new contract	Acknowledge the end of the old contract (celebrate good features of old contract).
	Create transitional structures (cross-functional task forces to manage change).
Contract generation	
Sense-making	Evoke 'new contract' script (have people sign on to 'new company').
Veterans become new	Make contract makers (managers) readily available to share information.
	Encourage active involvement in new contract creation.
Living the new contract	
Reality checking	Be consistent in word and action (train everyone in new terms). Follow through (align managers, human resource practices etc.). Refresh (re-emphasize the mission and new contract frequently).

Source: Rousseau (2003, 241)

of the above is typical of what we have previously described as the top-down approach to the management of change.

ACTION RESEARCH AND ACTION LEARNING

We referred earlier in this chapter to the emergent approach to the management of change. We can now look more closely at some of the suggestions offered by the practitioners who have developed these approaches. Kurt Lewin is sometimes seen as the father of the attempt to offer an opportunity for workers to express their views about their job, work, career and the organizational context, which encompass day-to-day experience.

Parallel with this movement in America was the Human Relations school and its work in the UK, which was focused on work problems and involved those working in the immediate area. So, both in coal mining and in nursing local workers were confronted with problems that, in some cases, threatened the very continuance of the work itself. The purpose of the change agent is to facilitate the process of addressing the problem together and devolving the options available to solve it. Following from this comes the implementation plan, which again the team devises with assistance from the facilitator (Trist and Bamford, 1951; Revans, 1980). Some authors offered a succession of action steps to guide those wishing to follow the stages (see Figure 8.9).

The types of action research are sometimes subdivided into technical, practical and emancipatory, depending on the knowledge, medium and science that are the focus of the research (Carr and Kemmis, 1986; Grundy, 1987). A full illustration of these different categories can be found in Darwin *et al.*, 2003, 298). The values required to be successful depend on the equal acceptance of the relevance of the experience of all the participants and are based on a variation of Kolb's learning cycle (Kolb *et al.*, 1971) adapted to a group context (see Figure 8.10).

How such change fits into the strategic context of organizational change is something that varies among different theorists and researchers. Burnes summarizes this aspect as follows:

Figure 8.9 *Cyclical processes in action*
Source: Cassell and Fitter (1992, 294)

> Change can be viewed as running along a continuum from incremental to transformational (Dawson, 1994; Stickland, 1998; Wilson, 1992). Incremental or fine-tuning forms of change are geared more to changing the activities/performance/behaviour/attitudes of individuals and groups, whereas transformational change is geared towards the processes/structures and culture of the entire organization. Obviously there are differences in how these writers construe these concepts. Some writers see fine-tuning or incremental change as being relatively isolated and/or relatively unimportant (Dunphy and Stace, 1992; Pettigrew, 1992), whilst others see it as being part of an overall plan to transform an organization (Kanter, *et al.*, 1992; Senior, 1997). In contrast, all seem to view transformational change as being strategic and important; though there are those who see it as being a relatively slow process (Kotter, 1996), those who see it as being a relatively rapid one (Peters, 1989) and those who argue that it can take both forms (Kanter *et al.*, 1992; Stace and Dunphy, 1994).
>
> (Burnes, 2000, 305)

Managing change projects may, of course, involve using a mix of people from different parts of the organization and particular reference to this can be found in Hayes (2002, 166ff.). Similarly, drawing up a framework for data analysis will become more critical for the control of a complex change project. Dawson offers useful advice on this topic (2003, 45ff.). Finally, for a comprehensive overview of what he calls 'Chance Architecture', there is a full chapter in Carnall (2003a, 258ff.). In his smaller book *The change management toolkit*, published in the same year, Carnall offers two useful checklists for evaluating the elements he sees as encompassing and summarizing that architecture as a tool for change agents (2003b, 81).

EVALUATING CHANGE

Among the books relating to the management of change, little is included on evaluation. The tools of validation are readily available and governments seem to like to identify targets

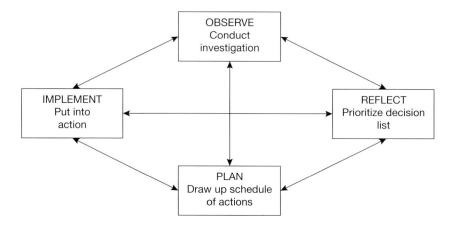

Figure 8.10 *Action research and action learning*
Source: Based on Kolb (1974, 307)

207

which are measurable and testable, perhaps because such metrics of performativity seem easy to access and can therefore be used more readily as a comparator in before–after assessment exercises at work. If we examine the rhetoric that surrounds Human Resource Management, then it reminds us, as we have seen, that HR outcomes are intended to impact on the return on investment, profitability of the company and yield on the share price (Guest, 1989).

Making changes within a workforce involves the biggest risk to the much vaunted goal of organizational commitment and, although that concept has been identified as being diffuse and largely inaccessible to researchers (Coopey and Hartley, 1991), yet nonetheless the likely effects of change on individual feelings of security and goodwill could be considerable. And yet, the question of evaluation is rarely mentioned in the literature surrounding the management of change. It is as if the subjects of change themselves do not merit the kind of feedback that would be de rigueur in any change exercise affecting the other major stakeholder, customers.

In many organizations, as we have noted, particularly in the public sector, initiatives for change often follow each other in annual succession. In one such organization with which I worked there was the government initiative, Next Steps, a policy paper from the Chairman, market testing, and personnel and efficiency review all in successive years. This culminated in 20 per cent of the staff being made redundant. So, however hard individuals worked to implement the new policies as they impacted on the organization year-on-year, the result at the end for one in five members of staff was arbitrary termination of employment. I am sure there will be many people who can recount similar anecdotal material.

The point to be made here is not the usual one about the intensive nature of change initiatives and how thoughtlessly they impact on the unsuspecting victims charged with implementing them. Rather, the point is that very little evaluation is conducted on any of the initiatives before the next is embarked upon. And yet, most theories of stepped change often contain an evaluative phase (Bullock and Batton, 1985; Nadler, 1993). It should be said that other change schemas sometimes suggest a final phase, which can be differently worded as 'conclusion' (Jacobsen, 1994, 302), 'monitor the change and reinforce it' (Pugh, 1984) or 'reinforce and institutionalize the change' (Kanter, 1992). However, the sense of these terms, while reflecting the need to seat change effectively, is not quite the sense in which 'evaluation' is used.

The range of roles, objectives, techniques and skills involved in evaluating how effective personnel managers are at achieving change is charted by one of the few volumes written specifically to address this somewhat specialist subject (see Table 8.2).

We might see here an attempt to identify particular areas in which personnel people could intervene in the organization in order to identify the outcomes of change. It is a very functional list and would coincide with a traditional Organizational Development approach to the subject. However, it begins to open out the considerations which might be needed to underwrite an attempt to discover how far management interventions have effected successful change.

What individuals feel about change might be a useful summarizer of the effective outcomes of change. We have seen in earlier chapters that the attempt to reframe what individuals do is always open to their own interpretation of the change imposed and that

Table 8.2 *Relative position of roles, objectives, techniques and skills*

Effectiveness		Technical efficiency (examples)	
Functional roles	Typical personnel objectives	Techniques	Skills
Adapt to environment	Manage change	Organization develop-ment ER strategies Job redesign Planning, coordinating	Interpersonal Social Consultancy
Goal attainment	Business objectives expressed as specific tasks	Budget control rations (from corporate plan) Planning, organizing	Financial Business management Decision-making
Integrate	Core values implied in policies	Employee relations strategies Organization design	Communication Persuasion Negotiation
Maintain roles	Personnel systems agreed with line management	Management of internal labour markets	Interpersonal Statistical/ administrative

Source: Tyson and Fell (1985, 83)

this interpretation may well be dependent on the basic assumptions that they hold about the aspects of their working life that are affected by enforced change. Discovering what these expectancies might be and the current perception of change would be an important aspect of any evaluation initiative.

Carnall (1999) offers two instruments for assessing opinions and perceptions within a group, both before the programme is embarked upon and when it is published just prior to implementation. The first survey contains questions focused on current expectancies (see Box 8.1).

The questions reproduced here are just a selection, which allows the reader to sample the question coverage and the possible responses available to respondents. It offers more clearly delineated answers than the Likert scale allows and should give at least a measure of expectancy within a workforce.

Evaluating responses to proposed project plans can be equally illuminating for the change agent (see Box 8.2).

It could be said that results might be dispiriting for the initiators of change. However, the exercise could have two major benefits: the first is that change agents will be alerted to areas of concern prior to embarking on any intervention – and this, as we have seen, can be about the content of the programme in detail. It might at least give the opportunity to modify parts of the programme or the option of interviewing individuals or groups to discover more fully the causes of concerns or objections. But the second point to make is that any measurement of change requires that some attempt be made to monitor conditions prior to the change and ensure that similar measurements be made afterwards and the results compared.

BOX 8.1 READINESS FOR CHANGE

3 The most recent and widely known change in the organization is viewed as	A success	Moderately successful	Had no obvious impact	Not successful
7 Present work procedures to be affected by the change are seen as needing	Major change	Significant alteration	Minor	No change
8 The problems to be dealt with by the changes were first raised by	The people directly involved	First-line management and supervision	Senior management	Outside consultants
9 The proposed change is viewed by end users as	Crucial to the organization's future	Generally beneficial to the organization	Beneficial to only part of the organization	Largely a matter of procedure
10 Top management support for the proposed change is	Enthusiastic	Limited	Minimal	Unclear
15 The proposed change is technically	Similar to others already under way	Similar to others undertaken in the recent past	Novel	Unclear technically

Source: Carnall (2003b, 98)

Reprinted with kind permission of Thomson Learning

Specific measurements of personnel functions have been accepted practice in most organizations and can include such items as:

Employee retention and turnover rates
Absenteeism rates
Ratio of suggestions received to number of employees
Frequency/severity of accident rates
Ratio of grievances to number of employees
Time lost through disputes
Number of references to industrial tribunals on unfair dismissal, equal opportunity, equal pay, harassment, racial discrimination issues etc.

(Armstrong, 2001, 121)

The problem with using such generalized measures may be that they do not relate specifically to the reasons for change and, similarly, the outcome following the change programme

BOX 8.2 STYLES OF MANAGEMENT

Little discretion	Some discretion, within	High discretion
Short-term planning horizon	limits	Long-term planning horizon
Gives service to junior line managers	Medium-term planning horizon	Acts as consultant to senior managers
Cycles administrative support	Gives service plus advice to middle management	Conceptualizes
Follows routines	Provides knowledge of systems and IT practice	Inventive, creative problem solver
Looks for leadership from fellow managers	Follows systems and modifies to some extent	Changes routines/ systems as necessary
	Gives leadership within existing structures	Copes rapidly with change and leads/ participates with top management team

Source: Tyson and Fell (1985, 23)

may have nothing directly to do with the change intervention. However, if no measurements are being taken then there is no opportunity to monitor any outcomes following a programme of change.

EMERGENT CHANGE STRATEGIES

We have already noted the contention of emergent change proponents that more open approaches to a workforce should be adopted if change is to have any chance of gaining support and consensus. Gaining commitment depends on asking open questions and listening to the answers. Such questions might include:

> Definition of corporate philosophy – what kind of business do we want to be? How do we want to be regarded by customers, employees and the other stakeholders in society?
>
> Environmental conditions are scanned – what is likely to happen for example, in government policy, unemployment, interest rates, inflation and the appropriate industrial sector?
>
> Evaluation of corporate strengths and constraints. This involves a SWOT (strengths, weaknesses, opportunities, threats) analysis of the company. The strengths and weaknesses are usually internal, the opportunities and threats external to the company.
>
> Objectives and goals emerge from the three stages above, answering the question what business are we in, what should we be in.
>
> Strategies are developed to meet these objectives.
>
> (Tyson and Fell, 1986, 75)

Similar questions precede the introduction of Business Process Re-engineering according to some of its proponents (Champy, 1995, 60). However, in these examples the ultimate

211

imposition of radical change is never in doubt as far as their authors are concerned and the ability of the subjects to modify the change programme may be rather limited.

EVALUATING TRAINING INTERVENTIONS

The theory and practice of evaluating training includes all those who have taken part, but also all those who receive and work with trainees after the training event is completed. Validational aspects we have referred to already and it would be fair to admit that testable and measurable factors have lent themselves more readily to such attempts than the more diffuse areas of affective response. However, there is no reason why such attempts should not be made. Indeed, our earlier example of constant change initiative suggests that failure to evaluate in this way may mean less learning of what was effective and what was not. This can only mean that there is a real risk of failure being revisited because conclusions of what has not worked in past initiatives have not been drawn by the agents and managers of change. Here, we can admit that an opportunity for organizational learning has probably been missed.

However, one aspect that does arise from the different practices of personnel concerns the role and function of its practitioners and the discretion that they have to intervene and relate to those undergoing change. The writers we have referred to earlier offer a three-fold distinction between what they refer to as the clerk of works, the contracts manager and the architect. The differences are delineated in Box 8.2.

We may find the distinction dated in terms of the levels of management, which have perhaps become less structured than they might once have been. However, the question of the different sources of influence, such as referent, expert information (French and Raven, 1959), is relevant to the change agent today and we will examine those different roles more closely in the next chapter.

Suffice it to say that the change agent is not invisible in the change process and the expertise that he or she brings to its implementation will influence the response of those who have to undergo enforced change at work.

DISCUSSION QUESTIONS

It may be a relief to know that few questions appear on this topic in papers on the Management of Change. However, occasional case studies are offered to candidates. Here is one that has featured in a recent paper:

Case study question

A change management consultant has been appointed by a local healthcare organization to provide advice on ensuring the smooth adoption of a new software system. A national team of information technology (IT) specialists, working in partnership with doctors' representatives, has developed the new software. Its dual purpose is to assist doctors with the diagnosis of patients' symptoms and provide a single database record for each patient; the latter will be accessible by all approved clinicians throughout the healthcare system via a 'healthnet'. The benefits for the patient are said to include better diagnosis (which is no longer totally reliant on the memory of the doctor) and better care for patients (all clinicians will be able to access quickly a full health record for each patient).

The change management consultant has conducted initial interviews with key stakeholders in the healthcare organization. Despite the advertised benefits, many concerns were raised in these interviews.

- Doctors are concerned about the effect of the IT system on the patient–doctor relationship:

  'I cannot concentrate on the patient and fiddle with a computer at the same time.'

  'When I use a computer it detracts from the consultation and it seems there are three of us in the room.'

  'I don't trust the proposed healthnet. What if patient information gets into the wrong hands?'

  Several doctors cited research by Sullivan and Mitchell (1995) which found an increase in the length of the patient consultation when IT is used.

- Nurses are concerned about the time it would take to both deal with patient needs and interact with the IT system. Many do not think that there is a need for the proposed change.

- Administrators are concerned about the potential loss of expertise. They are the main operators of the existing IT system:

  'If doctors and nurses start to use the computer the job will be different and I might be made redundant.'

In the light of these initial findings the general manager of the local healthcare organization has asked the change management consultant to produce a brief report on how this change should be managed. The general manager has also requested that the report provide an evidence-based rationale for the recommendations that are made.

POINTS TO EXAMINE

If we begin by identifying the approach taken thus far we might comment on the usefulness of the emergent strategy employed. The replies from the three constituent user-groups at least allow us to examine the concerns and objections foreseen by the users. It looks as though we have a combination of user concern about need; lack of belief by practitioners that time will be saved; a belief that using computers detracts from the consultation; concerns about patient confidentiality; and, for one potential user group, a belief that job security could be threatened.

It begins to look as though some research needs to be conducted into the time taken not just on the consultation, but also on the access to archived records in paper format and their return to the carousel or filing system after the consultation. This could present the team with a more accurate picture of diffuse tasks – labour intensive ones for the ancillary staff, which could be cut out by using the direct link, thus freeing administrators to welcome patients, answer phone calls and book consultations and prescriptions.

Some thought will need to be given to the patient responses to the doctor's use of a computer during the consultation. As so often happens, the surveys thus far have included only the voices of the health team members. Perhaps we may find that the patients actually admire doctors who are familiar with modern methods of linking ongoing diagnosis with patient records and the future treatment needs of hospital waiting lists and available bed-space.

Finally, we will need to address the question of training, help and support to the users themselves. Perhaps the users might like to examine the options available for acquiring new computer skills using software applications in this new context. The team may be small enough to allow one-to-one training, which will allow trainers to assess threshold knowledge and the skill of the users and tailor individual programmes of support and help.

Concerns and objections are best addressed by calculating interference costs. The survey should reveal how much it costs in time and effort to continue with the old system and the saving that could be yielded under the computerized system. The question of skill development can best be addressed by identifying individual programmes based on the individual needs of members of the team.

Overall, then, the answer can address the individual concerns by targeted questionnaires and combine the findings with more general conclusions about the impact of such computerization on the productivity factors of the practice and its key role holders.

REFERENCES AND FURTHER READING

Ahituv, N. and Neumann, S. *Principles of information systems for management*. Dubuque, IA: W.C. Brown Publishers, 1986.

Armstrong, M. *A handbook of human resource management*. London: Kogan Page, 2001.

Attwood, M. Pedler, M., Pritchard, S. and Wilkinson, D. *Leading change: a guide to whole systems working*. Bristol: The Policy Press, 2003.

Belson, W.A. *The design and understanding of survey questionnaires*. Aldershot: Gower, 1981.

Birchall, D. *Job design*. Aldershot: Gower, 1975.

Boddy, D. *Managing projects: building and leading the team*. London: *Financial Times*/Prentice Hall, 1992.

Brown, A.D. *Organizational culture*. London: Pitman Publishing, 1995.

Buchanan, D. (1979) *The development of job design theory and techniques*. Aldershot: Saxon House, 1979.

Buchanan, D. and Boddy, D. *The expertise of the change agent*. New York: Prentice Hall, 1992.

Bullock, R.J. and Batton, D. It's just a phase we're going through: a review and synthesis of OD phase analysis. *Group and Organizational Studies*, 1985, *10* (4): 383–412.

Burke, W.W. *Organizational development*. New York: Addison-Wesley, 1992.

Burnes, B. *Managing change: a strategic approach to organizational dynamics*. London: *Financial Times*/Prentice Hall, 2000.

Carnall, C.A. *Managing change in organizations*. London: *Financial Times*/Prentice Hall, 1992.

Carnall, C.A. *Managing change in organizations*. Harlow, FT: Prentice Hall, 1999.

Carnall, C.A. *Managing change in organizations*. London: *Financial Times*/Prentice Hall, 2003a.

Carnall, C.A. *The change management toolkit*. London: Thomson Learning, 2003b.

Carr, W. and Kemmis, S. *Becoming critical*. Lewes: Falmer Press, 1986.

Casey, C. *Work, self and society*. London: Routledge, 1995.

Cassell, C. and Fitter, M. Responding to a changing environment, in D.M. Hosking and N. Anderson (eds) *Organizational change and innovation*. London: Sage, 1992.

Cassell, C. and Fitter, M. Cyclical processes in action, in J. Darwin, P. Johnson and J. McAuley *Developing strategies for change*. Harlow, FT: Prentice Hall, 2002.

Champy, J. *Reengineering management: the mandate for new leadership*. London: HarperCollins, 1995.

Coch, I. and French, J.R.P. Overcoming resistance to change. *Human Relations*, 1948, *1*: 512–532.

Collins, D. *Organizational change: sociological perspectives*. London: Routledge, 1998.

Coopey, J. and Hartley, J.F. Reconsidering organizational commitment. *Human Resource Management Journal*, 1991, *1* (3): 18–32.

Darwin, J., Johnson, P. and McAuley, J. *Developing strategies for change*. London: *Financial Times*/Prentice Hall, 2003.

Dawson, P. *Organizatonal change: a processual approach*. London: Paul Chapman Publishing, 1994.

Dawson, P. *Understanding organizational change*. London: Sage, 2003.

Dinsmore, P.C. *Human factors in project management*. New York: American Management Association, 1990.

Dunphy, D.C. and Stace, D.A. Transformational and coercive strategies for planned organizational change. *Organization Studies*, 1988, *9* (3): 317–334.

Dunphy, D.C. and Stace, D.A. *Under new management: Australian organizations in transition*. Roseville, CA: McGraw Hill, 1992.

Fayol, H. *General and industrial management*, London: Pitman, 1949.

Fletcher, C. *Appraisal*. London: IPM, 1993.

French, J.R. and Raven, B. The bases of social power, in L. Cartwright and A. Zander (eds) *Group dynamics research and theory*. London: Tavistock, 1959.

Georgiades, N. A strategic future for personnel. *Personnel Management*, 1990 (February): 43–45.

Gerswick, C.J. and Davis, M.D. Task forces, in J.R. Hackman (ed.) *Groups that work and those that don't*. San Francisco, CA: Jossey Bass, 1989.

Grundy, S. *Curriculum: product or praxis*. Lewes: Falmer Press, 1987.

Guest, D.E. Personnel and HRM: can you tell the difference? *Personnel Management*, 1989 (January): 48–51.

Guest, D.E. Is the psychological contract worth taking seriously? *Journal of Organizational Behaviour*, 1998, *19*: 649–664.

Gunton, T. *Inside information technology: a practical guide to management issues*. New York: Prentice Hall, 1990.

Harrison, J.F. *Strategic management: of resources and relationships*. New York: John Wiley, 2003.

Harvey, D.F. and Brown, D.R. *An experiential approach to organizational development*. Englewood Cliffs, NJ: Prentice Hall International, 1992.

Hayes, J. *The theory and practice of change management*. Basingstoke: Palgrave, 2002.

Hood, C. *Making sense of management*. Oxford: Clarendon Press, 1998.

Jacobsen, I. *The object advantage: business process reengineering with object technology*. Reading, MA: Addison-Wesley, 1994.

Jick, T.D. and Peiperl, M.A. *Managing change: cases and concepts*. New York: McGraw Hill, 2003.

Kanter, R.M. The change masters. London: Routledge, 1992.

Kanter, R.M., Stein, B. and Jick, T.D. *The challenge of organizational change: how companies experience it and leaders guide it*, Free Press, 1992.

Kearney, A.T. *Barriers to the successful application of information technology*. London: Department of Trade and Industry and CIMA, 1990.

Kim, W.C. and Mauborgne, R. Tipped for the top. *People Management*, 2003, *9* (15): 27–31.

Kolb, D., Rubin, I. and McIntyre, J. *Organizational psychology: an experiential approach*, Englewood Cliffs, NJ: Prentice Hall, 1971.

Kolb, D.A. in J. Darwin, P. Johnson and J. McAuley *Developing strategies for change*. Harlow, FT: Prentice Hall, 2002.

Kotter, J.P. *Leading change*. Boston, MA: Harvard Business School Press, 1996.

Kotter, J.P. and Schlesinger, L.A. Choosing strategies for change. *Harvard Business Review*, 1979, *57* (2): 106–114.

Lawler, E.E. Reward systems and strategy, in J.R. Garner and H.W. Sweeny (eds) *Handbook of strategic planning*, New York: Wiley, 1986, pp. 10.1–10.24.

Lazarus, R.S. and Folkman, S. *Stress, appraisal and coping*. New York: Springer, 1984.

Leigh, A. and Walters, M. *Effective change: twenty ways to make it happen*. London: IPD, 1998.

Lewin, K. Frontiers in group dynamics. *Human Relations*, 1947, *1*: 5–41.

Louis, M.R. Surprise and sense making: what newcomers experience in entering unfamiliar organizational settings. *Administrative Science Quarterly*, 1980, *25*: 226–251.

Morgan, G. *Images of organization*. London: Sage, 1986.

Morley, L. Expense account. *Computing*, 1991, *2* (May): 18–19.

Nadler, D.A. Concepts for the management of organizational change, in C. Mabey and B. Mayon-White (eds) *Managing change*. London: Paul Chapman, 1993.

Oppenheim, A.N. *Questionnaire design, interviewing and attitude management*. London: Pinter, 1992.

Paton, R.A. and McCalman, J. *Change management: a guide to effective implementation*, London: Sage, 2000.

Pearson, B. and Thomas, N. *The shorter MBA*. London: HarperCollins, 1991.

Peters, T. *Thriving on chaos: handbook for a managerial revolution*. London: Pan Paperbacks, 1989.

Pettigrew, A.M. *The awakening giant: continuity and change in ICI*. London: Macmillan, 1985.

Pettigrew, A.M. *Shaping strategic change*. London: Sage, 1992.

Pollitt, C. Justification by works or by faith: evaluating the New Public Management. *Evaluation*, 1995, *1* (2): 133–154.

Porter, L.W. and Steers, R.M. Organizational commitment, job satisfaction and turnover. *Journal of Applied Psychology*, 1974, *59*: 603–609.

Pugh, D.S. (ed.) *Organization theory*. Harmondsworth: Penguin, 1984.

Randall, J.A. *Enforced change at work: the reconstruction of basic assumptions and its influence on attribution, self-sufficiency and the psychological contract*. Unpublished Ph.D. thesis, University of St Andrews, 2001.

Robinson, R. and LeGrand, J. *Evaluating the NHS reforms*. London: Kings Fund, 1994.

Rousseau, D.M. The problem of the psychological contract considered. *Journal of Organizational Behaviour*, 1998, *19*: 665–671.

Rousseau, D.M. Changing the deal while keeping the people, in T.D. Jick and M.A. Peiperl (eds) *Managing change: cases and concepts*. London: McGraw Hill, 2003.

Revans, R. *Action Learning*. London: Blond & Briggs, 1980.

Rusbult, C.E. and Farrell, D. A longitudinal test of the investment model: the impact of job satisfaction, job commitment and turnover of variations in rewards, costs, alternatives and investment. *Journal of Applied Psychology*, 1983, *68*: 429–438.

Schein, E.H. *Process consultation: lessons for managers and consultants*. Reading, MA: Addison-Wesley, 1988.

Senior, B. *Organizational change*. London: Pitman, 1997.

Stace, D.A. and Dunphy, D.D. *Beyond the boundaries: leading and recreating the successful enterprise*. Sydney and NJ: McGraw Hill, 1994.

Stickland, F. *The dynamics of change*. New York: Routledge, 1998.

Sullivan, F. and Mitchell, E. Has General Practictioner computing made a difference to patient care? A systematic review of published reports. *British Medical Journal*, 1952, 311: 848–852.

Trist, E.L. and Bamford, K.W. Some social and psychological consequences of the Longwall method of coal-getting. *Human Relations*, 1951, *4* (1): 3–38.

Tyson, S. and Fell, A. *Evaluating the personnel function*. London: Hutchinson, 1986.

Watson, G. *Resistance to change*. Washington, DC: National Training Laboratories, 1966.

Weick, K.E. *The social psychology of organizing*. Reading, MA: Addison-Wesley, 1979.

Wheatley, M.J. *Leadership and the new science*. San Francisco, CA: Berrett-Koehler, 1994.

Wilson, D. *A strategy for change*. London: Thomson Business Press, 1992.

Chapter 9

Change agency

Managing change or changing managers?

TOPIC HEADINGS

- Leadership and management
- The different roles of change agents
- The context of change agency/managing the culture
- Stages involved in change agency
- Process consultation

INTRODUCTION

There are several issues often taken for granted in much popular writing on the key people who make change happen in organizations. It would be easy to read some of the better-written passages that appear in the serious press and pass over the assumptions they sometimes contain without giving them a second glance.

The purpose of this opening section is to allow you to consider one such article section by section with time to consider what assumptions are being made by the writer and whether the reader is expected to agree with the common sense view expressed by the author of the article. It is always worth asking whether any evidence is offered to support the conclusion which the author is attempting to make.

We begin with an article from the *Financial Times*:

'Wanted: ruthless axeman with people skills'
The 1994–95 restructuring of Scott Paper, under the leadership of Al Dunlap, is an extreme example. Mr Dunlap made clear from the start that his mission was to increase shareholder value. On assuming control in May 1994 he immediately jettisoned 11,000 employees and sold several business units. Non-core functions were outsourced and middle management was purged. His cost-cutting zeal was reflected in the nickname 'Chainsaw Al'.

(*Financial Times*, 14 November 2001.
Reprinted with kind permission of *Financial Times*)

219

Consider the following questions:

1   What assumptions may have been behind Mr Dunlap's actions?
2   Which of his stakeholders was he likely to have been seeking to appease?
3   What do you think might have been the outcome of such a radical intervention?

You probably noted that the assumption implicit in the new Chief Executive's decision was that overheads had to be cut drastically to make the company viable.

You could have gone on to consider that perhaps Mr Dunlap had his eye on the demands of investors or financial backers, considering these as his primary stakeholders, perhaps to the exclusion of the many other stakeholders – particularly the staff.

The evidence of the research on the effect on staff left behind following mass redundancies is not encouraging (Hallier and Lyon, 1996). Low morale and disillusion for those remaining at work might well outweigh the initial benefits of cutting headcount to reduce overhead.

The article continues:

> In some ways the operation was an unqualified success: Scott Paper's market value tripled during his twenty months in charge. But the brutal restructuring arguably sapped the company's capacity for sustained performance. Scott Paper was sold to Kimberley-Clark, its long-time rival, in 1995. Whether it could have prospered as an independent entity is open to question.
>
> The lessons are two-fold. First, managing in a period of adversity requires senior executives to act as leaders – communicating, setting direction and generating a sense of purpose.
>
> Second, corporate restructuring needs to be accompanied by a coherent strategy and continuous investment in human capital – training, team building and management development.
>
> (*Financial Times*, 14 November 2001.
> Reprinted with kind permission of *Financial Times*)

Here are some more questions to consider:

1   What significance would you draw from the tripling of the company's market value?
2   Need this have had anything to do with company's subsequent failure?
3   Do you agree with the first lessons drawn from this narrative?
4   What caveats might you make about the second set of lessons drawn by the author of the article?

You might have commented that values are a function of perception and that, in the case of markets, those perceptions are likely to be comparative – in other words such valuations can be fluctuating as changes occur in the stock market and comparisons are made with other companies in the same sector offering different performance and results. In other words, a valuation may tell us little or nothing about the efficiency or effectiveness factors of the newly restructured company, merely its value compared with other competitors at the time.

The first set of lessons drawn seems unexceptionable. Yes, of course most people would agree that leadership is necessary as classically defined. However, in fairness to Mr Dunlap, there is no evidence to suggest that he did not offer this as part of his leadership style, in terms, say, of decisiveness. If he did, however, then we might reasonably ask whether doing things according to leadership theory always leads to the right decisions for a floundering company.

The assumptions embedded in the second set of lessons are more interesting in that they would be considered as main-stream good practice in management theory. Continuous investment in the staff has been a consistent watchword among both theorists and practitioners of HRM. We might, however, make the point that there could be circumstances where such investment might not be the immediately critical factor for the company's success. In other words, increasing efficiency by investing in people may not affect the overall effectiveness. Poor products or failing markets, for example, may make it impossible to revive a company's fortunes using such a management development route.

The article continues to outline possible theoretical assumptions underwriting good leadership practice:

> Warren Bennis, Professor at the University of Southern California and the eminence grise of leadership studies has argued that good leaders require seven distinct sets of skills. Almost all senior managers possess the first three: technical competence, a faculty for abstract thought and a record that commands respect.
>
> But, he argues, only corporate leaders of the highest calibre combine these with:
>
> - Taste – the ability to identify and cultivate talent;
> - Judgement – the knack of making difficult decisions in a short time frame with imperfect data;
> - People skills – the ability to communicate, motivate, delegate;
> - Character – integrity, drive, optimism, curiosity and courage.
>
> (*Financial Times*, 14 November 2001.
> Reprinted with kind permission of *Financial Times*)

Again, consider some questions arising from this excerpt:

1 What evidence is there that senior managers possess the three sets of skills suggested?
2 How do we know that only corporate leaders possess the final four attributes?
3 How could these attributes be evaluated?

If we ask on what evidence the writer has derived the seven 'distinct sets of skills', the article does not provide an answer here. The technical skill required, for example, is not specified, so we do not learn whether a CEO requires all core technical competencies essential for the company's efficient operation, or just those that pertain to his or her own job.

We might make the same point about the evidence that a person had a faculty for abstract thought. There is no evidence that this has been identified in the case of all the examples investigated. In the same way, the respect commanded by the CEO's record would be difficult to quantify in any way that would offer a role model for a successor to emulate.

Of the four skills that Bennis alleges distinguish corporate leaders of the highest calibre we can make similar comments:

- It could be argued that these factors are subjective or vague.
- Their relevance would be dependent on the context in which the defined skills were exercised and, as such, might be difficult to transfer successfully into another organization.
- Is a 'knack' an intuitive ability born of experience or merely inspired guesswork?
- How could the factors of character be measured at, say, an interview or selection process?

We receive no further information to answer these questions. The author continues:

> The 'emotional intelligence' school of management studies makes a similar point: empathy and a flair for managing human relationships are at least as important as analytical skills.
>
> 'The most important aspect of leadership is accurately reading the emotional reality. In a downturn it is important to recognise that fear and doubt are real and adjust your leadership style appropriately,' says Annie McKee, director of management development at the Hay Group, the human resources consulting firm.
>
> The good news, argues Ms McKee, is that emotional intelligence can be learnt. As a start, she suggests asking subordinates for confidential feedback on your listening skills. Professor Bennis has a more pithy recipe for managing in adversity: 'Tell the truth and communicate obsessively. Give people a sense of long-range perspective. Help them focus on the point of arrival rather than the pain and uncertainty that are now being felt.'
>
> (*Financial Times*, 14 November 2001.
> Reprinted with kind permission of *Financial Times*)

Consider what sorts of assertions are being made here and what evidence is offered in their support. In particular:

1 What definition of emotional intelligence is offered?
2 Why it is more important than analytical skills?
3 What is management style?
4 How can it be adjusted to counter fear and doubt?
5 How can 'emotional intelligence' be learned?
6 What evidence is there for asserting that giving people a 'long-range perspective' somehow relieves pain and uncertainty?

The article offers no evidence to the reader for answering any of the questions posed. It offers several examples of CEOs who have dealt with change successfully and outlines some learning points to be derived from the anecdotal evidence, but specific assertions of best practice are not empirically grounded here as the following account demonstrates:

> Cisco, the California-based networking equipment company, which has been hit by the slowdown in capital spending by telecommunications companies, is putting many of these ideas into practice.
>
> First, it acted quickly: the group noticed a sharp fall in demand in January and announced its restructuring plan in March. Second, restructuring was backed up by a revised strategy: capital spending has been focused on core growth markets with the aim of taking market share from weaker competitors.
>
> Third, management has been broadcasting a consistent, long-term message: although the scale of the downturn caught the company by surprise, it offers a chance for Cisco to 'break away' from its weaker competitors.
>
> Fourth, Cisco continues to invest in its internal management and processes. In August, it announced a new divisional structure aimed at sharpening its engineering and product development.
>
> Last, Cisco is led by a chief executive, John Chambers, who scores highly for emotional intelligence or the soft leadership skills identified by Prof. Bennis. When announcing redundancies in March, Mr Chambers appeared close to tears. He had vowed publicly on many occasions to avoid job losses at all costs. Now he had to break that promise. 'From a personal point of view, it is the worst thing I have ever done,' he later told journalists.
>
> The confessional style is not to everyone's taste. It is hard to imagine Mr Welsh or Mr Norman wearing his heart on his sleeve in this way. But Mr Chamber's personal touch seems to play well within Cisco and few doubt his authenticity. Chainsaw John he ain't.
>
> (*Financial Times*, 14 November 2001.
> Reprinted with kind permission of *Financial Times*)

Consider what logical connections are being made in this final excerpt from the article.

We may accept the need to respond to the slowdown in capital spending. We may accept identifying sectors where core growth is most likely to occur. We may also accept that targeting weaker competitors has a rationality that is unexceptionable. Restructuring to achieve the aims of a refocus in the market makes sense, too. What remains is to direct the message to those inside the organization about how to implement the change strategy.

However, it is the claims made about the CEO, Mr Chambers, that bring us back into the area of assertion unsupported by evidence. First, the required qualities previously attested by Professor Bennis are affirmed but not demonstrated by any evidence. Second, the CEO's tears may or may not have convinced those made redundant. However, the phrase 'playing well' sounds more appropriate for an actor on stage, but we could be forgiven for wondering whether it is a desirable attribute in a senior manager.

SUMMARY

It may seem that we have taken a rather extended introduction to a chapter on change agency. We might agree that leadership is a vital element in the 'toolkit' often alluded to by commentators and writers as essential to the change agent. But we can also see from reading a popular article in a serious broadsheet, which addresses a specialist and knowledgeable readership, that there are factors here that it is easy to confuse and assertions that it is easy to make at the superficial level of observing successful operators which are difficult to connect with a comprehensive underlying theory of managing change effectively. Challenging assumptions is still important and valid in our search for the skills required in the effective agent of the management of change.

We can all accept that what managers say should reinforce what they actually do and that managers should do what they say they are going to do: the one is the gauge of good communication and the other the gauge of integrity. But how far has all this to do with the person a manager is?

Underlying this attempt to clarify what ought to govern good management practice is another question: can what I am as a person be somehow managed to accord with some preset need in the company? How far can any individual change his or her behaviour radically enough to be the person required by the shifting needs of organizational change?

As we have seen, the context of management that we are now talking about is the most difficult to make sense of during enforced change at work. For many practitioners there is a series of steps which can be followed in a predictive way to ensure success, as we have seen with n-step approaches. Many of these changes involve disruption of job, work, career and even organizational membership. How can workers on the receiving end of this kind of change be managed in a way that retains a sense of goodwill or an undisturbed 'psychological contract' – whatever elements it may be thought to contain (Rousseau, 1998; Guest, 1998)?

In other words, as we have seen, at the heart of most change there will be resistance, conflict and probably alienation for many people and we are sometimes asked to believe that the way in which a leader responds in public can somehow be tailored to suit a general mood of grievance in a way that makes the victims realize that he or she is only human and feels bad about such disruption, thereby alleviating grievance, anger and betrayal. It would seem unrealistic to expect this to be an outcome that can be as simply managed as this.

So, as we examine the factors affecting successful management of change by any active participant or agent of change, we will need to examine what those agents can and cannot do in any attempt to alleviate emotional anger or grief. How far can managers or their agents of change recover goodwill with workers or restore loyalty and trust after they have been threatened or lost?

Finally, we will need to have a clear idea of the evidence acquired from interviews with those who have survived such imposed change at work. What actually changes for them? Do all individuals undergo a similar process of coping with change? If there are differences between the responses of such individuals, how are those differences demonstrated? Can managers somehow intervene to secure a better outcome by evincing 'emotional intelligence' or the seven factors, which characterize the role models offered in the article above?

We will look for an answer to these questions in two ways: first, we will examine how leadership skills are applied in an organization not facing change, before looking at how these skills and qualities should be deployed in a situation of enforced change at work; and, second, we will look at how different roles are defined in the implementation of enforced change at work.

LEADERSHIP AND MANAGEMENT

There is considerable reliance on notions of both management and leadership in the literature on the management of change. When we get to the subject of the change agent it is therefore not surprising to find that often assumptions are made about what factors of behaviour and belief are required from successful managers and leaders during enforced change at work.

The distinction between management and leadership has had a long history and ranges from a hierarchical view that only the person at the very top is the leader and, while others may manage discrete parts of the organization, they are also led by the CEO. In more recent years writers have come to view leadership as part of a manager's life, depending on the role he or she may be asked to play. One popular distinction suggests that 'managers are people who do things right and leaders are people who do the right thing' (Bennis and Nanus, 1985, 21). This last definition seems to suggest that leaders have a more strategic view, whereas managers merely repeat prescribed procedures and policies.

If we accept that leadership is more to do with the visionary or the strategic overview then intervention in the detail of management can be left to more functional staff to provide (Alvesson and Sveningsson, 2003, 970). Indeed, intervention in micro-management could in some circumstances be seen as bad leadership. In the pharmaceutical sector examined by the authors, managers suggested that a leader's intervention is unavoidable in strategic issues, but avoidable in operational issues.

Defining leadership as a strategic function moves us away from leaders as having super-human or above-average attributes and the discussion that such gifted or charismatic individuals are born not made (Adair, 1984). Indeed, getting followers to do what you want using knowledge, skills and attributes could be as much the responsibility of any manager as it is the leader's (Barker, 1997, 344). We could summarize such interventions as being necessarily motivational if they are to be effective and part of achieving required outcomes at work – arguably a requirement of management as well as leadership.

More current now is the view that leadership is an outcome of social construction requiring the complicity of others (Smircich and Morgan, 1982, 260). As such, it is an emergent process dependent on the shared meanings which have emerged from the framing of experience (Goffman, 1974). Such leadership consolidates, confronts and changes prevailing wisdom (Peters, 1978). It attempts to frame and define the reality of others (Smircich and Morgan, 1982, 258). As such, it is concerned with the management of meaning (Alvesson and Sveningsson, 2003, 967). Whereas it is the function of management to create stability, it is the function of leadership to create change. This may be through making sense of what other individuals experience during change, through roles, practices and typifications, or through the leader embodying the aspirations, values and practices thought to be needed in the new dispensation of change. More challengingly, one writer suggests that the leader is responsible for that 'process of change where the ethics of individuals are integrated with the mores of the community' (Barker, 1997, 352). This would suggest the leader's undertaking the role of a moral arbiter. These different perceptions suggest that the relationship between management and leadership is by no means as clear as some theoretical definitions suggest.

THE MANAGEMENT AND LEADERSHIP CONNECTION

So, if the relationship between management and leadership is difficult to establish within day-to-day company practice, it would be fair to ask how this debate fares under the conditions of change. In the opinion of some writers, leadership is little different from management (Rost, 1991). And, increasingly, managers need leadership skills, just as leaders cannot afford to be without management skills. In the context of change it could be argued that all managers will need to be able to exercise proactive leadership skills. In the words of one writer well known for his contribution to the development of leadership training and development:

> Good management is both art and science: it involves analysis and emotion. People respond to other people, not just to arguments in favour of a proposal; this is why leadership is important. Managers in times of change need to be leaders as well as good managers: indeed, if they are good leaders others will forgive their failings and seek to compensate for them.
>
> A leader is someone who believes in what he or she is trying to accomplish and is able to get others to believe it, too. Managers have subordinates: leaders have followers because people believe in them, trust them and admire them. The chief executive has a key leadership role to play in major restructuring and cultural change. Other managers also have to be able to lead their staff if the changes are to succeed.
>
> (Adair, 1984, 53)

So, what is it that the leader/managers have to understand about an organization facing change in order to be able to approach change with any chance of success?

First, there are the functional elements of any job which must be familiarized, some brought in from past experience, some learned from key colleagues (Stewart, 1991).

Second, there are strategic considerations: the question of why we are doing things the way we do them.

Third, there is the cultural context: a context of expectancies not just of those who are managed, but of colleagues and significant others outside the organization. It is debatable whether we can just learn this culture and absorb it by being around for a certain time (Deal and Kennedy, 1982). In some professional environments, such as the public sector, fellow professionals may need to be reassured that the new leader shares their concerns and knows the critical judgements that are expected of all professionals in virtue, perhaps, of being such a professional him or herself (Pollitt, 1995).

In the following sections we will examine how far these insights about the distinct functions of leaders and managers apply in the context of enforced change at work.

DIFFERENT ROLES OF CHANGE AGENTS

We will begin with an article which I believe offers an overview both of the different roles that may be being exercised during change in organizations and of the context within which they are played. Buchanan and Storey offer a comment that illustrates the point well:

Commentators who advocate a pluralist perspective on organizational change typically point to the plurality of actors engaged in the process. This useful but oversimplified notion is extended in this chapter to a consideration of 'four pluralities'. Pluralist accounts of change, it is argued, must consider first, the plurality of organizational actors; second, the plurality of change drivers; thirdly, the plurality of change phases; and fourthly, the plurality of roles that change drivers are required to perform.

(Buchanan and Storey, 1997, 128)

We will examine the points raised in turn.

As we have seen, accounts of change and change agents are often drawn up by gurus or hero-managers (Collins, 1998). They do not always acknowledge the critical contribution of other actors in effecting the change they describe. Particularly when outside consultants are brought in, we need to examine carefully the kind of roles they are required to carry out both wittingly and unwittingly by those who have engaged their services.

We will need to look closely at the critical function played by the internal author of the change. Significant change agents are sometimes the leader within, sometimes key members of staff who have the far-sightedness and commitment to see the need for change and respond to it at their own local level, sometimes an incoming outsider who rescues a failing organization.

This relates well to the second point: who is responsible for which parts of the change? At the individual level there may be particular skills which need to be assimilated in different parts of the organization. At group levels there may be reorganization and restructuring. At organizational level there may be refining company philosophy and strategy, rewriting company policies and procedures and revisiting key company documents from staff contracts, terms and conditions to the staff handbook itself. These functions may well require different change agents. One contributor lists these as follows:

- The advocate who proposes change
- The sponsor who legitimises it
- The targets who undergo it
- The agents who implement it
- The process owner – typically the most senior target.

(Davenport, 1993, 173)

The roles of change agency are various and those undertaking them will need to be chosen carefully to ensure they have the necessary competence and commitment. But, overall, this list suggests a team of people operating at different parts of the change programme with distinctive and essential roles.

WHAT CHANGE AGENTS NEED

Wherever they are employed and in whatever capacity, change agents need a raft of skills that will be the vehicle for their success throughout the phases of the change programme. Here is one such list:

- Sensing needs
- Amplifying understanding
- Building awareness
- Creating credibility
- Legitimising viewpoints
- Generating potential solutions
- Broadening support
- Identifying indifference and opposition
- Changing perceived risks
- Structuring needed flexibilities
- Putting forward trial concepts
- Creating pockets of commitment
- Eliminating undesired options
- Crystallising focus and concern
- Managing coalitions
- Formalising agreed commitments.

(Quinn, 1980, 51)

Such a list might be summarized as the role of facilitator: a change agent tasked with drawing out micro-change in an interactive way in different groups. Sometimes the particular techniques and styles of management are summarized in particular detail:

- Problem finding
- Map building
- Janusian thinking
- Controlling and not controlling
- Humour that oils
- Charisma.

(McCaskey, 1988)

Such a list begs the question of how far this is comprehensive and whether these elements need to be learned or to have been demonstrated prior to employment as a change agent. We are being offered a list whose content varies between techniques, skills and knowledge, which could be open to training, and personal qualities, which may not be so open.

If we assume 'problem finding' to be a skill, we might probably agree that it could be taught, though it would be fair to say that problems often relate to a particular context or technology, in which case we might reasonably ask how transferable they might be to a different sector and whether the past experience gained by a change agent is applicable in a new business context.

'Map building', too, could be construed as a skill. McCaskey defines this as 'ability to generate fresh ways of conceptualizing problem situations'. Something of the inspirational and subjective may be involved here. Again, probably only someone with wide experience could offer the fund of relevant examples necessary to convince the subjects of change that the agent has credible experience.

228

'Janusian thinking' is something every change agent and management consultant would like in good measure. McCaskey defines it as 'ability constructively to join apparently contradictory views and beliefs'. Again, can that be taught, or is it a function of subtlety and experience combined with perceived relevance by the subjects of change?

'Controlling and not controlling' might suggest the facilitative skills we commented on earlier – in the sense of playing advantage and letting the individuals be creative, while keeping in mind the overall goal/objective and never letting participants lose sight of that.

'Humour that oils' is described as 'using the restorative power of laughter'. We may well agree with this assertion, while noting that humour arises from the group and cannot be entered into by artificial means (joke telling, funny stories etc.). However, such an ability is rarely learned and would be dependent on the context in which the skill is exercised and responded to by the receiving group.

'Charisma', as we know, comes from the Greek word originally meaning 'gift'. McCaskey defines it as 'ability to stir enthusiasm, confidence and commitment in others'. All who have tried will usually admit to the two-way aspect of such interaction between change agent and the subjects of the change. Just as leadership is often described as charismatic, the gift must be demonstrated by the leader and acknowledged and responded to by the led.

Thus far, then, we have been offered a daunting list of a variety of skills and aptitudes whose relevance is as much a function of the context and the individuals in receipt of the change as of the natural talent of the change agent. Inspired choice in the formation of this team will be as much a function of its success as assessed competence and past experience.

SO, HOW MANY CHANGE AGENTS ARE NEEDED?

Most commentators identify different change agent roles within what, for most organizations, will be complex and interconnected functions. Breaking down these functions Buchanan and Boddy offer three issues to guide a possible division of labour:

- Content
- Control
- Process.
         (1992, 55)

Put simply, we might say that we need to define:

- What we want to do
- Who is in control
- How it is going to happen.

A combination of external advisers and the senior management group may define the first point in the list. Alternatively, a more emergent approach might have involved a larger constituent group. The implications of who is responsible overall for the change will then need to be addressed. Some writers refer to a leader or flag-bearer role and there may be an argument for that individual being an insider, at a senior level of responsibility – perhaps the CEO (Carnall, 1999).

However, as we have seen in previous chapters, the implementation of a change programme may require many different interventions over many stages in different areas of the business. Each of these roles will require knowledge and expertise to deliver their part of the programme. Such individuals will be change agents in their own right operating within a sphere of influence and dependent on discrete competencies and functions.

But, however many experts are needed to complete the change agents' team, there will still be the need for one leader to coordinate a complex programme and such an individual may have responsibility for people and budgets for the duration of the project and require significant project management skills (Dawson, 2003).

The literature on BPR offers a list of such roles for individuals involved in implementing a re-engineering programme. Certainly, the scope of radical change may well require a variety of roles and a set of responsibility links to show how these roles complement each other to achieve the objectives of the change management programme:

- Leader
- Process owner
- Reengineering team
- Steering committee
- Reengineering czar.

The leader appoints the process owner who convenes the reengineering team with assistance from the czar, under the auspices of the steering committee.

(Hammer and Champy, 1995)

What the literature is less clear about is the change of roles that may be required during the process of change and whether it is possible or appropriate for one individual to fulfil more than one role. Responsibility for changes in job functions may be difficult for an external change agent to undertake. On the other hand, it may sometimes be easier for an external change agent to broker change or institute training than it would be for an internal change agent (Graetz *et al.*, 2002).

There are no easy answers here. However, a clear distinction between roles with a logical linking of responsibilities to connect strategy and tactics will be important. Any confusion or overlap will be exploited by those who want to take advantage of any confusion to suggest that the change programme is failing to achieve its targets (Buchanan and Badham, 1999).

THE USE OF EXPERTS AS CHANGE AGENTS

There is sometimes a belief that experts may better succeed in persuading individuals and groups to accept change. The logic might be that anyone who has achieved a level of success in a required area of learning will find it easier to convince less expert or sceptical individuals that the change is achievable and that the relevant techniques may bring transition more easily into the task of establishing newly required behaviours.

Indeed, for some authors, there is a list of competencies that such experts need to possess, which may make them more effective in managing change at the functional part of the programme:

- Experts excel in their own domains
- Experts work in large and meaningful patterns
- Experts solve problems quicker and with less errors
- Experts have superior memories
- Experts use deep conceptualisations of problems
- Experts spend more time qualitatively analysing problems
- Experts have strong monitoring skills.

(Buchanan and Boddy, 1992)

Such assertions sometimes find support from the research literature in cognitive psychology (Kahney, 1986). However, it may be that the assumptions made do not necessarily apply to the management of change. Indeed, it could be argued that virtually every point in the list might equally alienate such an expert from a non-specialist audience being asked to adapt to or adopt different behaviours at work. Certainly new expertise is often a prerequisite of change. However, change agents may need to have credibility in front of specialist audiences and this might favour the use of internal change agents who have themselves achieved success in the newly required knowledge and skills and are therefore more credible exemplars of change.

Indeed, commentators suggest that involving willing internal participants may increase commitment and make use of inherent local talent to combine required competence with prior knowledge of the cultural background of the organization. As one writer puts it:

- Everyone is now a change agent.
- Opportunities are presented for individuals to self-select themselves into change agency roles.
- Change agency requires no special consideration for selection.

(Doyle, 2002)

What matters here is that between them the team of change agents can offer the necessary skills and qualities required to broker change among working groups. The list of qualities required for these generalists is extensive and demanding, but with prior training such candidates may present to others a combination of both competence and credibility. The bridge between competence and commitment is sometimes laid out as an extensive list of facilitative factors:

1 Sensitivity
2 Clarity
3 Flexibility
4 Team building
5 Networking

231

6 Tolerance of ambiguity

7 Communication skills

8 Interpersonal skills

9 Personal enthusiasm

10 Motivation and commitment

11 Selling

12 Negotiating

13 Practical awareness

14 Influencing skills

15 Helicopter perspective.

(Buchanan and Boddy, 1992)

Those chosen for the role of change agent may not have the exhaustive list of prerequisite skills and qualities suggested here. However, a team of individuals might well be able to mobilize between them the diverse skills, knowledge and experience, provided they operate flexibly and complement one another's abilities effectively. A knowledgeable and perceptive project team leader would be needed to broker such flexibility.

CONTEXT OF CHANGE AGENCY

Once we have looked at the phases, actors and drivers within the change process itself, we can look at the variation which may exist between organizational cultures and contexts. There will be differences in organizational structure, roles and responsibilities, hierarchies, power and the way it is exercised. Sometimes these are illustrated as a range of opposites (see Box 9.1).

Perhaps part of the objective of enforced change could be to bring about change across the descriptors offered here – and, let it be said, in either direction. For, though the lean and risk-averse school has made the running in the public sector with government initiatives for compulsory competitive tender and outsourcing to external providers, we could equally well see a move from small, discrete divisions to a more structured, bureaucratic form of organization (Hood, 1998).

BOX 9.1 MECHANISTIC VERSUS ORGANIC CULTURES

MECHANISTIC vs ORGANIC

MECHANISTIC	ORGANIC
■ Fixed job descriptions	Loose
■ Clear hierarchies	Vague
■ Lines of responsibility	Negotiational
■ Positional power	Expert power
■ Bureaucracy	Adhocracy

Source: Toffler (1970)

Similarly, change agents seeking to intervene in an organization to bring about change may want to consider the implication of the content and context of change. This is an aspect which is often associated with the contribution of UK literature associated with emergent change (see Box 9.2).

We can relate these headings to the drivers affecting the need for change in an organization and sometimes enable individuals and groups to appreciate and prepare for the likely impact of change. The gap between content and context may sometimes relate to the classic difference between efficiency and effectiveness: managing the gap between the two being a constant challenge to management. However, in certain extreme cases a more radical approach may be necessary and change agents need to be aware if this is the case.

For some writers a summary of possible approaches to change is offered, linked to the sort of challenge faced by the organization and suggesting that different styles are appropriate for different demands in a market (see Table 9.1).

Such diagrams suggest a normative approach to change strategy that may not appeal to the proponents of more emergent types of change. A more discursive approach might be found more helpful. For such commentators these factors might include the items listed in Box 9.3.

We might question how far meaning can be managed. If we look at the elements offered in the list then certainly symbolism, language, ideology and myth belong to the peer group or staff within the company. It might be argued that it is difficult for an outsider to penetrate such levels of shared meaning, let alone manage them. If we go back to Chapter 5, then we can say that, for some writers, the foundation of such elements is deeply rooted in the common beliefs or basic assumptions of individuals (Schein, 1985). The question will always remain: how can any individual or group manage such beliefs during enforced change?

MANAGING THE CULTURE

If we go back to the examples at the beginning of this chapter, then we can see that, for some leaders, change will mean defining different priorities. We could cite similar examples from the practice of Japanese companies sited in the UK. A single staff dining room and unreserved parking spaces were deemed to be significant changes to what would have been considered necessary concomitants of management status necessary in British industrial practice (Wickens, 1987).

BOX 9.2 INNER AND OUTER CONTEXTS OF CHANGE

Inner context	Outer context
■ History of the organization	Competition
■ Structure	Customer demand
■ Culture	Technology
■ Politics	Innovation

Source: Pettigrew (1987)

There is a secondary question, too, about change agents who come in from outside. How far is it important for them to be seen as sharing the profession or core activity the company is engaged in? Does a change agent in the medical sector need to have been a doctor or nurse him- or herself to be an effective change agent? If he/she is, will that make their interventions for change more acceptable to other members of the profession?

There are no simple answers to such questions. However, some consideration may well be given to those who are to be asked to embark on the role of the change agent from a position outside the company with no previous relevant experience of current practice and

Table 9.1 *Approaches to change and their uses*

Approach to change	Use
Task-focused -strong bottom line -workforce planning/job design/work practice reviews -focus on tangible reward structure -strong business unit culture	Major change in markets
Developmental Individual and team development -intrinsic rewards -strong emphasis on corporate culture	In growing markets
Turnaround -major structural change -downsizing -recruitment from outside -executive team building -breaking with old culture	Business environment changes dramatically
Paternalistic HR practices -precedent/procedures/uniformity -O & M -inflexible internal appointments policy -operator and supervisory training -individual awards and agreements	Very limited mass production situations

Source: Stace and Dunphy (1991, 259)

BOX 9.3 SIGNIFICANT FACTORS DURING CHANGE

- Processes of legitimation
- The management of meaning
- Symbolism
- Language
- Ideology
- Myth

Source: Pettigrew (1987)

its basic assumptions, for most change agents will hear an announcement from the body of the peer group quite early which goes something like: 'If you had done this job yourself, you would not be telling us to do it the way you are suggesting.' Without inside knowledge, such objections may be difficult to counter convincingly.

STAGES INVOLVING CHANGE AGENTS

We have already looked at the stepped approaches offered to analyse the stages of change in Chapter 6. We can accept that the term 'phases' may be a better descriptor of what often are overlapping elements, which will need careful project management to permit the many different actors to interface in a successful and coordinated way. These phases may, indeed, require a staged approach, each phase being broken down into its particular elements (see Table 6.1 on p. 149). As we have seen in the previous chapter, there may be a benefit in completing the change cycle and evaluating its impact for an initial group so that lessons learned early on may be implemented in subsequent groups going through the phases.

Finally, we return to the roles that change drivers are required to perform. Here, we come back to a literature, discussed earlier, which seeks to define different roles presumably used in a flexible way as required by the situation (see Box 9.4).

The list of attributes required by change agents could be seen as mirroring the phases themselves. Once again it suggests that there may be a need for a variety of skilled practitioners to carry out a programme of change effectively.

CRITICAL CHANGE SITUATIONS

Not all change is as controllable as the theory may sometimes suggest. The pitfalls included here remind us that the n-step approaches often reinforce the need to have top managers and key leaders on side in the change process. The cost of not achieving this is pointed out here in situations where the change agent will be most vulnerable (see Box 9.5).

We might consider these as being the likely background in many change situations. Each factor highlights the challenging nature of change and the threat that can be perceived by individuals and groups. Here, we approach the heart of likely resistance and the blocking response that can sometimes be triggered by enforced change at work.

BOX 9.4 CHANGE AGENT ROLES

- Visionary, catalyst, 'mover and shaker'
- Analyst, compelling case builder, risk assessor
- Team-builder, coalition former, ally seeker
- Implementation planner, action driver, deliverer
- Fixer-facilitator, wheeler-dealer, power broker
- Reviewer, critic, progress-chaser, auditor

Source: Buchanan and Storey (1997, 140)

BOX 9.5 FACTORS AFFECTING CHANGE ADVERSELY

- Strategic changes
- Rapid change – quick results
- Significant resource commitment
- Disinterested top management
- Unrealistic top management expectations
- Fickle support
- Uncertain Means
- Complex interdependencies
- Dependent on third parties
- Conflicting perceptions
- Multi-purpose changes
- Unstable goals
- Confused responsibilities for process and outcomes

Source: Buchanan and Boddy (1992, 54)

One author highlights the possible blocks to problem-solving and change that may occur during change programmes. He addresses the same phenomenon from the viewpoint of the individual:

- Perceptual blocks
- Emotional blocks
- Cultural blocks
- Environmental blocks
- Cognitive blocks.

He offers a useful list of actions to encourage creativity during problem solving:

- Stay loose and fluid in your thinking until rigour is needed
- Protect new ideas from criticism
- Acknowledge new ideas, listen, show approval
- Eliminate status or rank
- Be optimistic
- Support confusion and uncertainty
- Value learning from mistakes
- Focus on the good aspects of an idea
- Share the risks
- Suspend disbelief
- Build on ideas
- Do not evaluate too early.

(Carnall, 1999, 92–96)

Such suggestions would be considered good practice by any facilitator seeking to encourage emergent change through involvement of groups and individuals.

GAINING AND MAKING ALLIANCES

How then does an outside change agent gain supporters to the cause of change? Individuals often diverge because they interpret change in different ways, some positively and others less favourably. Some writers offer a list of possible responses from individuals being subjected to enforced change at work:

- Partners
- Allies
- Fellow travellers
- Fence sitters
- Opponents
- Adversaries
- Bedfellows
- Voiceless.

(Egan, 1994)

Identifying the positive contributors and proactively dealing with the sceptical or negative individuals may well be defining interventions in the implementation of a change programme.

As an inside change agent, we might well find the first three categories almost instantly identifiable. Opponents and adversaries might base their opposition on the grounds that they disagreed for reasons of detail in the change proposal. Their ability to adduce evidence to refute the relevance of change would need to be more thoroughly demonstrated to gain the credibility of their peer group. This knowledge will find the insider in a better position to address the problem of resistance.

In contrast, if the change agent does not share the core employment experience, it may be harder to find partners, allies and fellow travellers and the opponents and adversaries may find it easier to gain support within the group.

Some writers offer a list of suggested responses for coping with the sceptical and negative. As we remember from the n-steps approach offered in Chapter 6, the outsider can adopt a series of tactics:

- Wait them out
- Wear them down
- Appeal to higher authority
- Invite them in
- Send emissaries
- Display support
- Reduce the stakes
- Warn them off.

(Kanter, 1983)

Leaving aside the hype, the author still admits by implication that, without higher authority in evident support, the task may well be impossible. It would be kinder to suggest that such models 'are post-hoc rationalisations, accounts of change after it has happened rather than planning the implementation process in advance' (Buchanan and Storey, 1997, 139). Such tactics may work, but the question of how long to live with persistent dissenters may be difficult to avoid and will perhaps need to be addressed.

For some writers the question of different roles raises issues like team-building, networking and the tolerance of ambiguity. There is a literature which addresses manager behaviours and effectiveness, including political considerations together with classical management communication skills. These include things that can be taught – suggesting an underpinning knowledge and skill enhancement together with much that could be described as a function of personality. One such list recommends that managers:

- Exhibit a high tolerance of frustration.
- Encourage full participation and are able to permit people to discuss and pull apart their decisions without feeling that their personal worth is threatened.
- Continually question themselves but without being constantly critical of themselves.
- Understand the 'laws of competitive warfare' and do not feel threatened by them.
- Express hostility tactfully.
- Accept victory with controlled emotions.
- Are never shattered by defeat.
- Understand the necessity for limits and for 'unfavourable decisions'.
- Identify themselves with groups, thereby gaining a sense of security and stability.
- Set goals realistically.

(Argyris, 1952; Stewart, 1985, 63)

We can accept that such lists apply to all who want to exhibit outstanding management behaviours. But how to acquire such an array of qualities is another question. And we are still left with the problem of cultural fit. Indeed, if we go back to Chapter 5 on culture, we can acknowledge that how far a manager or change agent is acceptable depends on the basic assumptions of the receiving group. 'Is he/she one of us?' is a valid question, which is bound to be asked and even those with similar beliefs may find their credibility questioned if they suggest unacceptable courses of action resisted by a peer group.

PROCESS CONSULTATION

One attempt to address this corporate culture or shared assumptions was proposed by Edgar Schein. It is no surprise to learn that he worked with Kurt Lewin in the early days of changing the perceptions of groups of workers by engaging them in the sensitivity or T-groups in which individuals and groups are facilitated to assess and come to terms with their own perceptions and beliefs with a view to modifying them to more acceptable or currently required attitudes. He summarizes his programme in diagrammatic form (see Table 9.2).

Such change programmes enable people to take charge of their own change – an early form of emergent change, perhaps, because it seeks to address culture as a set of beliefs

Table 9.2 *Process consultation*

Model	Task	Interpersonal
Content	Formal Agenda	Who does what to whom
	GOALS	
Process	How the task is done	How members relate to each other
Structure	Recurrent processes	Recurrent interpersonal relationships
	Standard Operating Procedures	ROLES

Source: Schein (1988, 63)

and bring them to the surface in discussion groups. Its proponents harbour no doubts as to its efficacy:

> It helps the organisation to improve its inherent capacity to cope by helping it diagnose itself, select its own coping responses and determine its own progress.
>
> The process consultant is an expert in organisational processes and can help the client develop diagnostic and intervention skills in these areas.
>
> Uncovers organisations and group cultural assumptions.
>
> Assumption: if the client can begin to solve his/her own problem, he/she will also have learned something about the process of how to solve problems.
>
> (Schein, 1969)

The process approach seems to assume that individuals and groups will become aware of their own need for the change defined with the help of the facilitator. It also assumes that the change agent and the peer group define a problem in the same terms or with the same result. Perhaps we need to accept that both individuals and groups can be remarkably impervious to suggestions that change is a necessary response to outside threat.

Rather harsher is the recommendation of the proponents of BPR. The question of what to do with persistent dissenters is not avoided in these precepts:

1 Don't live too long with people who refuse to change their behaviour, especially if their work is important to achieving your reengineering goals. Your tolerance of old behaviours signals that you are not serious about change.

2 The above applies to all people, managers as well as workers. This is a new democracy!

3 Don't expect people to change how they behave unless you change what they do; that is their work must be designed to allow them to act differently.

4 Don't expect cultural change to happen immediately. Although you may achieve some early results, a complete cultural change is usually measured in terms of years (hopefully just a few) rather than months.

5 Don't articulate a new or updated set of values and then delay reengineering your management process to support them.

> (Champy, 1995, 109)

239

RETURN TO LEADERSHIP

We began this chapter with a consideration of classical leadership texts. We saw that leadership behaviours are offered as capable of training and many organizations offer such training or list the qualities as a requirement in their senior officers or executives.

However, the question of the perception of those who are led is less clearly enunciated in the literature. If we accept the key role of basic assumptions in the cultural literature and the important and central role of frames and references in individual cognition, then finding the link between the personal and corporate constructs becomes very important to the leader and manager of change.

We are here at the crossroads of what is held to be important personally and as a member of a group. On top of this link between personal and corporate constructs is an area of uncertainty, which must exist during any enforced change: can we resist by appearing to accept, without losing our position of power or control, either as individuals or as a group? If so, how do leaders of change know whether the content of the change has been assimilated or not?

We have seen the many different approaches to the theory and practice of change. Some focus on the techniques that the leader of change should adopt in order to be successful. Others focus on the context of change: how far the culture, or commonly held set of beliefs within the working group can be adjusted to enable it to come to terms with outside change.

We have seen the breakdown of tasks within a management of change programme, which ranges from the strategic overview of the group to individual change interventions and the expertise required to make it happen.

Underlying these considerations, which are capable of logical analysis and planning, there remain moral issues, which will be affected by basic assumptions in the minds of those to be subjected to the change. How far will they accept the change and be persuaded by the blandishments of the change agents? In all honesty, any experienced change agent would have to admit that we cannot predict who will change willingly and who will resist.

All that we can say is that change agents who share the basic assumptions of the subjects of change are in a better position to understand and appreciate the concerns and objections that individuals and groups may have and be prepared to handle these sympathetically. Perceptive leadership includes an acceptance that it may not be possible to reach agreement or negotiate in the face of fear or intransigence.

WHAT THE GOOD LEADER DOES

One book that we have already mentioned is *The skills of leadership* by John Adair. It is unusual in that the author has attempted to identify from their own writings the ways in which leaders might consider the task that lies before him or her. One such example is Field Marshall Lord Slim, who brought the British Fourteenth Army in Burma back from defeat to victory against the Japanese in the Second World War.

Slim drew up his own account of assessing the needs of his ordinary soldiers to guide him in assessing need for change and his role as the principal agent of change:

I remember sitting in my office and tabulating these foundations of morale something like this:

1 Spiritual

(a) There must be a great and noble object.

(b) Its achievement must be vital.

(c) The method of achievement must be active, aggressive.

(d) The man must feel that what he is and what he does matters directly towards the attainment of the objective.

2 Intellectual

(a) He must be convinced that the object can be obtained; that it is not out of reach.

(b) He must see, too, that the organization to which he belongs and which is striving to attain the object is an efficient one.

(c) He must have confidence in his leaders and know that whatever dangers and hardships he is called upon to suffer, his life will not be lightly flung away.

3 Material

(a) The man must feel that he will get a fair deal from his commanders and from the army generally.

(b) He must, as far as humanly possible, be given the best weapons and equipment for the task.

(c) His living and working conditions must be made as good as they can be.

(Adair, 1984, 23)

Slim then describes how he went about achieving these objectives and those who want to read his account will find it in his own book *From defeat to victory*. What is significant here is the setting of objectives based on principles clearly set down. It demonstrates an aspect of this leadership, which was not delineated quite as clearly in many accounts given by hero-managers: the significance of perception and judgement concerning the beliefs of the individuals to be led.

We have already examined in Chapter 5 the role that culture plays as a context of management and leadership. We can also recall that, for many contributors to the literature, the significance of norms, values, beliefs and basic assumptions lie at the heart of this evaluation of the individual working in the context of an organization. It is this aspect that we will look at briefly now.

One contributor to the research on what makes a good manager has been writing on the subject for nearly 30 years. Rosemary Stewart stands in a long line of research, which sought to examine what makes an effective manager and how different managers adapt to and adopt a new job at a senior level in an organization. She cites studies of such individuals, getting into the work, learning about the job, but also being tempted to do what has worked last time or what they know they are good at. We might call this the functional part of the job: what do I need to know; what must I do myself; whom do I need to work with to become effective?

But once this familiarity with the daily job demands has been mastered there is the strategic overview that Slim demonstrated so clearly above. Stewart refers to this, as do many popular writers, as the helicopter approach: the ability to see things in some sort of overview – a concerted, holistic approach to people, the structure of the organization and the context in which they operate with its daily changing demands.

Listening to what change managers and agents say about their work can be an interesting exercise in spotting beliefs about human beings and the way they are expected to respond to change. It should enable the reader or listener to identify assumptions being made about people and the processes of change they may embark on to achieve success.

Our chapter can only offer tentative conclusions, as the outcome will be dependent on the balance achieved between the change agents and the bottom-up involvement of those affected by the enforced change.

Sympathy, in its original sense of suffering with those affected by such change may well be increased in change agents who share the same basic assumptions and professional experience as those on whom the change will be visited. For, however empowering and bottom-up the change process is, we have to admit that the final management responsibility for the change, wherever it lies, will have to be exercised sensitively to bring it to a successful conclusion, requiring, as it does, a combination of front-of-house and back-stage skills.

DISCUSSION QUESTIONS

Here are two examination questions you might like to consider:

1   Describe the skills needed by a change agent. How can the change agent deploy these to overcome the most likely and significant blocks to change in the organization?

The first part of your answer will need to identify the skills. Certainly there is no lack of lists available in the textbooks. Perhaps it would be worthwhile addressing the different roles that the change agent may be expected to play and fitting the skills into the roles identified. This will allow you to explore the strategic roles, the managerial roles and the functional or tactical roles involved.

The second half of the question raises the question of blocks. Again, we have seen at least one list of individual perceptions which may act as a block to acceptance of a change programme. However, we could broaden the answer to include situations which make change more critical and the outcome more uncertain. Again, we have seen such a list of factors and they may be worth commenting on individually.

We might conclude by pointing out that a change agent is unlikely to feel comfortable attempting to fill all the roles required. Personal experience and aptitude might find most people struggling to fill less familiar roles. As we also pointed out, the team approach should offer complementary skills, knowledge and experience together with a mix of internal and external change agents whose variety of skills combined with unity of commitment may be the strongest and most convincing experience for those subjected to enforced change at work.

2   Define the styles of management required of an effective change agent. Show how his or her success might be dependent on using different styles throughout the stages of a planned change with:

- Senior managers
- First-line managers
- Members of staff.

The second question shares some similarity with the previous question given that different roles and functions within the category change agent are now required to be demonstrated in the answer.

A decision will have to be made about styles of management – whether, say, the traditional styles of directive, coaching, supportive and delegational styles might make a useful starting point to illustrate the different application of roles to functions that the change agent might require.

This might then link up naturally with the levels of responsibility represented by the traditional roles offered in the question. So, senior managers might require a discussive style to enable them to explore the strategic aims of the programme and the issues which this may raise within the company, for and against. First-line managers may need to be convinced by a demonstration that new procedures, policies and systems can work to improve the demands being made on them in fulfilling day-to-day demands. Finally, members of staff will have their own concerns which will mirror the basis of resistance outlined by Nadler: the loss of control, status and power over jobs that they had previously attained competence in but may now have to learn anew.

In each case different skills may be needed by the change agent, applied in each different context. However, even this difference of context may not obviate the human concerns, which any person facing change may have. This brings us back to the traditional blocks to change, which we discussed earlier, and reinforces the need for all change agents to have a facility for handling concerns and objections.

REFERENCES AND FURTHER READING

Adair, J. *The skills of leadership*. Aldershot: Wildwood House, 1984.

Alvesson, M. and Sveningsson, S. Good visions, bad micro-management and ugly ambiguity: contradictions of (non-)leadership in a knowledge-intensive organization. *Organizational Studies*, 2003, *24* (6): 961–988.

Argyris, C. *Personality fundamentals for administration: an introduction for the layman*. New Haven, CN: Yale University Labor and Management Center, 1952.

Attwood, M. Pedler, M., Pritchard, S. and Wilkinson, D. *Leading change: a guide to whole systems working*. Bristol: The Policy Press, 2003.

Barker, R.A. How can we train leaders if we do not know what leadership is? *Human Relations*, 1997, *50* (4): 343–362.

Bennis, W.G. and Nanus, B. *Leaders: the strategies for taking charge*. New York: Harper & Row, 1985.

Buchanan, D. and Badham, R. *Power, politics and organizational change: winning the turf game*. London: Sage, 1999.

Buchanan, D. and Boddy, D. *The expertise of the change agent: public performance and back-stage activity*. New York: Prentice Hall, 1992.

Buchanan, D. and Storey, J. Role taking and role switching in organizational change: the four pluralities, in I. McLoughlin and M. Harris (eds) *Innovation, organizational change and technology*. London: International Thomson, 1997.

Bullock, R.J. and Batten, D. It's just a stage we're going through: a review and synthesis of OD phase analysis. *Group & Organization Studies*, 1985, *10* (4): 383–411.

Carnall, C.A. *Managing change in organizations*. London: *Financial Times*/Prentice Hall, 1999.

Champy, J. *Reengineering management: the mandate for new leadership*. London: HarperCollins, 1995.

Collins, D. *Organizational change: sociological perspectives*. London: Routledge, 1998.

Davenport, T. *Process innovation: reengineering work through IT*. Boston, MA: Harvard Business School, 1993.

Dawson, P. *Understanding organizational change: the contemporary experience of people at work*. London: Sage, 2003.

Deal, T.E. and Kennedy, A. *Corporate cultures*. Reading, MA: Addison-Wesley, 1982.

Doyle, M. From change novice to change expert: issues of learning, development and support. *Personnel Review*, 2002, *4*: 465–481.

Egan, G. *Working the shadow side: a guide to positive behind-the-scenes management*. San Francisco, CA: Jossey Bass, 1994.

Goffman, E. *Frame analysis*. New York: Harper, 1974.

Graetz, F., Rimmer, M., Lawrence, A. and Smith, A. *Managing organizational change*. Sydney: John Wiley Australia, 2003.

Guest, D. Is the psychological contract worth taking seriously? *Journal of Organizational Behaviour*, 1998, *19*: 649–664.

Hallier, J. and Lyon, P. Job insecurity and employee commitment: managers' reactions to the threat and outcomes of redundancy selection. *British Journal of Management*, 1996, *7*: 107–123.

Hammer, M. and Champy, J. *Reengineering the corporation*. London: Nicholas Brealey Publishing, 1995.

Hood, C. *The art of the state*. Oxford: Clarendon Press, 1998.

Kahney, H. *Problem solving: a cognitive approach*. Buckingham: Open University Press, 1986.

Kanter, R.M. *The change masters: corporate entrepreneurs at work*. London: George Allen & Unwin, 1983.

McCaskey, M.B. The challenge of managing ambiguity and change, in Louis R. Pondy, R.J. Boland and H. Thomas (eds) *Managing ambiguity and change*. Chichester: John Wiley, 1988.

Peters, T.J. Symbols, patterns and settings: an optimistic case for getting things done. *Organizational Dynamics*, 1978, *7*: 3–22.

Pettigrew, A.M. Context and action in the transformation of the firm. *Journal of Management Studies*, 1987, *24* (6): 649–670.

Pollitt, C. Justification by works or by faith: evaluating the New Public Management. *Evaluation*, 1995, *1* (2): 133–154.

Quinn, J.B. *Strategies for change: logical instrumentalism*. Homewood, IL: Richard D. Irwin, 1980.

Rost, J.C. *Leadership for the twenty-first century*. New York: Praeger, 1991.

Rousseau, D.M. The problem of psychological contract considered. *Journal of Organizational Behaviour*, 1998, *19*: 665–671.

Schein, E. *Process consultation*. Reading, MA: Addison-Wesley, 1969.

Schein, E. *Organizational culture and leadership*. San Francisco, CA: Jossey Bass, 1985.

Schein, E. *Process consultation: lessons for managers and consultants*. Reading, MA: Addison-Wesley, 1988.

Smircich, L. and Morgan, G. Leadership: the management of meaning. *Journal of Applied Behavioural Science*, 1982, *18* (3): 257–273.

Stace, D.A. and Dunphy, D. Beyond traditional paternalistic and developmental approaches to organizational change and HR strategies. *International Journal of HRM*, 1991, *2* (4): 263–283.

Stewart, R. *The reality of management*. London: Pan Books, 1985.

Stewart, R. *Managing today and tomorrow*. London: Macmillan, 1991.

Toffler, A. *Future shock*. London: Pan Books, 1970.

Wickens, P. *The road to Nissan*. London: Macmillan, 1987.

Chapter 10

Conclusions

TOPIC HEADINGS

- Introduction
- Rethinking organizational change
- The deeper theoretical debate
- The way ahead

INTRODUCTION

The final word on any subject is rarely spoken unless the subject matter has reached its own conclusion and cannot be revisited in any way. It seems unlikely that change at work will be in that situation at any time. The first part of the title, *Managing change*, will always be part of the ongoing agenda of any organization, driven at very least by technology and the desire to achieve continuing productivity improvements to provide profit opportunity ahead of the competition. But, as we have seen, much of the prescriptiveness contained in the 'to do' literature assumes that change will be a simply structured or a structural programme, easy to implement and driven by a logic that ought to be apparent to all reasonable people with any knowledge of business need. There may be an occasional flurry of unease or resistance among the workers subjected to such change, but they will quickly realize that newly implemented efficiency factors will make their working life easier and, provided they are supported through the change with the appropriate training, they will soon be quiescent, if not enthusiastic about the change.

The second half of our title, *Changing managers*, should alert us to the human dimension which is always inherent and indeed deeply held by those involved – including managers themselves. As we have seen in the debates surrounding New Public Management, there are still deeply held reservations about imposing productivity and efficiency targets on health professionals. This clash of basic assumptions about where the service exists seems likely to remain the more insuperable obstacle to change. Here, we may encounter the

247

prescriptions of culture change assumptions and, as we do, we are alerted to the various different meanings of this word which are not always clarified by those who espouse the need for such change.

Perhaps we should not be too hard on the users of the concept of culture, for, indeed, there remains a difficult fault-line between individual attitudes and group perceptions in the context of change. How far the one influences the other is rarely accessible to change agents and is equally difficult for researchers to clarify with subjects, too. What we can see is that the impact of enforced change at work affects not just surprise and sense-making, but also the very identity and discourse underwriting previously held basic assumptions about self, work and society.

There are continuing debates which address the practical approaches and concerns now current among practitioners and underlying that discussion there are deeper and more enduring debates about organizations, individuals and the knowledge that is possible in the interactions that take place at work. We will as a postscript offer a sample of both to guide students embarking on continued research.

RETHINKING ORGANIZATIONAL CHANGE

A recent International Research Workshop held at the University of Sydney addressed the above topic and included several contributions whose findings both summarize some of the points we have discussed here and also draw conclusions about the priorities that can guide future research. The range of papers is not dissimilar from the direction taken in the chapters of this book.

First, there is a summary of the styles of change management and the approaches that are often espoused by writers and practitioners. The authors state that 'what unites them is an optimistic view of achieving intentional change' (Palmer and Dunford, 2002, 245). Interestingly, they note that change management is about interpreting and suggest that managers have a role in 'creating meaning for other organizational members and helping them to make sense of the differing meanings attached to events' (Palmer and Dunford, 2002, 247). Such assertions exhibit a touching belief that human beings are always as suggestible as this.

The question of meaning and whether it can be managed in the way suggested exercises practitioners and researchers alike. Here, we are often placed back in the debate on culture and how far we can define it, access it and then intervene in a way that could be described as managing it. It should be noted that more thoughtful contributions suggest caution and care in approaching this underlying aspect of change. 'Effective change management is not just about the "hard" structural aspects of organizations, but also requires actions based on an in-depth appreciation of their cultural and human aspects' (Grant et al., 2002, 238).

For some writers, discourse remains a critical point of access to the ongoing search for meaning inherent in human experience and the effect of enforced change on subsequent reinterpretation. The search for this continuing account by those involved suggests that emergent change will remain the favoured vehicle for change initiatives, given that it offers the most available opportunities for all participants in the change process to share ideas, thoughts and feelings about the impact of impending change and its interpretation. In this sense, then, 'Discourse itself becomes action that can either aid or hinder change processes and paying insufficient attention to organizational discourse also means foregoing the richness that this lens can provide' (Heracleous, 2002, 255).

For some, the enduring belief in the efficacy of metaphors is offered as a way of engaging and promoting images that enable or facilitate different interpretations of change interventions. 'Change agents can employ an organization's prevalent metaphors as a diagnostic tool that reflects actors' ways of thinking about their organization and its need for change' (Heracleous, 2002, 258). It may well be that this is true. However, we would still need to ascertain how far the new imagery has been accepted and whether the change events are being interpreted according to the new metaphor or not. For most researchers that can be a difficult point of access and for managers and change agents almost impossible to know.

The question of the agents of change is much more carefully addressed and the step approach is happily less obtrusive in current writings. Indeed, there are even references 'stressing the inherently ambiguous nature of consulting work' (Wright and Kitay, 2002, 272). However, there is a welcome move towards evaluation of work undertaken by change agents. Such developments 'form part of a shift away from the traditional approach to consultancy as an advice-giving activity to one in which consultants are actively engaged in the process of organizational change' (Morris, 2000).

Overall, the discussion on the nature and significance of change continues to underwrite the management of change topic. For some writers, that requires revisiting the meaning of change itself and also the context in which change takes place. Specifically, the attempt to deal with change-related issues in organizations may require addressing three challenges:

- Ambiguous and imprecise ways of talking about organizational change.
- Changing organizational contexts that require new ways to think and talk about change.
- The reliance on implicit assumptions about change that may not be relevant in a world of continual change.

(Marshak, 2002, 239)

The emphasis remains a reflexive and shared endeavour which makes no assumptions about the impact that change may have, nor the significance of the changing context in which such interventions take place. Once again the favoured means for achieving the optimum outcome would seem to be bottom-up change initiatives.

THE DEEPER THEORETICAL DEBATE

The practical debate of how best to manage change needs to be grounded in a wider-ranging discussion on the nature of reality and how individuals can make sense of what they experience during change events. The steady-state theories of structural functionalism offered the stepped approach, incremental change or punctuated equilibrium as models for thinking about change.

The focus on individual interpretation and the reinterpretation required by the challenge of enforced change requires the researcher to consider the more subjective construction of experience. Thus 'organization itself is a question and not yet a given. In this regard,

249

Foucault's (1986) technique of "problematization" and Derrida's (1981) "deconstruction", when applied to organizational analysis, turn the given into a question and the familiar into the unfamiliar' (Chia, 1995, 592). The beginnings of research invite an exploration of the breakdown of basic assumption triggered by enforced change at work.

As we saw earlier, this challenge to deconstruct basic beliefs and the need to reconstruct around an intervention occasions a 'general or organizational "conversation" (Lyotard 1984) composed of a multiplicity of plot lines that individuals and groups elaborate, refine, accept and discard as they seek to make sense of their work and themselves' (Humphreys and Brown, 2002, 436). At this point we cross the line between individual perception and group attempts to rationalize the meaning of change initiatives. In these ways 'individuals, groups and organizations continuously create and re-create themselves in what are highly reflexive processes of interpretation and enactment' (Goffman, 1959).

For the change agent there may be the temptation to pragmatic approaches drawing on different research findings applied to techniques imposed on the subjects of change. Gabriel refers to such stratagems as 'paragrammes' – 'the image of practitioners using theories to tame irregularity and achieve control [is] severely at odds with the precarious qualities of life in contemporary organizations' (Gabriel, 2002, 143). Such imposition can give rise to confusion and suspicion in those on whom it is visited. As one writer explains:

> This notion [of multiple discourses] occurred to me the other day as I was making notes after a meeting in a factory at which I had been struck by the way one manager had responded to another's question about whether a new managing director would be likely 'to speak our language.' The second man asked, 'What the hell is our language? Which language do we speak these days?' It occurred to me that it was possible to develop an interpretation of what was going on in the organization by utilizing a concept of alternative languages or discourses which could be said to be current in an organization.
>
> (Watson, 1994, 813)

However astute the choice of metaphors, the interpretation of meaning and imputation of value lies solely with the individual and may or may not be shared with the group.

The search for meaning, both at individual and group levels, will continue and is required, almost, by the experience of enforced change at work. It can presage a deconstruction of previously held basic assumptions about self, life, work and organization. But, if that is the case, there is an opportunity to think again, to make sense, to reconstruct in ways that would have been impossible before:

> Information, argues Baudrillard (1983 and 1988), destroys meaning and signification, distinctions between media and reality collapse, and, in a society saturated by media messages, meaning implodes into meaningless noise. By contrast my research into organizational storytelling suggests that even within data-dominated environments, we continue to read meanings into the event of our daily lives and to essay interpretations on those who broadly share our experiences.
>
> (Gabriel, 1995, 492)

250

Such a search for new meaning is not just the province of the researcher. It is the forum of contestation lying at the centre of human self-awareness. It sometimes seeks to share itself and may be always on the move. The researcher, change agent and manager will benefit from entering into this exercise of sense-making which accompanies change whether managed or not, for, 'as soon as one can no longer think things as one formally thought them, transformation becomes very urgent, very difficult and quite possible' (Townley, 1994, 17).

THE WAY AHEAD

The topic of change and its possible management will always have a currency with general readers, practitioners and researchers, perhaps for different reasons, but ultimately with a similar purpose: to find out what people experience and whether there is any transferable learning to be derived. There will be those whose focus is managerial and who welcome opportunities to explore strategies that can be applied to achieve successful change at work, and there will be those who believe that a more evaluative approach opens up a reflective vein of research, which is not to be traduced by pragmatic considerations of facilitating change techniques for managers.

We may accept that the more hortatory and prescriptive approaches to change management are viewed with more reserve than during the days of programmed and n-step approaches. If so, it is more likely that the emergent stream of research will offer the reflective approach to change with continued emphasis on the individual subjects of enforced change at work. The petits recits that are the foundation of individual discourse enable the researcher to examine the response to change, which includes challenged basic assumptions, possible deconstruction and even reconstruction of perceptions about self, work and society.

However, this reflexivity does not take place in a vacuum and is in a sense a crossroads at which the subject reflects not just on his or her responses to enforced change and its implication for sense-making and meaning, but also a point of connection with other influences and other reconstructions surfacing at the same time.

The organizational identity discourses referred to in some research is a central concern for individuals in the group and organizational context (Knights and Morgan, 1991, 267). The search to make sense of shared experience may well be the source not just of metaphors confected by managers and change agents, but other significant groups as well. Following this tradition of research, then, suggests that metaphors may themselves assume or evoke paradigms (Boland and Greenberg, 1988, 18) and that these paradigms may denote not just differentiation but also ambiguity requiring resolution (Martin and Meyerson, 1988, 93ff.).

The path suggested here could open the way to connections between individuals, groups, ideas and significance, which see the individual as the crossroads between reflexivity and indexicality. A traditional discourse is perhaps threatened by enforced change and the ensuing sense-making may be a focus of an opportunity for the individual to explore a new identity emerging from the deconstruction of previously taken-for-granted basic assumptions.

Always the context of individual sense-making is the voice of the other. There is a resonance that may be found here which alerts the individual to either the possibility of reassessed identity and a different discourse or resistance and continued self-assertion in the face of challenge and change.

251

REFERENCES AND FURTHER READING

Boland, R.J. and Greenberg, R.H. Metaphorical structuring of organizational ambiguity, in Louis R. Pondy, Richard J. Boland and Howard Thomas (eds) *Managing ambiguity and change*. New York: John Wiley & Sons, 1988, pp. 17–36.

Chia, R. From modern to postmodern organizational analysis. *Organization Studies*, 1995, *16* (4): 579–608.

Derrida, J. *Positions*, trans. A. Bass. London: Athlone Press, 1981.

Foucault, J. *Positions*. Chicago, IL: Chicago University Press, 1981.

Gabriel, Y. The unmanaged organization: stories, fantasies and subjectivities. *Organization Studies*, 1995, *16* (3): 477–502.

Gabriel, Y. Essai: on paragrammatic uses of organizational theory – a provocation. *Organization Studies*, 2002, *23* (1): 133–153.

Goffman, E. *The presentation of self in everyday life*. New York: Doubleday, 1959.

Grant, G., Wailes, N., Michelson, G., Brewer, A. and Hall, R. Rethinking organizational change. *Strategic Change*, 2002, *11*: 237–242.

Heracleous, L. The contribution of a discursive view to understanding and managing organizational change. *Strategic Change*, 2002, *11*: 253–261.

Humphreys, M. and Brown, A.D. Narratives of organizational identity and identification: a case study of hegemony and resistance. *Organization Studies*, 2002, *23* (3): 421–450.

Knights, D. and Morgan, G. Corporate strategy, organizations and subjectivity, *Organizational Studies*, 1991, *12* (2): 251–273.

Lyotard, J.F. *The postmodern condition: a report on knowledge*, trans. G. Bennington and B. Massumi. Minneapolis: University of Minnesota Press, 1984.

Marshak, R.J. Changing the language of change: how new contexts and concepts are challenging the ways we think and talk about organizational change. *Strategic Change*, 2002, *11*: 279–286

Martin, M. and Meyerson, D. Organizational cultures and the denial, channeling and acknowledgement of ambiguity, in Louis R. Pondy, Richard J. Boland and Howard Thomas (eds) *Managing ambiguity and change*, New York: John Wiley & Sons, 1988, pp. 93–125.

Morris, T. Promotion policies and knowledge bases in the professional service firm, in M. Perpeil, M. Arthur, R. Goffee and T. Morris (eds) *Career frontiers: new conceptions of working lives*. Oxford: Oxford University Press, 2000.

Palmer, I. and Dunford, R. Who says change can be managed? Positions, perspectives and problematics. *Strategic Change*, 2002, *11*: 243–251.

Townley, B. *Reframing human resource management*. London: Sage, 1994.

Watson, A.J. Rhetoric, discourse and argument in organizational sense making: a reflexive tale. *Organizational Studies*, 1994, *16* (5): 805–822.

Wright, C. and Kitay, J. 'But does it work?' Perceptions of the impact of management consulting. *Strategic Change*, 2002, *11*: 271–278.

Index